BACKPACKER.

HIDDEN GEMS
100 GREATEST UNDISCOVERED
HIKES ACROSS AMERICA

FALCONGUIDES®

An imprint of The Rowman & Littlefield Publishing Group, Inc.
4501 Forbes Blvd., Ste. 200
Lanham, MD 20706
www.rowman.com

Falcon and FalconGuides are registered trademarks and Make Adventure Your Story is a trademark of The Rowman & Littlefield Publishing Group, Inc.

Distributed by NATIONAL BOOK NETWORK

Cover photo by Stephen Yocom
Back cover photo by Harry Hitzeman
Maps by Melissa Baker © The Rowman & Littlefield Publishing Group, Inc.

British Library Cataloguing-in-Publication Information available

Library of Congress Cataloging-in-Publication Data

Names: Horjus, Maren, author.
Title: Backpacker Hidden Gems : 100 greatest undiscovered hikes across
   America / by Maren Horjus.
Description: Guilford, Connecticut : Falcon, [2018] | "Distributed by
   NATIONAL BOOK NETWORK"—T.p. verso.
Identifiers: LCCN 2018002523| ISBN 9781493033867 (Paperback) | ISBN
   9781493033874 (e-book)
Subjects: LCSH: Backpacking—United States—Guidebooks. | Hiking—United
   States—Guidebooks. | Walking—United States—Guidebooks. | Trails—United
   States—Guidebooks. | United States—Guidebooks.
Classification: LCC GV199.4 .H67 2018 | DDC 796.510973—dc23 LC record available at https://lccn.loc.
gov/2018002523

∞™ The paper used in this publication meets the minimum requirements of American National Standard for Information Sciences—Permanence of Paper for Printed Library Materials, ANSI/NISO Z39.48-1992.

Printed in the United States of America

Photo: John McCormick

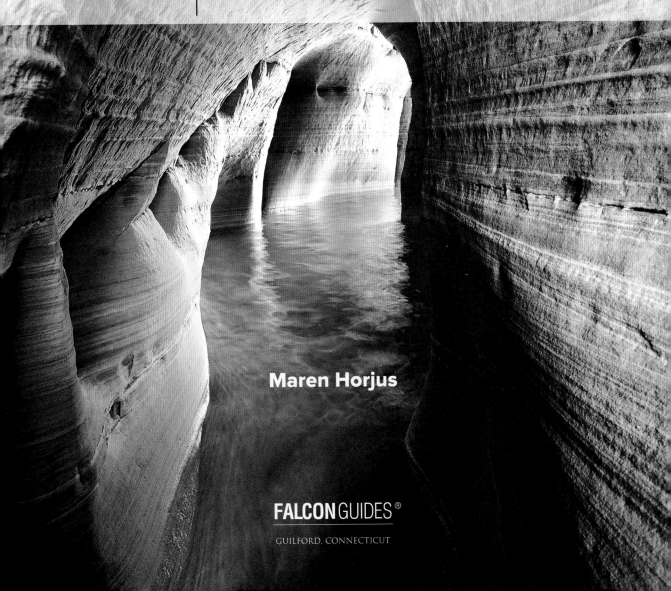

BACKPACKER

HIDDEN GEMS

100 GREATEST UNDISCOVERED HIKES ACROSS AMERICA

Maren Horjus

FALCON GUIDES ®

GUILFORD, CONNECTICUT

CONTENTS

Introduction: Spoiler Alert, xi

Photo: iStockphoto

Photo: iStockphoto

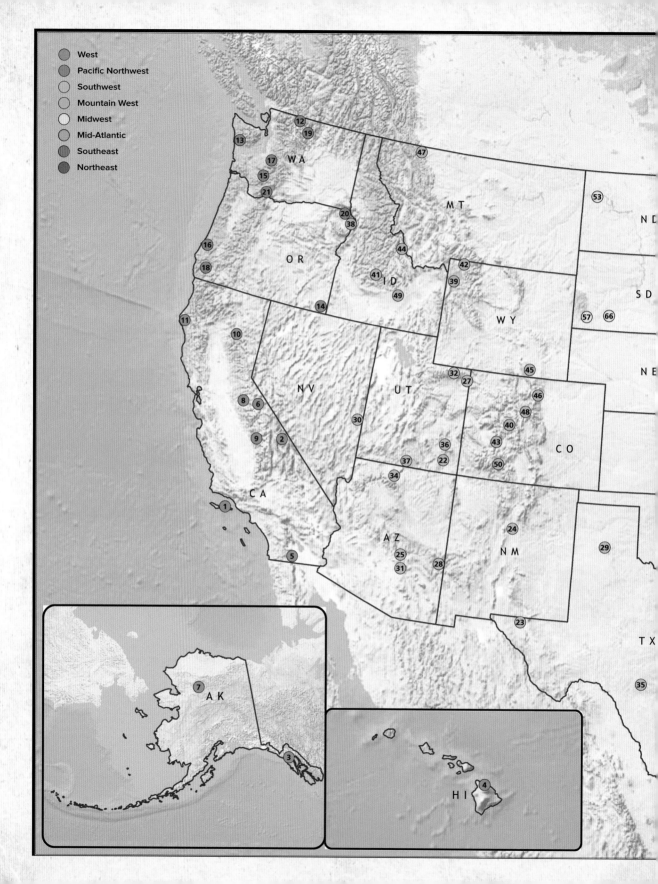

West
Pacific Northwest
Southwest
Mountain West
Midwest
Mid-Atlantic
Southeast
Northeast

MN

65 51 55

63

WI 58

MI

60 64

67

IA

61

IL

IN

52 56

MO 59

KY

73 78

TN

AR 88 91 85
80 82

26 92 81

MS AL GA

SC
79

89

87

83 LA FL

84 86

90

OH

54

WV
74 76
69

VA

PA

72

NY

68 75 71

77

VT 99
94
NH
97 98
93

ME 100

MA
95 CT 96 RI

NJ

70

MD
DC DE

NC

See 180-foot-tall Deer Creek Falls (and swim in its depths) on the Thunder River-Deer Creek Loop, page 102.

INTRODUCTION

SPOILER ALERT

Yes, we're into oversharing when it comes to the outdoors. Here's why.

"WHERE YOU HEADED?" asks the silver-haired man, slightly incredulously, as he hoists a wobbly external-frame pack near where ice-blue Tapeats Creek spills into the silty Colorado, deep in the belly of the Grand Canyon. I'm a two-day walk from the nearest trailhead, an overgrown user path on the national park's North Rim, itself a day's drive away from the nearest incorporated town. I'm surprised to see him down here, and apparently he feels the same about me.

"Deer Creek," I reply, pointing downriver to where the chocolate-colored Colorado disappears between sky-kissing walls of orange sandstone.

"The *BACKPACKER* hike, huh?"

I smile and nod. I'm midway through the Thunder River-Deer Creek Loop, a 26-mile epic scouted—and somewhat popularized—by *BACKPACKER*. The man who held my post at the magazine more than a decade ago had heard rumblings about a spectacular (and tough) loop on Grand Canyon's seldom-visited North Rim that descended to the Colorado River on the Thunder River Trail and back out on the Deer Creek Trail. The catch was that you had to get a little creative on the in-between because no official trails connected the two. He, along with a few other former *BACKPACKER* editors, put boots to (very faint) trail and did it. It was a gem in every sense: challenge, scenery, and solitude.

And then they did what we've been doing since 1973. They shared it. Some would say they "spoiled" it by publishing directions for other hikers to follow, but after more than four decades of scouting and writing about undiscovered routes, we know what it really means: Others would get to see the Mars-like Esplanade fall off into the chasm of the Big Ditch and witness freshwater Thunder Spring burst through a limestone amphitheater into an emerald oasis. Others would get to ford a route through rocky rubble above where the Colorado River sluices through the cliff-pinched Granite Narrows, and then ride a natural flume that time and Deer Creek have made so smooth it rivals any water park slide.

I stood at the bottom of the Grand Canyon that day because I wanted to see it—*feel* it—for myself. I wanted a lifetime's worth of desert highlights packed into a single trip, and I didn't want to throw elbows with the hordes on the Bright Angel Trail to get it. It worked: I encountered just three parties on that three-day circuit, and they were all there on *BACKPACKER*'s recommendation. You can try it, too. Find an exact trip description for the Thunder River-Deer Creek Loop on page 102. I've updated some of the logistics, but I promise

The Colorado River courses through the Grand Canyon.

you'll savor the same challenge, scenery, and, yes, solitude that made the hike a must-do epic when *BACKPACKER* first put it on the map.

The same is true of the other ninety-nine hidden gems in this book. Each one has been vetted by one of our editors or field scout who explored a wild lake, a quiet canyon, a lonely peak, or a secluded hideaway and chose to "spoil" it on you. That's because the miserly pleasure of holding a secret spot to yourself isn't anywhere near as gratifying as sharing outdoor joy. And we're confident that you—as a wilderness steward of the highest order—will protect these places so they're truly unspoiled for others to discover. So head out and try one of our favorites. Start small with the 6.6-mile trip through Texas's Lost Maples State Natural Area (page 105) or the easy, 3.2-mile walk through Wyoming's Snowies (page 141). Go nuts and tackle an off-trail ridge walk in Washington's North Cascades (page 36) or a forgotten route to a beachy oasis in Hawaii's Kohala Forest Preserve (page 11). No matter where you end up, I guarantee you'll find mind-melting scenery worthy of the classics—but a lot less crowded.

I guarantee you won't be disappointed, and I should know.

UPGRADE YOUR SUNSET PHOTOS

Master exposing these high-contrast scenes to capture the outdoors at its best.

GET READY Figure out when and where the sun will set. Best bet: The Photographer's Ephemeris app will tell you the exact angle for any spot and date. The iOS version includes an option to forecast whether the clouds will light up (this usually happens after the sun is down). Low-tech option: Find west with a compass, and look for high clouds with a clear horizon. Start getting in position to shoot an hour before sunset.

GET SET Compose a wide shot to include points of interest such as flowers, a tent, or a lake, but avoid framing any of them (or the sun itself) smack in the center. If conditions are right for colorful clouds, fill two-thirds of your frame with sky. Otherwise, compose with more land.

SHOOT Since the light will be low, use a tripod and expose for the brightest part of the scene (on smartphones, tap the sky). The land will seem really dark, but that's OK. Keep shooting; the colors will evolve up to 45 minutes after the sun is down. Later, use the shadows slider in photo-editing software to lighten the dark sections until the images look like what you remember. App to try: Adobe Photoshop Express (free for Android, iOS, and Windows).

DON'T FORGET SUNRISE The technical details and end result are very similar, except the best colors are often just *before* the sun rises.

EMBRACE HDR High dynamic range (HDR) imaging combines multiple shots with different exposures into one image to help capture scenes with a big spread between dark and light spots, a common challenge with sunset scenes. Using a tripod, take three to seven images at varying exposures, capturing color in the brightest areas and full detail in the darkest. In a photo-editing program like Adobe Lightroom, find an HDR option from the drop-down menus, then fine-tune. Be wary of adding so much brightness that it looks like full daylight in shadowed areas, and keep an eye out for halos where dark and light meet and ghost effects where something moves between images. Shortcut: Use an HDR smartphone app or built-in camera function like the iPhone's.

Text: Genny Fullerton

California's giant sequoias (page 27) are the most massive trees in the world. Photo: iStockphoto

WEST

01: RETURN OF THE NATIVES
CHANNEL ISLANDS, CALIFORNIA

Shannon Davis

The waves at Santa Cruz Island roll shoreward in gentle sets of 3-foot swells. I wait until the tide is lowest and paddle hard, jabbing at a couple barnacle-encrusted rocks for balance on my way out of an SUV-size sea cave, one of 326 on the island's cliff-riddled shore. Out on the open water, I steer my 12-foot sit-on-top kayak into a tiny inlet near Scorpion Rocks, pausing to watch a gang of California brown pelicans take flight. Two harbor seals surface and blink their bulging eyes. Neon-orange garibaldis dart through the seaweed below my boat. The weather is golden, and just yards away, the island appears so quiet and pristine with California buttercups in bloom, I have a hard time imagining that this place was ever anything but a perfectly preserved haven.

But Santa Cruz Island, located 19 miles off the Southern California coast, wasn't always so achingly gorgeous. In fact, it used to be a pigsty. Literally. Thousands of feral pigs, brought here first as livestock in the 1800s, rooted through the soil, feasting on native plants, leaving barren slopes vulnerable to invasive weeds. Golden eagles followed the pigs, which were easy pickings for the large raptors. Soon, the eagles began preying on island fox, a species living nowhere else in the world.

By 2004, the pigs had all but decimated nine of the island's twelve endemic plants, and the fox population, once in the thousands, had dipped below ninety. It looked like the pigs wouldn't stop until they'd chowed right through this delicate ecosystem—an environment so unique that biologists often call it "America's Galapagos."

In most places, it's impossible for land managers to eradicate an invasive species completely, but on an island it's feasible to hunt down every last one. Thanks to a joint effort between The Nature Conservancy and the National Park Service (which own 76 and 24 percent of the island, respectively), the pig looting was stopped in one of the biggest and fastest species eradication projects ever conducted. Between April 2005 and July 2006, gunners-for-hire killed 5,036 pigs. After more than a year of subsequent monitoring for stray swine, officials declared biological order restored in August 2007.

I'm visiting Santa Cruz Island to explore a place biologists say is more pristine than at any time in the last 180 years. I came to observe a rare phenomenon: an ecosystem reborn.

AFTER PADDLING BACK TO THE ANCHORAGE, I head to camp at eucalyptus-scented Scorpion Ranch and find only two of forty sites occupied. The camp is on the northeast corner of Santa Cruz, one of five isles in Channel Islands National Park. It's day one on my journey, and the truth is I can't help feeling a little piggish myself. Before the 7-mile paddle along the coast, my sea-kayaking guide, Andy Babcock, had wheeled a handcart full of falafel, pale ales, tuna steaks, and Peet's coffee over to his favorite campsite. No sufferfest this weekend. Babcock stashed the grub into steel lockers near the site's picnic table. He said the lockers were called "pig boxes" because the park service installed them to keep the porkers from ravaging campers' supplies back when they had the run of the place.

In the evening, we feast on the ferry-packed groceries, then turn in early to recharge for the next day. Come first light, I'll walk 15 miles southeast to Del Norte Camp on the island's isthmus. I'll gain 1,200 feet, crossing the highest point on the national park side of the island and pass through ten different biomes. It's a traverse, Babcock tells me, that's rarely done. But it's the best way to see the island's rugged interior.

Early the next day, just fifty steps down the Scorpion Canyon Trail, I spot two island foxes playing in a dry creekbed, and I pause to watch the cute, 4-pound predators pounce on grasshoppers in the morning sun. A quarter mile later, the route makes a sharp turn and I begin a steady climb, gaining 700 feet along grass-lined clay trails to a junction with an old ranch road and a barren, sepia-tone ridgeline. The views here are postcard perfect— bristly, green grass giving way to cliffs and a deep-blue ocean with islands that seem to hover above the whitecapped waves. About 4 bazillion Southern Californians live within eyesight on the mainland, but I won't see a soul here all day. Santa Cruz is popular with dayhikers and paddlers, but walk a couple hours in any direction, as I'm doing, and you'll be the only human.

I cruise another 5 miles along Montañon Ridge, a craggy spine with patches of prickly pear and rooftop views into sandy coves. Campo Del Norte lies another 6 miles away in a small, shaded grove, and I'm starting to think of dinner and the flask of scotch in my pack. But after a confusing trail junction (mid-island paths tend to be overgrown due to the lack of regular hoof traffic), I'm jarred back into the moment by the sight of a decomposed pig. It's hairy, the size of a Labrador, and must have had some serious dental problems.

THE ORIGINS OF SANTA CRUZ'S ECO-RAMPAGE CAN BE TRACED BACK TO 1839, when Spanish diplomat Andres Castillero moved onto the island and subsequently built one of the biggest sheep ranches in California. Docile farm pigs, originally brought here for food, broke through their fence lines and escaped into the wild. Once on the loose, they became a menace—pretty much overnight. "Feral pigs are devastating," Babcock tells me. "It only takes two years for them to turn from a fat, pink farm pig to fearless, longhaired animals with tusks that can pierce metal."

That a tame porker with a future no brighter than the glint from a butcher's cleaver can go completely primal seems pretty inspiring in a weird way. I can be soft and pink myself from time to time, but I like to think I'd harden up if left to fend for myself, just like those rampaging pigs.

That's not to say I'd like to take on well-armed conservationists intent on restoring order. "We did triage on the island," says Rachel Wolstenholme, when I meet her on my third day, at Prisoners Harbor, a 3.5-mile hike from Del Norte. Wolstenholme is the island restoration manager for The Nature Conservancy, and she's accompanying me on a 4-mile out-and-back on the Pelican Bay Trail, from Prisoners to a pristine arc of white sand. (Wolstenholme left her post with The Nature Conservancy in 2009.)

The path crosses Nature Conservancy land, and a group of volunteers who'd come to pull invasive weeds for the weekend wave hello as we pass. We cover the rolling terrain at a decent clip, dropping into steep drainages, climbing tight switchbacks, and finally rising onto a grassy plain where we head off-trail toward a carpet of yellow blooms. Wolstenholme graciously ignores my bad pig jokes on the way.

The conservancy started its island overhaul in 2002. "We bred island foxes and bald eagles in captivity while trapping the golden eagles and transporting them to Northern California," Wolstenholme explains. And they started getting rid of the pigs, too. Unlike the feral sheep that also once roamed here, the pigs couldn't be trapped and shipped elsewhere. State regulations forbade it because of their potential to spread disease. So The Nature Conservancy hired a New Zealand company called ProHunt to "dispatch" the pigs, fencing the island into five sections and shooting them from helicopter and on foot. By the end of ProHunt's work, there were enough dead pigs to feed an army.

"There was a lot of bacon," Wolstenholme says self-consciously. The carcasses fed hunters and other islanders, and The Nature Conservancy used some to feed bald eagle chicks. But most decomposed and were recycled into the ecosystem.

With the pigs gone, native plants are springing back to life. The coreopsis bloom, the biggest in a century, is such a bright, electric yellow that you can see the biggest patches from the mainland. On top of that, Wolstenholme says bald eagles are nesting here for the first time in more than fifty years, and the island fox has rebounded, its population now topping 1,300. The island is in full rebirth; it just needed a little tough love.

As I hike back to the pier to wait for the ferry, I recall something Babcock said when I first arrived. I'd asked him why there were so few visitors; the island seemed so empty. "No locals ever come out here," he said. "They say there's nothing out here. Well, yeah! That's the point."

TRIP PLANNER

SEASON Year-round

PERMIT Required for overnight stay ($15 per party per night for Del Norte Campground); reserve at recreation.gov

COMMERCIAL FERRY Island Packers; book a round-trip ferry ride from Ventura at islandpackers.com

CONTACTS Channel Islands National Park; nps.gov/chis & The Nature Conservancy; nature.org

I'd argue that there's plenty out here. Miles of rugged shoreline, trails lacking only hikers, secluded campsites galore, and stunning island wildlife—there's simply nothing that doesn't belong.

DO IT

DISTANCE: 22.6 miles (out and back)

TIME: 2 days

DIFFICULTY: ★★★✦

THE PAYOFF: Explore the rugged interior of Santa Cruz Island to secure ocean views and wildlife sightings.

TRAILHEAD: Scorpion Anchorage (34.0499, -119.5563); a ferry will drop you off at the pier.

MILES AND DIRECTIONS

FROM SCORPION ANCHORAGE:

1. Hike to the trailhead kiosk and head west.
2. Continue on the **Scorpion Canyon Trail** (keep an eye peeled for island foxes frolicking in the underbrush) as it climbs out of the canyon to its terminus near mile 2.2.
3. Head west on the **Montanon Ridge Trail,** which climbs to big views on its route to an intersection near mile 4.9.
4. Stay straight on the **Del Norte Trail,** which passes short spurs to ocean views, en route to mile 10.3.
5. Split north toward **Del Norte Camp,** .9 mile away.
6. If you gain permission to enter Nature Conservancy land, visit Pelican Bay on a 10.2-mile out-and-back from camp before retracing your steps to Scorpion Anchorage.

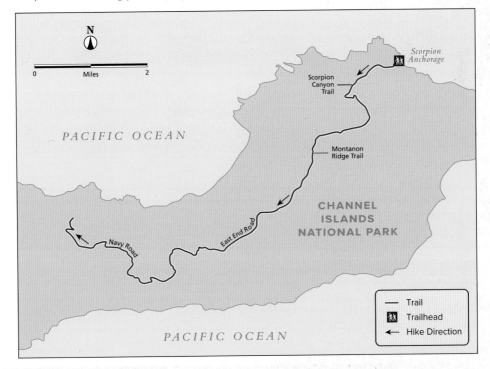

02: DO IT YOURSELF
GRAPEVINE MOUNTAINS, DEATH VALLEY NATIONAL PARK, CALIFORNIA

A backpacker's wonderful dilemma: where to go in the largest national park in the continental United States? If you follow the available beta, you'll inevitably end up at the Racetrack, Telescope Peak, or Devil's Golf Course, where visitors funnel every day. Those spots are worthy, sure, but why limit yourself in a park so full of raw wilderness? Instead, head into the trailless, maze-like Grapevine Mountains, a range that conceals more canyons than have names. At first, as you trudge across the sunbaked alluvial fan between road and range, you may curse the decision to target this godforsaken nothingness. But soon, you'll enter your own private slot canyon and realize that nothingness is exactly the point.

TRIP PLANNER

SEASON October to April

PERMIT None

CONTACT Death Valley National Park, www.nps.gov/deva

DISTANCE: 2-plus miles (out and back)

TIME: 2 days

DIFFICULTY: ★★★↗

THE PAYOFF: Camp in an unnamed slot canyon, where exploration opportunities are endless.

TRAILHEAD: Scotty's Castle Road (36.8365, -117.2264); 26 miles north of the Stovepipe Wells Ranger Station off CA 190

MILES AND DIRECTIONS

FROM SCOTTY'S CASTLE ROAD:

1. There are no rules here: Drive north along Scotty's Castle Road from CA 190—paralleling the Grapevine Mountains—and park when you spy a canyon that looks inviting. The coordinates listed above set you up to venture into Red Wall Canyon, one of only a few named features here, though the unnamed wash east of 36.8908, -117.2739 is a fine alternative. Once you land on a starting point, head east through the desert and up rocky washes, picking a path of least resistance to the foot of the range, roughly 1 to 2 miles away from the road, depending on where you start. From there, head into the mountains as far as you like.

2. Retrace your steps to the trailhead.

DON'T MISS THIS CAMPSITE: RED WALL CANYON (MILE 2.2)

We'd be remiss to tell you where to go in this trackless desert wonderland, but the bend in the wash up Red Wall Canyon near 36.8616, -117.2018 is hard to beat. Crumbly redrock walls soar 600 feet overhead in spots, and the flat basecamp sets you up well to stage day missions into the heart of the mountains. But, no matter where you end up, pleasant nighttime temperatures and Death Valley's legendary dark skies almost require camping without a tent.

GEAR TIP: PACK IN WATER

You won't find any water here, so be sure to haul it in (one gallon per person per day in mild conditions). The approach from Scotty's Castle Road isn't long, but it will feel interminable on a hot day, so start early.

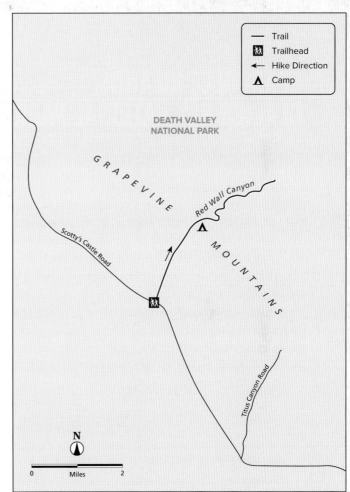

Legend:
— Trail
🏃 Trailhead
← Hike Direction
▲ Camp

DEATH VALLEY NATIONAL PARK

GRAPEVINE MOUNTAINS

Red Wall Canyon

Scotty's Castle Road

Titus Canyon Road

N

0   Miles   2

BEARDSLEE ISLANDS, GLACIER BAY NATIONAL PARK, ALASKA

For backpackers, Alaska is the deep end of the pool. It's a dazzling place that's a little scary, a bit mysterious, and completely exhilarating in its magnitude. Grizzlies lurk there, winds howl through the jagged mountains, vast glaciers offer a humbling sense of scale. But you don't need to take the plunge if you're not ready. Instead, hang tight to the wall and visit the Beardslee Islands, just an easy, 20-minute paddle north of the visitor center at Glacier Bay. The grandeur of the setting—picture secluded beach campsites set between stranded icebergs in the shadow of snowcapped peaks—belies the fact that you don't need a guide or, frankly, a lot of time to get there. Expect to see humpback whales, sea otters, bears, moose, and bald eagles. Among these private islands, solitude beckons—with adventure close behind.

TRIP PLANNER

SEASON May to September

PERMIT Required for overnight stay (free); obtain from the Bartlett Cove Visitor Information Station

COMMERCIAL FERRY While private vessels are permitted to dock in Glacier Bay, your best bet is to visit via the Alaska Marine Highway ferry system, a cruise ship, a tour vessel, or a jet service; visit the park website to find an itinerary that best suits your plans.

CONTACT Glacier Bay National Park, www.nps.gov/glba

DISTANCE: 4-plus miles (out and back)

TIME: 2 days

DIFFICULTY: ★★

THE PAYOFF: Inch into wild Alaska with an easy paddle to a private island in Glacier Bay.

TRAILHEAD: Glacier Bay Lodge (58.4542, -135.8853); a ferry or plane will drop you off at the pier.

MILES AND DIRECTIONS

FROM GLACIER BAY LODGE:

1. Launch your boat in Bartlett Cove and paddle around Lester Island to take your pick of private beaches among the Beardslees.

2. Retrace your strokes to the put-in at Glacier Bay Lodge.

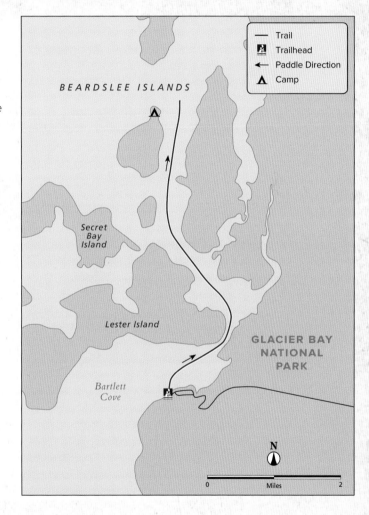

ALL THE EXTRAS

DON'T MISS THIS CAMPSITE: BEARDSLEE ISLANDS (MILES 2 TO 6)

Point your bow to the Beardslee Islands, where an absence of designated back-country campsites means you should let fate and whimsy dictate where you pull your boat ashore. Some fifty unoccupied islands cluster in the water here, so feel free to be selective; look for one with a grassy meadow above the beach ideal for tenting. Wherever you end up, set up as far back from the waterline as you can, and note that the tidal exchanges are massive here.

GEAR TIP: RENT A BOAT

Need to rent a boat? Glacier Bay Sea Kayaks (glacierbayseakayaks.com) in Gustavus rents kayaks for about $45 per day.

KEEP YOUR EYES PEELED: FAUNA

Scan for ripples on the water's surface to spy sea lions, harbor seals, otters, porpoises, and humpback whales. The latter grow to be nearly 50 feet long, weighing well over 30 or 35 tons, and may be the most prized quarry for a wildlife lover in this park. Humpbacks spend spring, summer, and fall gorging themselves on small schooling fish in Glacier Bay.

EXTRA CREDIT: ADD A HIKE

You could spend the better part of a week paddling among the Beardslees and exploring the small islands on foot, but you won't find any developed trails. To tack on a hike to your multisport adventure, budget time in Bartlett Cove, the launching point of the paddle. From there, explore a tidal lagoon on the 4-mile Bartlett River Trail or set aside a day for the 8-mile Bartlett Lake Trail, an unmaintained path that leads through temperate rainforest to a jade pool at the foot of the snow-capped Chilkat Range.

04: WET AND WILD
WAIMANU VALLEY, KOHALA FOREST RESERVE, HAWAII

Nestled below 2,000-foot-tall ramparts shellacked in emerald ferns, tucked in a grove of palms fed by surging cascades on the edge of the Pacific, Waimanu Valley does a good job masquerading as a hiker's Eden. It's the sort of scenery that has the power to convert even the most nature-averse—if they ever got here. Separated from the nearest resort town by 40 miles and a steep 4WD road, even the trailhead does a decent job of keeping the crowds at bay. But beyond that, it's just silly: Relentless ups and downs (including grades as steep as 40 degrees), a dozen gulches, and river crossings that creep up to chest high keep Waimanu Valley nothing more than a Google image search for all but the hardiest hikers.

TRIP PLANNER

SEASON Year-round

PERMIT Required for overnight stay (free); obtain online at camping.ehawaii.gov

CONTACT Division of Forestry and Wildlife, dlnr.hawaii.gov

DO IT

DISTANCE: 18 miles (out and back)

TIME: 2 days

DIFFICULTY: ★★★★★

THE PAYOFF: One of the most punishing approaches in the country means you have full license to get lazy in this little-visited oasis, with its perfect weather, trees laden with tropical fruit, and the Shangri-la of swimming holes.

TRAILHEAD: Waipio Valley (20.1186, -155.5882); 8 miles west of Honokaa on Waipio Valley Road

MILES AND DIRECTIONS

FROM THE WAIPIO VALLEY:

1. Descend the rugged Waipio Valley as far as your car can handle, then continue on foot to the Wailoa Stream.

2. Pick up the **Muliwai Trail,** which switchbacks 7.6 miles up and over the gecko-green, waterfall-streaked valley before dropping down to the sometimes chest-high Waimanu Stream. (There's an installed rope, which lets hikers move hand-over-hand through the deepest sections.)

3. Cross and continue across the black-sand beach to find a perfect campsite.

4. Retrace your steps to the trailhead.

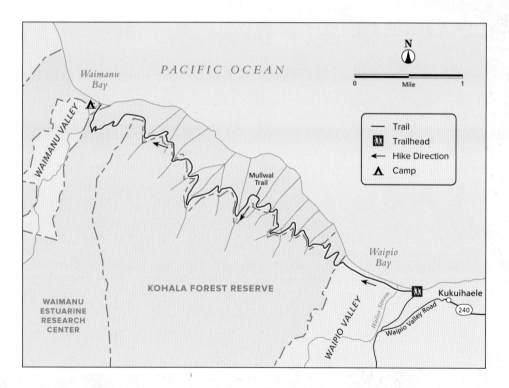

ALL THE EXTRAS

DON'T MISS THIS CAMPSITE: WAIMANU VALLEY (MILE 9)

Negotiate your way across the beach to find a shaded sandbar nestled between the Pacific Ocean and a wild deserted valley, complete with densely vegetated cliffs and thousand-foot waterfalls. Pitch your tent—or sling a hammock—under the palms, then head down to the black-sand beach to play in the surf.

KEEP YOUR EYES PEELED: RUINS

A tsunami chased the area's last inhabitants out in 1946. Wander upstream to explore what's left of their village, then harvest hors d'oeuvres: Guavas, pear-like mountain apples, papayas, and avocados grow here.

EXTRA CREDIT: ADD A HIKE

Follow wild pig trails an hour upvalley to 1,000-foot Waiilikahi Falls, a two-drop cascade with a deep, sparkling pool, straight out of your favorite island fantasy.

Wild avocados

05: WARM HAVEN
ANZA-BORREGO DESERT STATE PARK, CALIFORNIA

Winter blues? This Southern California desert hideaway has the cure: With "cold-season" temperatures in the 60s and 70s, winter is the perfect time to wander its cactus-filled canyons, scramble rocky peaks, and scope for desert wildlife. Use these tips and trips from local expert **Robin Halford** to plan an unforgettable warm-weather getaway. By Elisabeth Kwak-Hefferan

THE INSIDER

Two guidebooks (*Hiking in Anza-Borrego Desert*, volumes one and two) weren't enough to exhaust Robin Halford's knowledge of the park: The volunteer hiking leader for the Anza-Borrego Desert Natural History Association and local gift shop owner is currently working on volume three.

1. FLORA-FILLED DAYHIKE

The wildflower blooms at Anza-Borrego are the stuff of legend, with hundreds of species lighting up the desert when conditions are just right (the best shows require the perfect combination of rainfall, temperature, and sunshine). "If it's a good bloom in the spring, Hornblende Canyon can be just fantastic," Halford says. To stroll among blossoms like apricot mallow, purple Canterbury bells, and orange apricot yarrow, hike the 3.8-mile loop up Hornblende, over a small saddle, and down Box Canyon in late winter or early spring. No flower explosion this year? No problem: In these canyons, iconic desert plants such as hedgehog cactus, barrel cactus, agave, and prickly pear are always a sure thing.

2. BEST OVERNIGHT

A lack of reliable water sources in the park makes backpacking in Anza-Borrego best for shorter trips, like the 10.4-mile overnight loop connecting Rockhouse and Butler Canyons in the Santa Rosa Mountains Recreation Area. Park where the road splits between the two canyons (4WD required; high-clearance 2WD cars can usually make it the first 7 miles, but you'll have to walk the final mile to the trailhead). Head into Rockhouse, where you'll have to scramble across several boulder fields to reach Hidden Spring, about 3.5 miles in. "It's more of a seep," Halford says, so pack in at least a gallon of water per person per day. Take a break here before backtracking roughly 100 feet from the spring to find an unsigned trail up to Jackass Flat, where you can scout a campsite on the wide bench (clear from flashflood danger). Next day, head through taller, narrower Butler Canyon to loop back to your car.

3. WILDLIFE SPOTTING

The park's canyons and rocky mountain slopes provide a refuge for 800 to 900 endangered Peninsular Range bighorn sheep (as well as kit foxes, bobcats, mountain lions, jackrabbits, and more than seventy species of reptiles and amphibians). For your best shot at glimpsing the elusive bighorns, head to the steep terrain they favor. Halford's favorite scoping spot is 3,657-foot Sunset Mountain, a 3.5-mile out-and-back trip. Drive 4.3 miles up Pinyon Wash (4WD required), park, and hike east, slaloming through boulders and cacti, to a saddle on the peak's western side (there's no official trail, but the route is straightforward). Skirt the northern flank and follow a ridge to a "sheep guzzler," or park-maintained seasonal water tank, then top out for views over the Vallecito Mountains and the Salton Sea.

4. CAR CAMP WITH A VIEW

The vista over miles of wrinkled badlands at Fonts Point draws crowds of wine sippers and sunset gazers most nights: "Fonts is beautiful, but everyone goes there," Halford says. Better: the similarly sweeping views from Vista del Malpais, just to the east. Best: You can drive to within about 0.1 mile of the overlook (high-clearance vehicle required; 4WD recommended) and set up camp for a solo sunset show chased with mind-blowing stargazing. "It's very unlikely you'll see anyone else," Halford says. (No reservations or permit are required, but keep your vehicle within one car length from the road.)

5. DESERT ESSENTIALS

Halford never leaves home without a multitool with pliers to extract cholla cactus spines. "No matter where you go, you learn fairly quickly that the cholla really do seem to jump on you," she says.

TRIP PLANNER

SEASON November to April

PERMIT None

CONTACT Anza-Borrego Desert State Park, bit.do/anza-borrego-desert-sp

---

06: HIGHLIGHT REEL
NYDIVER LAKES,
ANSEL ADAMS WILDERNESS, CALIFORNIA

With all due respect to John Muir's gospel-like ravings, the Sierras are actually *better* than he said. For proof, you need only tackle a long weekend in the Ansel Adams Wilderness, where you can combine primo stretches of the Pacific Crest and John Muir Trails with unmatched views of 13,150-foot Mount Ritter, what Muir himself deemed the "noblest mountain of the [Sierra]." The only problem is that the area is so astoundingly spectacular that it draws crowds. Think of that as a blessing, though, because the main corridors essentially funnel hikers to the same brand-name lakes and basins. Instead, venture a little ways—seriously, less than a mile should do—off the main trails and you'll secure deserted lakes, forgotten valleys, and solo summits that still look and feel like they did more than a hundred years ago when the grandfather of wilderness himself first laid eyes on them.

DO IT

DISTANCE: 22 miles (loop)

TIME: 2 to 3 days

DIFFICULTY: ★★★★⯪

THE PAYOFF: Venture off-trail to enjoy the bounties of the East Sierra without sharing.

TRAILHEAD: Agnew Meadows (37.6829, -119.0845); 9 miles west of Mammoth Lakes on Agnew Meadows Road

Adapted from text by William M. Rochfort, Jr.

MILES AND DIRECTIONS

FROM THE AGNEW MEADOWS TRAILHEAD:

1. For views that parade along the route like a procession, do the loop counterclockwise: Head 8.1 miles north on the **Pacific Crest Trail** (also called the **High Trail** here) to Thousand Island Lake.

2. Veer south onto the **John Muir Trail,** looping past Emerald, Ruby, Garnet, and Clarice Lakes to a junction near mile 12.5.

3. Turn west onto the **Shadow Creek Trail,** which is already a relative ghost town compared to the Pacific Crest and John Muir Trails, and trek another 0.8 mile toward Ediza Lake.

4. Before crossing the Nydiver Lakes drainage, leave the trail and follow the water roughly a mile upstream to a trio of sapphire-like tarns. ***Note:*** Only proficient navigators should attempt this.

5. Retrace your steps to the intersection of the John Muir and Shadow Creek Trails near mile 17.

6. Close the loop after 5 miles on the **Shadow Creek Trail.**

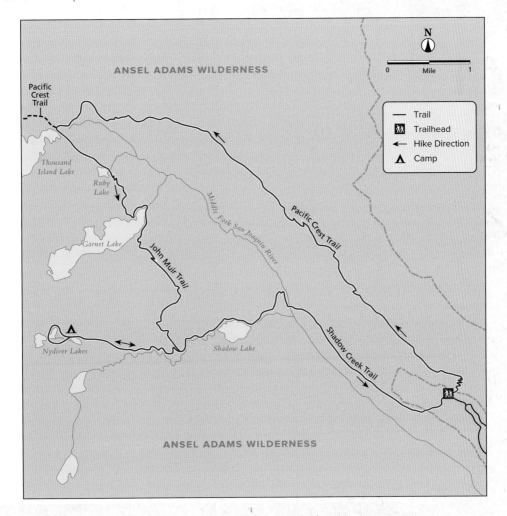

TRIP PLANNER

SEASON June to October

PERMIT Required for overnight stay ($5 per person); obtain from the visitor center or reserve at recreation.gov

CONTACT Inyo National Forest, www.fs.usda.gov/inyo

ALL THE EXTRAS

DON'T MISS THIS CAMPSITE: NYDIVER LAKES (MILE 14.3)

The Sierras' bountiful lakes and miles of alpine terrain are a perfect canvas for off-trail exploration. You can't go wrong wherever you end up, but the Nydiver Lakes basin may have the best sweat-to-reward ratio. An easy jaunt off the main drag lands you at a trio of lakes seated beneath Mount Ritter and its glacier-polished granite ramparts. To get there, peel off the Ediza Lake Trail near 37.6907, -119.1560 and point your compass to the Nydiver Lakes, just a mile away. The tarns offer (practically guaranteed) solitude and (definitely guaranteed) tent-door views of mountain majesty. Set up your tent on the broad, sandy bench just east of the land bar between the uppermost lakes and set an alarm for sunrise; you won't want to miss the reflections of Ritter and Banner Peak, all gold against still water, at daybreak.

GEAR TIP: PACK A ROD

Break out the flies at the Nydiver Lakes; the brookies here aren't used to them and practically jump onto the line.

EXTRA CREDIT: ADD A HIKE

Mount Ritter nearly killed John Muir on his first ascent in 1872—fortunately, there are more benign routes than the one he chose up the iconic peak, and the best is easily accessed from camp. Summit the 13,150-footer on a 4-mile, marked out-and-back from the Nydiver Lakes via the Southeast Glacier Route. The relatively easy Class 2 and 3 scrambling is nontechnical, but call ahead to check on the snowpack—you may need an ice axe and crampons. Either way, plan on an early start.

07: MOUNTAIN REFUGE
ARRIGETCH CREEK, GATES OF THE ARCTIC NATIONAL PARK AND PRESERVE, ALASKA

It's true: You won't find a hike more inconvenient in the pages of this book than this trek in the northern corner of Alaska. Also true: You won't find more solitude—or grander scenery—on this planet. Gates of the Arctic National Park and Preserve is like a 13,000-square-mile walk-in deep freezer—the door of which swings open for visitors for just a few months out of the year. There are no permits to apply for, no roads to putter down in an RV, no campgrounds, no official trails, and, for all intents and purposes, nobody else. In most respects America's second-largest national park is as quiet and wild as it was in the Pleistocene era, before humans set foot in North America. See for yourself at the headwaters of Arrigetch Creek, where chiseled summits, glacier-blue lakes, and sheer remoteness pin you into the landscape, making the enormous terrain oddly intimate. Consider paradise found.

TRIP PLANNER

SEASON July to September

PERMIT None

BUSH PLANE: Brooks Range Aviation; book a round-trip air taxi ride from Bettles at brooksrange.com.

CONTACT Gates of the Arctic National Park and Preserve, www.nps.gov/gaar

DISTANCE: 13.4 miles (out and back)

TIME: 3 days

DIFFICULTY: ★★★★

THE PAYOFF: Discover a private alpine paradise at the end of a wild river in the vast, trailless (and road-less) Gates of the Arctic, which has remained virtually unchanged from time immemorial.

TRAILHEAD: Confluence of the Alatna River and Arrigetch Creek (67.5035, -153.9285); a bush plane will drop you off near the confluence.

MILES AND DIRECTIONS

FROM THE CONFLUENCE OF THE ALATNA RIVER AND ARRIGETCH CREEK:

1. Find the rough climbers' trail and follow it some 6.7 miles southwest up Arrigetch Creek, through alder thickets and beneath granite massifs to the clearing where the Arrigetch and Aquarius Valleys meet.

2. Retrace your steps to the trailhead and your bush plane pick-up spot.

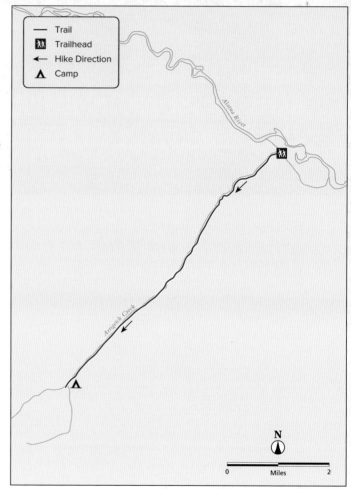

Legend:
— Trail
🚶 Trailhead
← Hike Direction
⛺ Camp

Alatna River

Arrigetch Creek

N

0 — Miles — 2

Adapted from text by Paxson Woelber.

ALL THE EXTRAS

DON'T MISS THIS CAMPSITE: ARRIGETCH AND AQUARIUS VALLEYS (MILE 6.7)

You can camp en route to the headwaters, but you'll want to budget multiple days for this spot in the glacial cirque where the Arrigetch and Aquarius Valleys meet. Set up a basecamp in the grassy clearing, tucked against some ground shrubs, then spend the following days exploring both veins.

EXTRA CREDIT: MAKE IT LONGER

Consider the Miles and Directions a general framework, but don't feel limited. You could spend a week in this corner of Alaska—and chances are, you'll want to. From your basecamp, hike about 4 miles up Arrigetch Valley to the headwaters of the creek, set beneath its eponymous spires: the 7,000-foot Arrigetch Peaks. Set aside another day to explore the Aquarius Valley, roughly 2 miles south of camp. There, five unnamed lakes sit amid sharply rising summits. Of course, if you're a rock climber or mountaineer, you'll want even more time to properly acquaint yourself with the mind-bending terrain.

KEEP YOUR EYES PEELED: WILDLIFE

North America's most charismatic beasts call Gates of the Arctic home. Consider it the Northern Hemisphere's Big 5: Grizzlies, black bears, moose, muskoxen, and caribou headline the roster (take proper precautions). Expect to see old antlers pockmarking the social path.

08: ALONE IN A CROWD
YOSEMITE NATIONAL PARK, CALIFORNIA

By Kelly Bastone

'm standing by myself on top of El Capitan with a lump in my throat as big as Half Dome, but heights aren't my issue: It's the complete absence of another person. *All alone on the most photographed rock face on the planet? Impossible.* Even crazier: I hiked here on a Muir-worthy trail that threads through the heart of Yosemite Valley and hasn't appeared on a map since 1990.

I'd always wanted to hike in the Valley, but had avoided joining the legendary throngs: Yosemite attracts 3.6 million visitors annually and sells out of popular backcountry permits from Memorial Day to Labor Day. My boycott would last until I discovered a way to find real solitude—not just smaller crowds. Then I caught wind of a secret trail, an unknown, heart-of-the-valley path that was dropped from park maps almost thirty years ago. It helps that I'm here in October, after the summer rush and before the late-autumn snows. But damned if I didn't find it: the perfect backpacking adventure—complete with starry skies, staggering views, and crowd-free streamside campsites—smack in the middle of America's third-busiest national park.

Since I arrived in Yosemite Valley yesterday, I've managed to elude the crush of humanity that's as much a part of this place as its supersize waterfalls and granite monoliths. Each summer some 95 percent of park visitors squeeze into the Valley's 7 square

Photo: Taylor Gray

miles—an area that amounts to less than 1 percent of the park's total size. That's 13,571 people per square mile, per day—and about 13,570 more than I like to include in my back-country adventures. But in two days of hiking I've passed just a couple other hikers, and I'll encounter only a handful more over the next several days. My secrets: a local named Pete Devine and that invaluable, out-of-date map.

A twenty-five-year resident and outdoor educator with the Yosemite Association, Pete had regaled me with stories of a secret trail known only to a handful of locals. With the flatulent name OBOFRT—for Old Big Oak Flat Road Trail—it isn't officially a trail at all, but an abandoned road. Once the main tourist route used by travelers coming from the west and dropping into the Valley, the OBOFRT became a secondary byway after the current Big Oak Flat Road was built in 1940. Then, in 1943 rockslides buried portions of the historic road beneath truck-size boulders, and the OBOFRT was retired. Today, occasional patches of asphalt are all that remain of this idyllic, unsigned footpath.

"Even in August, you'll almost never see a car parked here," Pete says, as he edges his minivan into a nondescript pullout off the main Valley road. A ranger had scrawled "Rock-slides" on our permit as our originating trailhead, but no sign marks the spot where we start our trip. We're just west of El Cap Meadow, where scores of people are gaping at the climber-dotted monolith. But here—no one. In fact, I'll see just twelve people on my entire four-day trek, which follows the OBOFRT for 4.5 miles before connecting with the infor-mally named North Rim Trail and heading east, past El Cap, Eagle Peak, and Yosemite Falls. Even without our sneaky start leg, though, this version of the North Rim traverse would be life-list-caliber: Solitude extends all along the North Rim, except for pockets of people at Yosemite Falls and North Dome, accessed by shorter spur trails from the opposite end. It also helps that most backpackers favor routes that beeline away from the Valley. But hike above the crowds instead of racing away, and you'll enjoy some of the most epic views in the park.

PETE AND I SET OUT ON THE ROADBED LATE IN THE AFTERNOON. We revel in its gentle grade (the rest of the trails out of the Valley are elevator shafts) and make good time striding along manzanita-covered hillsides. Berry-studded bear scat is everywhere, indicating Yosemite's bruins have been gorging themselves before winter puts the kibosh on good eats. Pete smiles as he points to the faint outline of a bear track headed in our direction.

Everything—not just bears—seems to thrill Pete, who possesses a scholar's curiosity about the entire natural world. But his muscular legs suggest his learning isn't all logged at a desk: His 6-foot 5-inch figure practically floats over the landslides we encounter, leading the way until we arrive at the hike's first overlook—a gem of a vista juxtaposing the impos-sibly sheer faces of Half Dome and El Capitan. "What I love about this view is the way it hides all traces of development," Pete says, pointing out how campsites, houses, and even the Valley Loop Road remain obscured from our vantage point.

Continuing on, we camp near Cascade Creek, still on the OBOFRT and not far from where John Muir himself traveled during his first visit to Yosemite. For nearly 150 years,

Sunrise in Yosemite

people have been coming here to admire this place—longer if you consider the Native American tribes that once migrated to and from this oasis along the Merced River. So after a dinner of Indian curry, as we perch on our bear canisters and count the stars, I ask Pete if he ever feels the Valley's many visitors are loving it to death.

"Oh, some people think there should be a daily quota on the number of visitors allowed in the Valley," he says. And yes, those crowds have an impact. But Pete says the bigger threat to the landscape is generated far beyond its granite domes. "Climate change has the potential to impact the park more negatively than the cars or hikers," he explains, adding that 25 percent of the park's pollution comes from China and its appetite for coal. He sees the effects of that carbon output every time he visits Lyell and Maclure Glaciers, where he's been measuring the ice's retreat since 1999. Compared to one hundred years ago, their surface area has shrunk by 60 to 65 percent. "The factors causing the biggest changes here may be the hardest for us to control," he reflects.

The next day we leave the OBOFRT and pick up the North Rim Trail, following it east toward El Capitan and Yosemite Falls. We cross open expanses of glacier-crushed granite where the blue sky blazes overhead, then enter a forest of giant sugar pines.

In a few hours, we arrive at the top of Yosemite Falls, the tallest verified fall in North America at 2,390 feet. Now, in mid-October, Yosemite Creek is a string of placid pools, and it's difficult to imagine it as a mammoth firehose capable of blasting me off the cliff. Yet even without the crushing torrents of water I'd see during peak runoff in May and June, I still shiver when I lean out over the precipice and gape at the falls. From below, when runoff is low, the water can break up into wispy curtains and blow across the granite face in a rainbow of colors.

At the top of the falls, I bid farewell to Pete: This is where he must peel off, hiking back to his car via the Yosemite Falls Trail so he can spend tomorrow in the office. Tonight I'll camp alone, a little upstream from the falls. "But tomorrow night," Pete says, "you're in for a treat. I wish I could stay out with you," he sighs before turning for home.

THE NEXT MORNING, I pack quickly and follow the cairns up to Yosemite Point, a smooth lump of granite that looms high enough above the falls to catch the morning's first rays. I bask for a minute to warm my chilly fingers, then continue east along an open ridge affording 360-degree views: On my right is the Valley, 3,000 feet below; to my left, the rounded mountains of the Sierra present a montage of gumdrop-shaped hills of granite. I don't meet another hiker for 4.5 miles, until I come to North Dome, a 7,542-foot promontory and a popular 9-mile dayhike from Tioga Road. A scant six people bask on the rock— a tiny fraction of the numbers you'd encounter on other, shorter dayhikes.

Continuing on, I travel another 6 miles through sun-soaked forest so dry my boots stamp puffs of dust from the trail. The afternoon's heat releases the pines' pleasant fragrance, but by the time I reach Snow Creek and the gravelly bench where I'll camp, salt and grit plaster my skin, so I strip for a bracing bath that's almost as invigorating as the scene from my tent.

Tomorrow, I'll descend into Yosemite Valley with its gridlocked roads and packed parking lots and milling crowds. But tonight, blissfully removed from the traffic, I camp at Snow Creek, a grandstand spot with the best view ever framed by nylon.

Like the moon enlarged 1,000 times, Half Dome fills the sky above me, its circular sweep of granite interrupted by impossible flatness. Its neighbor, Clouds Rest, contrasts Half Dome's massive plane with random bulges and ripples that look like liquid, not stone. I'd expect to be over granite by now, after admiring it all week, but I'm more mesmerized than ever. As the slanting sun turns those monoliths orange, then pink, then an ominous gray, I can't tear my gaze away. Maybe because there's no one else here to bear witness, I watch with the eyes of ten people.

TRIP PLANNER

SEASON May to November

PERMIT Required for overnight stay ($5 per party plus $5 per person); reserve online ahead of time or try for a walk-in at the Yosemite Valley Ranger Station

COMMERCIAL SHUTTLE The free Valley shuttle (operates year-round) will pick you up at the Mirror Lake trailhead and deposit you at Camp 4, from where you'll have a 3-mile walk west back to your car. In summertime you can pick up the El Capitan shuttle (also free) from Camp 4 and ride it to the El Capitan Picnic Area, a short walk from your car at the Old Big Oak Flat Road trailhead.

CONTACT Yosemite National Park, www.nps.gov/yose

DISTANCE: 30.4 miles (point to point)

TIME: 4 days

DIFFICULTY: ★★★✈

THE PAYOFF: Savor Yosemite's icons in solitude when you use a long-forgotten passage to the North Rim.

TRAILHEAD: Old Big Oak Flat Road (37.7239, -119.6450); 9 miles east of the Arch Rock Entrance on Northside Drive

MILES AND DIRECTIONS

FROM THE OLD BIG OAK FLAT ROAD TRAILHEAD:

1. Pick your way west up the now-defunct **Old Big Oak Flat Road Trail** to mile 4.5.
2. Veer north on the **El Capitan Trail,** which traces the North Rim 10.6 miles east to an intersection above Yosemite Falls. (Pass worthy spurs to El Cap's prow and 7,779-foot Eagle Peak en route.)
3. Head south on the **Yosemite Falls Trail** to a junction near mile 15.5.
4. Split east onto the **North Dome Trail,** taking it 11 miles on a high catwalk above the Valley to an intersection near the Snow Creek drainage. (Set aside time to tackle short spurs to Yosemite Falls Overlook, Yosemite Point, North Dome, and Indian Rock, a rare granite arch.)
5. Continue south into Tenaya Canyon on the **Snow Creek Trail** to mile 28.
6. Follow the **Valley Loop Trail** 2.4 miles southwest along Tenaya Creek to the road near the Merced River, where you can pick up the free park shuttle back to your car.

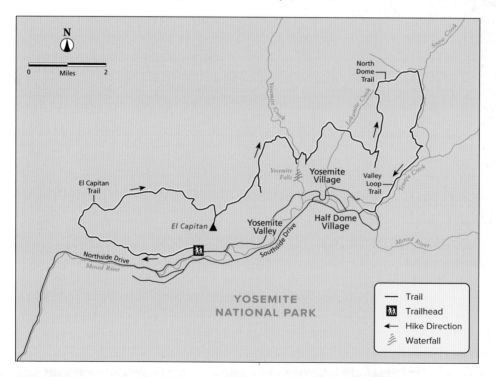

09: LAND OF GIANTS
REDWOOD CANYON,
KINGS CANYON NATIONAL PARK, CALIFORNIA

There aren't many places where you can sleep under the canopy of 2,000-year-old giant sequoias, making this trip into the world's largest such grove life-list material for backpackers of any skill level. Thanks to prescribed burning, the trees in the Redwood Mountain Grove vary widely in size and age—from 30-foot-tall juveniles to ancient behemoths that reach the heavens. And while the area is at least somewhat popular among dayhikers, you'll find surprising solitude when the sun sets: Even in summer, only about sixty people camp in this well-kept-secret corner.

TRIP PLANNER

SEASON May to October

PERMIT Required for overnight stay ($10 per party plus $5 per person); reserve online or obtain from the Kings Canyon Visitor Center

CONTACT Kings Canyon National Park, www.nps.gov/seki

Adapted from text by Elisabeth Kwak-Hefferan and Sarah L. Stewart.

DISTANCE: 6.5 miles (loop)

TIME: 2 days

DIFFICULTY: ★ꓹ

THE PAYOFF: Camp in a quiet redwood grove on an easy-but-underrated loop.

TRAILHEAD: Redwood Saddle (36.7075, -118.9210); 25 miles east of Squaw Valley off FR 14S75

MILES AND DIRECTIONS

FROM THE REDWOOD SADDLE TRAILHEAD:

1. For a shorter first day, do it clockwise: Trek south on the **Redwood Creek Trail,** paralleling the path's namesake 1.9 miles to an intersection.

2. Veer southwest onto the **Sugar Bowl Trail,** climbing 1,500 feet up Redwood Mountain for views of 8,000-foot granite monoliths rising above the treetops before looping north along the ridge back to the trailhead.

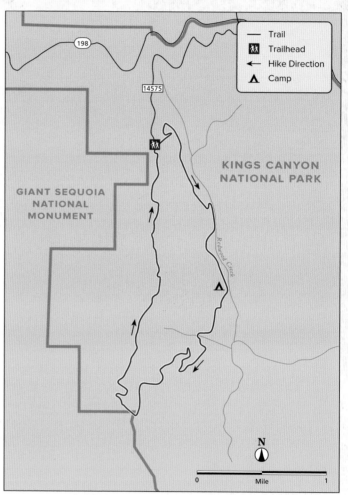

ALL THE EXTRAS

DON'T MISS THIS CAMPSITE: REDWOOD MOUNTAIN GROVE (MILE 1.9)

A dispersed camping policy means you can sleep anywhere you like in the heart of this canyon. But for a campsite with five-star amenities, pick a flat spot dwarfed by the massive conifers near the trail junction at mile 1.9. The tallest trees outrank sky-scrapers, reaching nearly 300 feet (and 20 feet in diameter), and the easy access to Redwood Creek is hard to beat. Set up your tent amid the ferns and thick duff—you won't find a softer bed for tree gazing.

KEEP YOUR EYES PEELED: FLORA

Sky-kissing trees aren't the only plant on the brochure here: Expect a glut of mid-summer lupine blooms in Redwood Canyon. The purple flowers grow calf-high in the shady groves, decorating the canyon's western slopes.

Giant sequoias

10: SPLASHDOWN
SUMMIT LAKES,
LASSEN VOLCANIC NATIONAL PARK, CALIFORNIA

Carved by fire and chiseled by ice, the southern Cascades have the chops to provide a lifetime of alpine highlights—mountain lakes, high meadows, lava fields, pine forests, and cinder cones—in a weekend trip. But more often than not, visitors to the area overlook Lassen in favor of its big-name neighbor, Mt. Shasta, or the northern Sierra highlights, like Tahoe and Yosemite. That leaves this lake-heavy loop for the few who are willing to venture deep into the national park's heart, where nature's long-running geologic drama is still center stage.

TRIP PLANNER

SEASON June to November

PERMIT Required for overnight stay (free); apply online or obtain from any of the ranger stations, the visitor center, or the Loomis Museum

CONTACT Lassen Volcanic National Park, www.nps.gov/lavo

DISTANCE: 19.1 miles (lollipop-loop)

TIME: 2 days

DIFFICULTY: ★★↗

THE PAYOFF: Pass eight lakes on this easy weekend through volcanic high country.

TRAILHEAD: Summit Lake at Dersch Meadows (40.4981, -121.4271); 10 miles east of Manzanita Lake on CA 89

MILES AND DIRECTIONS

FROM THE SUMMIT LAKE TRAILHEAD AT DERSCH MEADOWS:

1. Take the easy-to-find user trail 0.5 mile to Summit Lake.

2. Split east onto the **Summit Lake Trail,** which wends past Echo and Upper Twin Lakes to the start of the loop at mile 4.4.

3. For a shorter first day, do the loop clockwise: Continue on the Summit Lake Trail past Lower Twin and Rainbow Lakes and through a ghostly forest of bleached tree skeletons and charred trunks from a managed 2004 fire to the southwest shore of Snag Lake.

4. Veer south onto the **Snag Lake Trail,** trekking away from the sprawling pool alongside Grassy Creek, to Horseshoe Lake at mile 10.9.

5. Take the northern route around Horseshoe (keeping your head up to see Lassen Peak poking above the pines to the west) to connect with the **Pacific Crest Trail** in roughly 2 miles.

6. Close the loop on the PCT, which undulates through a shady forest back to Lower Twin Lake.

7. Retrace your steps 4.4 miles to the trailhead.

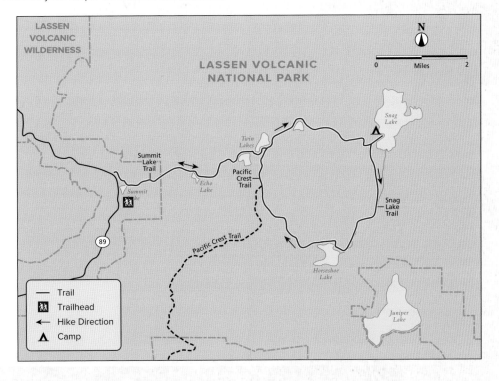

11. PUNISHING PARADISE
LOST COAST, CALIFORNIA

I n Northern California's remote King Range, the peaks rise thousands of feet from the sea along a stretch of coastline so precipitous that engineers rerouted the Pacific Coast Highway inland. Sure, it's hard to get to—but where else can you hit mountains, beach, and redwoods on one trip? Local expert **Paul Sever** dishes his best tips and tricks for tackling the prize of the Golden State. By Shelby Carpenter

THE INSIDER

Completing the Lost Coast Trail once is a badge of honor. Wilderness ranger Paul Sever has hiked it more than 50 times. "For being such a well-known piece of backcountry in California, the Lost Coast remains relatively untouched," he says.

1. THE CLASSIC

The 24.6-mile Lost Coast Trail links Mattole Beach (northern end) to Black Sands Beach (at Shelter Cove); you'll want a shuttle (info below). Plan it so the wind is at your back, and aim for a minus tide so you can explore the tide pools. "Venture out onto the rocks and look for pockets of water to find starfish and anemones," Sever says. Bring a knife to harvest mussels if there isn't a quarantine (check with the California Department of Public Health).

2. GEAR TIP

"Bring a tide chart," Sever stresses. Three sections of the Lost Coast Trail are impassable at high tide (mileage from Mattole): Punta Gorda (mile 2.4), between Sea Lion Gulch (mile 4.7) and Randall Creek (mile 8.8), and between Miller Flat (mile 16.6) and Gitchell Creek (mile 21.4). Begin the tricky sections within two hours after high tide.

3. TOP CAMPSITES

You can camp anywhere on the beach, but the best sites are beside mountain streams that flow into the ocean, which you'll find roughly every 2 miles. Many hikers stop at Randall Creek (mile 8.8 from Mattole), so Sever suggests pushing on to quieter Spanish Flat (mile 9; great for spring flora like lupine and California poppies) or hanging back at Cooksie Creek (mile 6.8; cool rock formations). **Note:** Be prepared to camp earlier than planned if a rising tide could prevent you from crossing one of the coast's narrow stretches.

4. BEST WILDLIFE VIEWING

Whether you're thru-hiking or just hiking part of the Lost Coast, stop off at Sea Lion Gulch (mile 4.7 from Mattole). Sever recommends going in June or July to see newborn sea lions or March or April for baby seals.

5. SECRET FOREST RAMBLE

Many hikers end at Shelter Cove, but the Lost Coast actually extends another 26 miles south in Sinkyone Wilderness State Park. This southern section offers an entirely different experience, as the trail winds up and over coastal bluffs and through old-growth redwood groves, descending only a few times to secluded coves. Explore the 16-mile section between Bear Harbor and Usal Campground for a sampler.

6. EPIC FOR GLUTTONS

Get it all—mountains, beach, *and* redwoods—on this three-day, 20.9-mile loop that tags 4,088-foot King Peak. From the Saddle Mountain trailhead, link the King Crest, Rattlesnake Ridge, Lost Coast, and Buck Creek Trails to create the loop that gains more than 4,000 feet of elevation. Sever recommends camping at Bear Hollow Creek (mile 8.2) on day one in the mountains for easy water access and Buck Creek (mile 16.4) on day two on the beach for wildlife viewing.

7. BEST CAR CAMPGROUND

"Car camping on the beach is a can't-miss California experience," Sever says. Get it at Mattole Beach, and, from there, try a 2.4-mile dayhike to the Punta Gorda Lighthouse. Sites are $8 per night and first-come, first-served.

TRIP PLANNER

SEASON Year-round, but early fall is best to avoid spring rain and summer fog

PERMIT Required for overnight stay (free); self-issue at the trailhead kiosk

COMMERCIAL SHUTTLE Lost Coast Adventures (lostcoastadventures.com) runs hiker drop-offs and pickups. Prices vary.

CONTACT King Range National Conservation Area, bit.do/king-range

Consider 14,410-foot Mt. Rainier (page 50) the crown jewel of the
country's top-left corner. Photo: iStockphoto

PACIFIC
NORTHWEST

12: THE HIGHEST ORDER
NORTH CASCADES NATIONAL PARK, WASHINGTON

By Christopher Solomon

Scott wakes us in the shivery predawn. He's waiting, pack on, unsmiling, ready to set off for the Challenger Glacier, while my toothbrush rattles in my mouth. I've seen this with other guides: They start out fun-loving enough, horsing around on the easy, early stretches of trail. And then, during the night, the martinet murders the joker. This time, though, it's understandable. The last available forecast before we headed into the remote Picket Range, in Washington's North Cascades National Park, promised just two weather-free days to get past these mountains' cruxes before showers turned this place into a lethal Slip-n-Slide. And this is the third day of our five-day adventure.

The Pickets are undeniably dramatic, a quiver of arrow-point peaks fashioned of such dark stone that one half expects to see the flying monkeys of Oz patrolling their gendarmes. The Pickets are also the least-visited section of one of the least visited national parks in the Lower 48. But anyone going in has to think carefully about the range's potentially problematic mix of weather and vertical terrain. A multiday trek through this broken landscape is both committing and hugely difficult—so much so that when I called to inquire about the area, one of the park's climbing rangers tried to scare me off, listing with unnecessary gusto the challenges we'd encounter: yawning glaciers, trailless valleys thick with hypodermic devil's club and slide alder as tight as prison bars, and a 7-mile jawbone of peaks that takes on at least 100 inches of precipitation annually. It wasn't until the 1960s

Photo: Stephen Matera

that pioneers blazed a high route along the west side of the Pickets' spine, and now, perhaps only a dozen or so ultrafit hikers try the 35- to 40-mile traverse each year—and the cautious ones, like us, hedge against the few dicey, technical sections by hiring a guide.

In our case, a guide who's now standing by impatiently while we break camp. "If it rains on you, you're hosed," Scott, 33, a hard-driving outdoorsman who works for a Seattle-area guide firm, had said earlier. "You'll be sidehilling on wet, glacier-polished slabs, and heather, and dirt." For today, at least, speed and efficiency equals safety.

But then, every hurried step toward the dangerously fractured Challenger Glacier and into the Pickets takes us deeper into solitude, and deeper into uh-oh territory if anything goes wrong. Now, striding past 40-foot-long crevasses, I think of General George Pickett, the Civil War Confederate whose name is forever yoked to any ill-considered rush over treacherous ground. Which is more or less what I've asked for with this expedition. I'm a seasoned backpacker who's grown weary of foot-polished trails, and I tend to be goal-oriented. If I set out on a hike, I generally finish. With the Pickets, I understood I was seriously upping the ante. My friends Steve and Adam gamely volunteered to come along.

TWO DAYS EARLIER, the trek toward the Pickets' sharpened fencerow of peaks had started off pleasantly enough. From the trailhead east of Mount Baker, the route climbed amicably, the sun warmed our shoulders, and huckleberries appeared near Hannegan Pass. At lunch, topos came out, and we recited names of the landmarks we'd see in the misty week ahead: Mount Terror. Mount Fury. The Chopping Block. Mount Despair.

"Where's Dead Baby Pass?" Scott deadpanned. We all laughed, like the crowd at a slasher film before the unkillable undead start making house calls. But why not? Our bellies were full of sun-ripe berries and a good trail lay before us. We dropped into Hobbity woods of big hemlocks, made 9 miles easily, and camped next to the Chilliwack River. That night our laughter bounced over the cobbles.

Something changed as soon as we waded across the river the next morning. The abandoned path up to Easy Ridge climbs a sharp 2,500 feet in 2.5 miles. Steve got stung by four bees. Rain fell harder and longer than forecast. Everybody was still goofing, if wet. But I couldn't help feeling that with the Chilliwack ford, we had crossed some Rubicon.

After gaining Easy Ridge and walking for a few hours along a cloud-shrouded ridgeline, we reached the first of several obstacles: Imperfect Impasse, a giant axe-cleft in the mountainside. Some climbers try to weave their way across on sketchy ledges, betting against a cartwheel into the void. Scott reconnoitered that idea and nixed it. Instead, we dropped several hundred feet downhill to where the Impasse broadens, then scrambled up the opposite slope, using vegetation belays and even the rope once, when the gully turned manky.

Ten hours and 6,200 feet of uphill after breaking camp, I slumped to the ground on a high col, thighs cooked at a spot called Perfect Pass. Fifty feet from the tents, the earth plunges twelve stories to the magnificently shattered Challenger Glacier, one of the Cascades' larger chunks of ice. The storm blew out. We drank cups of hot tea and chuckled over the day's funniest happening as the pink dusk morphed to purple.

AND NOW, AS THE SUN RISES, Scott is rousing us, infusing urgency. The mountains reflect his mood. Scrambling up the rocky edge of 8,248-foot Mount Challenger, the Pickets' northernmost peak, we spy bits of pipe, pieces of a zipper, a burn mark on a rock face: vestiges of a rescue helicopter that crashed here in 1980, killing five men. The setting moon is as white as a bleached skull. At the Challenger Glacier, crampons go on, and harnesses and rope. We snake upward in silence, pop over a saddle, and steal into the heart of the range.

We choose an L-shaped route through these massive granite amphitheaters, across cirques of talus that have yet to fully settle. When a piece of rock slides loose underfoot and crashes downhill, setting off sparks, the air smells of gunfire. We move fast but also with focus, because a single misstep among 10,000 will spell disaster—a torqued ankle, a shredded ACL. Eyes glued to feet, we pick our way down a steep face, cross two more glaciers, then move across two major cirques of restless stone. We set up tents at Picket-Goodell Pass.

Here there's finally a chance to lift our heads and see what our sweat has bought us. It's pretty grand. Even in sunshine, the west peak of 8,288-foot Mount Fury glowers, as drippy and freeform as a Gaudi cathedral. To the south, the Southern Pickets surge 6,000 feet up, looking black and menacing and impossibly crimped. And look—here's the sandy footprint of an anonymous mountaineer, already being dismantled by the afternoon breeze. No wonder some who love the Pickets are always lobbying to leave the range out of guidebooks. A hiker here can still feel like the first person who's ever found the place.

We sprawl in warm heather, toes in the dirt, feasting on turkey jerky and views and silence, and the feeling of being high up in the mountains under soothing sun. Only Scott paces the next ridge, scrambling up and down, scouting, ruminating.

THE NEXT MORNING BEFORE SUNRISE, we pick our way along narrow cliff bands. We only have to go 6 miles today, but we need to plunge into and cross the Goodell Creek drainage, ascend to Picket Pass, slither into adjoining McMillan Cirque, then dodge a rock fin called The Barricade as well as the Southern Pickets' hanging glaciers—all to get out of the range's most treacherous area before rain falls. Behind us, the horizon is milking over like a cataracted eye.

The steep heather steps disappear, replaced by twisty cedars that require limbo moves to negotiate. Once, at a tricky spot, Scott sets up a rope belay as a hedge against a slip. It seems unlikely, for the most part, that a fall itself would kill. But a fall followed by two or three rolls might end in an unintended cliff dive. Five hundred feet and two cliff bands later we're in the cirque, looking thankful for a bit of good balance and chutzpah. Then the whole process repeats in reverse, as we scramble, scuffed and heaving, up toward Picket Pass.

At treeline, Scott goes to check on a gully above that splits the cirque—the last obstacle before Picket Pass, and allegedly the platform for the trip's best views. We sit on talus, eating and joking, ahead of schedule.

When Scott returns, his mouth is a hyphen. In August, in this low-snow year, the plug of snow that makes the gully-crossing a cakewalk is missing. Without it, the ledge is "low fifth-class climbing—wet, with kitty litter sprinkled on it, above a 50-footer." A 50-foot drop, that is. We jump up and look for other options. There are none. We're done, Scott says.

"But . . ." I say, my competitive instincts kicking into overdrive.

The guide holds his palm out like a traffic cop. And just like that, this Pickets Charge is over. Silence falls—the silence of disappointment. Then it's the silence of four minds recalibrating our situation. The quest is over. Now it's all about finding a way out.

Which way to bail? The shortest distance to a cheeseburger is 10 miles down Goodell Creek, below us. One Pickets veteran's advice bellows in my head: Never retreat into a side valley. But none of us has the stomach, or the moleskin, to march back the way we came, when the North Cascades Highway lies tantalizingly close, and downhill to boot. After a quick discussion of our limited options, we reach a consensus: We'll drop into the jungle.

THE HARDSHIP OF THE NEXT DAY AND A HALF IS EXQUISITE. The slide alders greet us at the valley floor. They grab at packs and ice axes, toss us to the ground, grind progress to a quarter of a mile an hour. To rise above the groves of devil's club, we try to walk on massive fallen cedars, only to punch through rotting logs, the falls leaving us clutching at stinging nettles. Adam's forearms look like he's lost a steel-cage match with a saguaro. When things get much worse, Steve spots fresh bear tracks. Still, we bushwhack a respectable 5 miles by dinnertime, toss tents up on a bouldery streambed, pick out the biggest shrapnel, and fall into deep, bear-less dreams.

The next morning, Scott is a bloodhound at finding scraps of game trails. An abandoned logging road takes us the last 2 miles out. Seven bee stings, three blackened toenails, fourteen blisters, three savaged pairs of pants, and several trashed trekking poles later, we're drinking cold beer by the roadside, waiting to be delivered to red meat. There's plenty of time to pluck at thorns and think. Success is well and good, but when it comes to roaring campfire tales, victory can't hold a candle to epic failure. Only now does my goal-oriented brain begin to register that there's more to this than finishing. Rather than a one-time conquest, the Pickets might just be a work in progress.

In fact, Adam and Steve are already looking at the map, talking about other routes through the Pickets, talking about next summer. I take a long draw off my beer. I look at my bloated, bloodied feet. I look at my friends. Then I look at the map, too.

⇇ — ⟫ DO IT ⟪ — ⇉

DISTANCE: 27 miles (out and back)

TIME: 2 days

DIFFICULTY: ★★★★★

THE PAYOFF: Get a taste of Washington's toughest range—including the postcard scenery—without venturing into technical terrain.

TRAILHEAD: Hannegan Pass (48.9101, -121.5922); 54 miles east of Bellingham on FR 32

MILES AND DIRECTIONS

FROM THE HANNEGAN PASS TRAILHEAD:

1. Take the **Hannegan Pass Trail** 4.9 miles east over its namesake to a fork.
2. Veer southeast onto the **Chilliwack River Trail** and continue 5.4 miles to the river crossing.
3. Wade across the Chilliwack River and find the social path.
4. Head up Easy Ridge, going south. Camp (after landing one of four permits) anywhere that suits between mile 11.7 and 13.5 or so.
5. Retrace your steps to the trailhead.

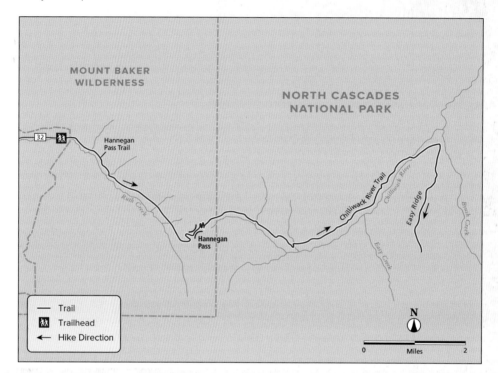

TRIP PLANNER

SEASON Late July to October

PERMIT Required for overnight stay (free); reserve at pay.gov or gun for a walk-in

GUIDE Only experienced mountaineers should continue beyond Easy Ridge unguided; the terrain is technical and requires savvy routefinding. To do it guided, inquire at Pro Guiding Service (proguiding.com). Prices vary.

CONTACT North Cascades National Park, www.nps.gov/noca

13: EMERALD CITY
QUEETS RIVER, OLYMPIC NATIONAL PARK, WASHINGTON

Like a moat around a castle, the 50-foot-wide, often-roiling Queets River guards one of Olympic's most spectacular old-growth rainforests. And because the nearby Hoh Rainforest offers similarly looming trees without the river crossing, it draws the neck-craners, saving the primordial Queets Valley for those willing to brave the trailhead ford. And what a ford it can be: Most of the time, rain and snowmelt feed an impassable torrent. But by late summer, levels usually dip to knee or waist height. If the flow is below 800 cfs and there's no rain in the forecast, wade across to the far bank, where miles of silent singletrack under ancient Douglas fir, Sitka spruce, and hemlock of Jurassic proportions await.

TRIP PLANNER

SEASON August to October

PERMIT Required for overnight stay ($5 per party plus $2 per person per night); obtain at the Wilderness Information Center in Port Angeles or at the South Shore Lake Quinault Ranger Station

CONTACT Olympic National Park, www.nps.gov/olym

DISTANCE: 32.4 miles (out and back)

TIME: 2 to 4 days

DIFFICULTY: ★★★↙

THE PAYOFF: An undiscovered rainforest awaits on the other side of a surging river.

TRAILHEAD: Sams Rapids (47.6240, -124.0156); 25 miles north of Quinault on FR 030/Upper Queets Road

MILES AND DIRECTIONS

FROM THE SAMS RAPIDS TRAILHEAD:

1. If conditions allow, ford the Sams and Queets Rivers east. (Find the slowest, shallowest section downstream of hazards, unbuckle your pack straps, and use a trekking pole or walking stick for stability.)

2. Continue east on the **Queets River Trail,** which parallels its namesake 16.2 miles to its terminus near the confluence with Alta Creek.

3. Retrace your steps to the trailhead.

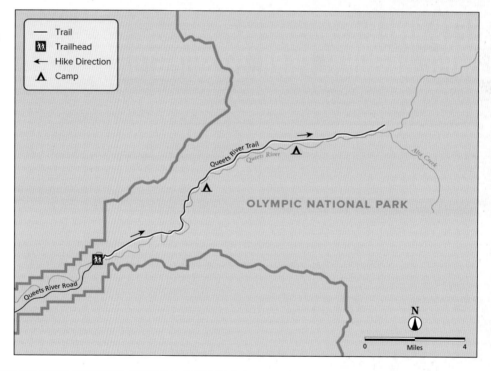

DON'T MISS THIS CAMPSITE: GRAVEL BAR (MILES 5.4 TO 11.6)

Camping is only allowed at Spruce Bottom (5.4 miles in), Bob Creek (11.6 miles in)—and at any gravel bar of your choosing. The flexibility of option C is hard to beat, so embrace your freedom and settle on whichever low-impact patch of soil suits you. You'll appreciate the easy access to the Queets, where five species of Pacific salmon—including steelhead—spawn. In the morning, take inventory of which animals left tracks.

14: MIDDLE OF NOWHERE
WEST LITTLE OWYHEE CANYON, OWYHEE CANYONLANDS, OREGON

By Elisabeth Kwak-Hefferan

Photo: Eli Cirino

When I finally crest the canyon rim, there's still nothing and nobody around. I didn't see a soul all six days of my trip. I didn't even see any sign people were ever here—hard to believe, given how the oh-wow moments piled up. There was the perfect campsite I found—a wide, sandy riverside beach with a killer view of the stars. Or the stretch of narrows I reached, where the canyon's wavy sides lean in to only 40 feet across. I rounded riverbends to discover grand rock amphitheaters and watched the canyon walls rise to 400 feet in spots. As I unlace my boots, I wonder if the new Oregon Desert Trail—or, let's be honest, this story—will let this cat out of the bag. I don't know. But I bet not. The West Little Owyhee Canyon is still too remote, too intense, too well-guarded by tire-popping access roads to attract the crowds. The river crossings that require swimming and the bushwhacking through spiky willows and wild roses will still be deal-breakers for most hikers. But this canyon will remain lonely for the few souls who will put up with all of that in search of a few days of solitude. You know who you are.

TRIP PLANNER

SEASON April to June and September to October

PERMIT None

CONTACT Oregon Natural Desert Association, onda.org

DISTANCE: 46 miles (point to point)

TIME: 5 to 7 days

DIFFICULTY: ★★★★★

THE PAYOFF: Steep climbs, long miles, and challenging terrain scare others away, leaving beach campsites, canyon narrows, and grand amphitheaters for adventure-seekers.

TRAILHEAD: Anderson Crossing (42.1307, -117.3159); 75 miles southeast of Burns Junction off Pole Creek Road

SHUTTLE CAR Three Forks (42.5446, -117.1619); 35 miles south of Jordan Valley on Fenwick Ranch Road

MILES AND DIRECTIONS

FROM THE ANDERSON CROSSING TRAILHEAD:

1. Pick up the true **Continental Divide Trail** and follow it 3.1 miles northbound along the ridgeline that separates Idaho and Montana. (The Salmon National Forest falls off to the west and the Beaverhead National Forest to the east.)

2. Instead of following the official CDT east off the divide (where it eventually traces the Jahnke Creek drainage east), stay high: Pick a path of least resistance along America's spine to mile 6 or so.

3. Above Skytop Lake, peel east off the Divide. Expect class 3+ climbing as you negotiate the scree to the Pioneer Lake basin near mile 7.2.

4. Find the official **Pioneer Creek Trail,** which wends 3.9 miles down the wooded drainage to reconnect with the CDT at mile 11.1.

5. Proceed northeast on the CDT 1.5 miles to where it splits north on singletrack. Instead of continuing northbound, follow the Jeep track 3.2 miles to your shuttle car at Van Houten Lake.

DON'T MISS THIS CAMPSITE: CANYON BEACHES (MILES 11 TO 14)

Every twist in this canyon brings a new shrub-shaded throne or sandy beach campsite. If you want warm sand between your toes, plan to stop in the straightaway section between miles 11 and 14, where the beach campsites roll out like a parade, each better than the last.

GEAR TIP: PACK FOR WATER

In addition to quick-dry clothes and sturdy water shoes, you will need trekking poles or a hefty walking stick. They save your knees and you can use them to probe in the water for safe footing.

N

0 Miles 10

OREGON
IDAHO

OWYHEE
RIVER CANYON
WILDERNESS
STUDY AREA

Continental
Divide Trail

─── Trail
🚶 Trailhead
← Hike Direction
▲ Camp

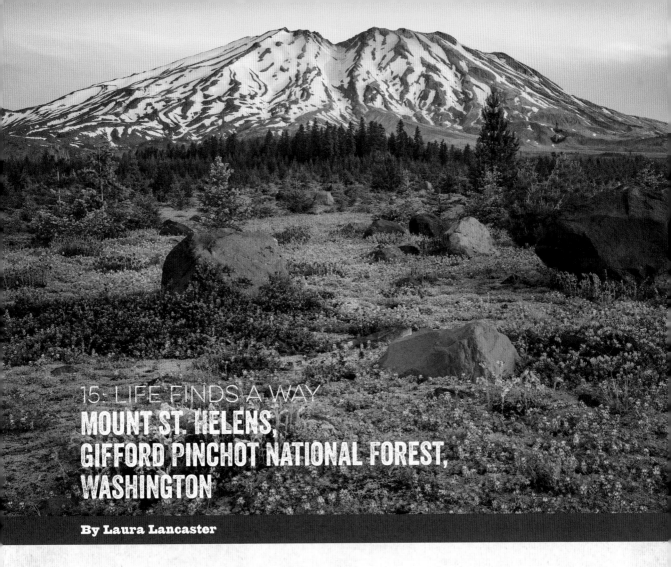

15: LIFE FINDS A WAY
MOUNT ST. HELENS, GIFFORD PINCHOT NATIONAL FOREST, WASHINGTON

By Laura Lancaster

From the top of Windy Ridge, it looks as if Mount St. Helens erupted yesterday. You can still see the steaming, gray wound on the side of the now-peakless mountain. Below, Spirit Lake is half hidden by a logjam built from the white ghosts of a long-dead forest. But the trek across the eastern slopes, which were wiped clean by the surge of rock and volcanic gas in 1980, reveals small signs of life hidden among the devastation, like smears of lichen and lupine. We leave the scorched earth behind for more signs of renewal: Knee-high pine saplings carpet the south side of the ridge, and, by the time the trail hits Smith Creek, the trees are 20 feet tall. Shiny new forest, in the blink of an eye.

DISTANCE: 22.8 miles (loop)

TIME: 3 days

DIFFICULTY: ★★↙

THE PAYOFF: Meander through the blast zone to see a forest reborn at the foot of Mount St. Helens.

TRAILHEAD: Ape Canyon (46.1654, -122.0922); 46 miles east of Woodland on FR 83

MILES AND DIRECTIONS

FROM THE APE CANYON TRAILHEAD:

1. Follow the **Ape Canyon Trail (#234)** 4.5 miles northwest up the forested flank of Mount St. Helens to the barren cinder plateau.

2. Turn north onto the **Loowit Trail (#216)** and take it 1.7 miles through the Plains of Abraham and into the heart of the blast zone to an intersection.

3. Stay north on the **Abraham Trail (#216D)** and hike 2 miles to its terminus at the **Truman Trail (#207)**.

4. Take the Truman Trail north to the parking lot at the Windy Ridge Interpretive Site at mile 10.

5. Continue clockwise, linking the **Windy Ridge (#227)** and **Smith Creek (#225) Trails** for 10.1 miles through new- and old-growth forest and past sporadic long-range views of the volcano to the Muddy River.

6. Veer west onto the **Lava Canyon Trail (#184)** and go 1.5 miles through the chasm to the Lava Canyon Interpretive Site parking area at mile 22.6.

7. Walk 0.2 mile west on FR 83 back to the trailhead.

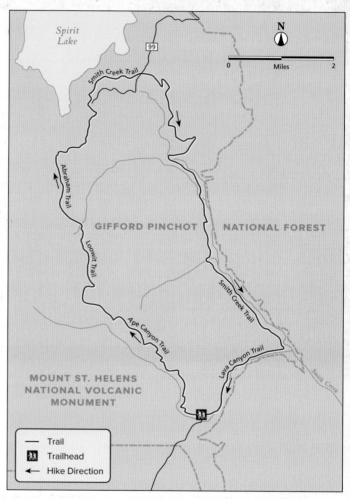

TRIP PLANNER

SEASON June to October

PERMIT Required for overnight stay (free); self-issue at trailhead kiosk

CONTACT Gifford Pinchot National Forest, www.fs.usda.gov/giffordpinchot

16: OCEAN AVENUE
OREGON DUNES, OREGON DUNES NATIONAL RECREATION AREA, OREGON

Most people will flock to the Olympic Peninsula in Washington in search of easy-access beach hikes. That's OK—good, even. Farther south, the quieter Oregon coast serves up prime seaside tent real estate without the crowds or permit hassles. And frankly, you won't know the difference when you're savoring a nylon-framed view of sea stacks looming in the fog-shrouded surf. This is a case when Plan B might actually outrank Plan A.

TRIP PLANNER

SEASON May to October

PERMIT None

CONTACT Siuslaw National Forest, www.fs.usda.gov/siuslaw

DISTANCE: 6.2 miles (lollipop-loop)

TIME: 2 days

DIFFICULTY: ★↗

THE PAYOFF: Evade national park crowds and beach-camp in the underrated Oregon Dunes.

TRAILHEAD: Tahkenitch (43.7952, -124.1495); 12 miles south of Florence off US 101

MILES AND DIRECTIONS

FROM THE TAHKENITCH TRAILHEAD:

1. Follow the main footpath 0.2 mile south to an intersection.

2. For a shorter first day, tackle the loop counterclockwise: Proceed north on the **Tahkenitch Dunes Trail,** which meanders 1.1 miles through stands of shore pine to an intersection.

3. Split south onto the **Tahkenitch Creek Trail,** paralleling its freshwater namesake 0.5 mile to where it spills into the Pacific Ocean.

4. Follow the ocean 1.3 miles south.

5. Loop 2.9 miles back to the original junction on the **Threemile Lake Trail.**

6. Retrace your steps to the trailhead.

DON'T MISS THIS CAMPSITE: CATARACT VALLEY CAMP (MILE 5.6)

Bed down in an electric-green understory beneath a canopy of western red cedars at this quiet, seven-site camp. Despite its name, you won't get waterfall views, but nearby salmonberries fruit in July and a stream makes water duty easy.

DON'T MISS THIS CAMSITE: IPSUT CREEK CAMP (MILE 11.4)

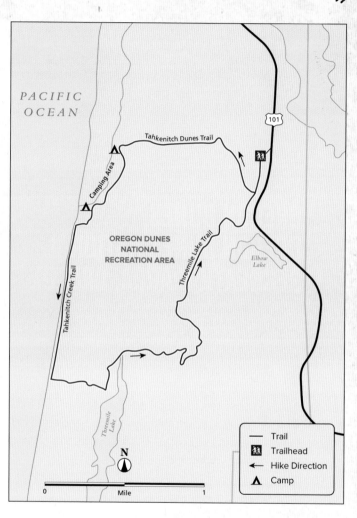

This temperate rainforest site on the ice-blue Carbon River was a car campground before a monster storm washed out the 5-mile access road. Without traffic, it's now a mellower destination for backpackers looking to linger another night on this loop.

ALL THE EXTRAS

DON'T MISS THIS CAMPSITE: TAHKENITCH CREEK (MILES 1.5 TO 2)

Set up your tent in prime, surfy solitude above the high-tide line anywhere near where the stream flows into the Pacific. The nylon-framed view to the ocean is hard to beat if you score clear weather, but even if you miss a fog-free window, don't fret: There's something dreamy about the way the mist mingles with the conifers and dunes, too. And you'll just have to come back.

KEEP YOUR EYES PEELED: WILDLIFE

Threatened western snowy plovers nest and roost in the Oregon Dunes most of the year (which is why this slice of the recreation area is closed to OHVs). Look for the small shorebirds skittering across the beach and, if you're lucky, spy the cotton ball-like chicks. Scan for mammal prints from black bears, elk, deer, and foxes in the soft sand; watch for the animals that produced the prints lurking in the forested dunes a bit back of the water.

GEAR TIP: PACK CORD AND STUFF SACKS

Best bet for pitching a tent on sand: Ditch tent stakes in favor of deadman anchors. To do it, tie cord to each of your tent's stake-out points. Lash the other end of each cord around a sand-filled stuff sack and bury the "deadman" at least a foot below the surface.

Western snowy plover

MOTHER MOUNTAIN, MOUNT RAINIER NATIONAL PARK, WASHINGTON

By Elisabeth Kwak-Hefferan

Call it the face that launched a thousand trips: The view of Mount Rainier's northwestern façade from Spray Park, where overflowing lupine and paintbrush blooms jostle each other to get into the frame, may just make for the most memorable photo op in the park. There's just one problem on my trip here—I can't actually see the peak. On this summer morning, chilled mist swirls among the wildflowers, blotting out the postcard view. But I don't mind: The fog lends an otherworldly vibe to the scene and keeps fair-weather hikers away, giving me a rare chance to savor the colorful meadow in solitude. Besides, as I'll be reminded over and over again on this loop around underappreciated 6,375-foot Mother Mountain, you don't have to see the bigger one to feel its power.

TRIP PLANNER

SEASON July to October

PERMIT Required for overnight stay ($20 for reservations, free for walk-ins); fill out a reservation request form online or obtain a walk-in from any ranger station.

CONTACT Mount Rainier National Park, www.nps.gov/mora

DISTANCE: 16.5 miles (loop)

TIME: 3 days

DIFFICULTY: ★★

THE PAYOFF: Think "Rainier," and "Mother Mountain" probably doesn't come to mind, but that just means you won't have to win a permit lottery, throw elbows for campsites—or share the views.

TRAILHEAD: Mowich Lake Campground (46.9325, -121.8633); 6 miles east of the Mowich Entrance on Mowich Lake Road

MILES AND DIRECTIONS

FROM MOWICH LAKE CAMPGROUND:

1. Take the **Wonderland Trail** 0.2 mile southeast.

2. Pick up the **Spray Park Trail** and take it 7.5 miles through blossom-filled subalpine meadows to a fork at mile 7.7. (Don't miss the view of 350-foot Spray Falls, a fireworks blast of a cascade, near mile 2.)

3. Follow the rerouted **Wonderland Trail** (a 2006 flood washed out the original) 3.3 miles along the roiling Carbon River to an intersection.

4. Veer 0.4 mile north to Ipsut Creek Camp.

5. Back at the junction, turn southwest to continue 4.7 miles on the Wonderland Trail (where it merges with the Ipsut Creek Trail), climbing over 5,100-foot Ipsut Pass and dropping down to the west shore of Mowich Lake and the trailhead.

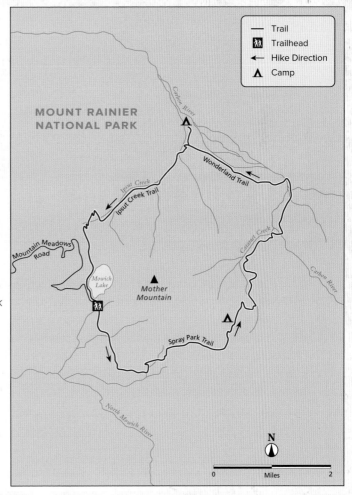

——	Trail
🚶	Trailhead
←	Hike Direction
▲	Camp

MOUNT RAINIER NATIONAL PARK

Carbon River

Wonderland Trail

Ipsut Creek Trail

Ipsut Creek

Cataract Creek

Carbon River

Mountain Meadows Road

Mowich Lake

Mother Mountain

Spray Park Trail

North Mowich River

N

0   Miles   2

18: GOOD AS NEW
ROGUE RIVER,
WILD ROGUE WILDERNESS, OREGON

By Laura Lancaster

It's late afternoon when I finally catch sight of the Rogue River—a quick glance between the peeling bark of the madrones. A wildfire roared through here a decade ago, so I thought open vistas on the recently restored Wild Rogue Loop would be plentiful. But between the dense Pacific Northwest mist and the rebounding forest, I haven't had much in the way of views. When the canopy eventually opens atop Panther Ridge, I can just barely make out the river twisting through the cloud-shrouded ravine 3,500 feet below. It's as if nothing ever changed.

TRIP PLANNER

SEASON April to November

PERMIT None

CONTACTS Rogue River-Siskiyou National Forest, www.fs.usda.gov/rogue-siskiyou & Rogue National Wild and Scenic River, bit.do/rogue-river-blm

DISTANCE: 28.1 miles (loop)

TIME: 3 days

DIFFICULTY: ★★★

THE PAYOFF: Explore the best and least visited gorges and virgin old-growth forests in the Wild Rogue Wilderness on this renovated route.

TRAILHEAD: Mule Creek (42.7221, -123.8773); 36 miles west of Glendale on Mule Creek-Marial Road

MILES AND DIRECTIONS

FROM THE MULE CREEK TRAILHEAD:

1. Do the loop counterclockwise and head 7.1 miles on the **Mule Creek Trail** through a narrow gorge and around to a dirt road on Panther Ridge.

2. Turn south and take the road 0.1 mile to the Buck Point trailhead.

3. Take the **Panther Ridge Trail** 6.4 miles southwest through primeval forests to an intersection.

4. Veer southeast onto the **Clay Hill Trail** and steeply descend 3.4 miles to the rapids of the Rogue River at mile 17.

5. Parallel the water downstream on the **Rogue River Trail** to the Marial trailhead at mile 26.3.

6. Follow the dirt road 1.8 miles to close the loop at the Mule Creek trailhead.

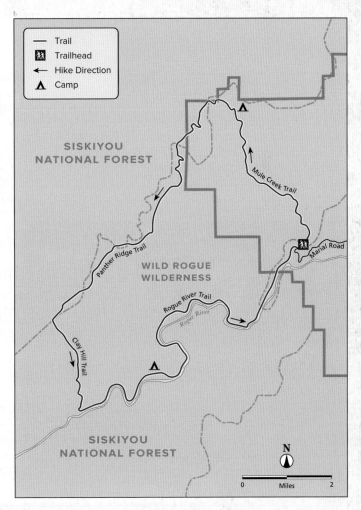

ALL THE EXTRAS

DON'T MISS THIS CAMPSITE: MULE CREEK (MILE 5.2)

Knock out the majority of the climbing on day one, then take a pit stop for the night at this flat spot near the offshoot of Mule Creek (look for it trailside upon exiting the canyon). Be sure to replenish your water supply before you take off the next morning: there's no more until you hit the Rogue at mile 17.

DON'T MISS THIS CAMPSITE: TATE CREEK (MILE 17.6)

Skip the first sites on the Rogue River Trail (where most folks will throw down) and continue to the spot just past Tate Creek. From camp, follow the short spur upstream to a deep pool at the end of a rock chute that doubles as a waterslide.

EXTRA CREDIT: ADD A HIKE

Panther Ridge is densely forested, but a unique outcropping—called Hanging Rock—near the high point of the trail provides a view of the Rogue River Valley. To reach it, look for an unmarked, 0.3-mile spur at mile 8.7.

Bleeding hearts

19: ABOVE IT ALL
SAHALE GLACIER CAMP, NORTH CASCADES NATIONAL PARK, WASHINGTON

You're not on top of the world when you reach this rock-protected site at 7,600 feet, but you'll think you are. Blame the views, which are crowded with mountains the way the night sky is crowded with stars. Or maybe it's the thundering crashes coming from the large towers of ice that drop from glaciers below you. Or maybe it's because you're sleeping on the edge of Sahale Glacier, which offers hours of adventures for those with crampons, ice axes, and ropes (and experience). Put it all together and you'll come to the conclusion: Modest elevation be damned, this is high-alpine camping at its finest.

TRIP PLANNER

SEASON July to October

PERMIT Required for overnight stay (free); obtain from the information center

CONTACT North Cascades National Park, www.nps.gov/noca

Adapted from text by Graham Averill.

DISTANCE: 11 miles (out and back)

TIME: 2 days

DIFFICULTY: ★★★★

THE PAYOFF: More than 4,200 feet of climbing keep the pikers away, leaving the unbroken skyline of the Cascades (and one of the best campsites in the entire National Park System) for the stout-legged.

TRAILHEAD: Cascade Pass (48.4754, -121.0751); 24 miles east of Marblemount on Cascade River Road

⟵————————————————————————————————⟶

MILES AND DIRECTIONS

FROM THE CASCADE PASS TRAILHEAD:

1. Switchback up the western slope of 8,681-foot Sahale Mountain on the **Cascade Pass Trail** to the saddle near mile 3.4.

2. Veer north onto the **Sahale Arm Trail,** which continues ascending talus and alpine meadows to its terminus at the Sahale Glacier at mile 5.5.

3. Retrace your steps to the trailhead.

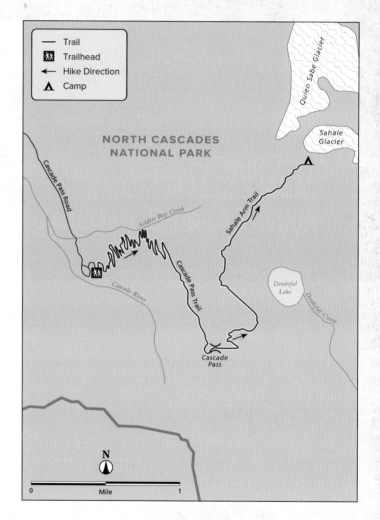

ALL THE EXTRAS

DON'T MISS THIS CAMPSITE: SAHALE GLACIER CAMP (MILE 5.5)

Nab one of the sites at the edge of the moraine—and make sure you pack an extra memory card. The wind-sheltered flat spots terrace across the slope, offering vantages south and east to a parade of name-brand peaks, like Mount Formidable and Mount Storm King. Below, the scree drops off 2,000 feet to Doubtful Lake, a Caribbean-blue alpine tarn.

KEEP YOUR EYES PEELED: FLORA

Yellow glacier lilies, pink mountain heather, purple lupine, and red Indian paintbrush cloak Sahale Arm in summer. In fall, enjoy trailside blueberries.

Lupine on Sahale Arm

20: LONELY CANYON
JOSEPH CANYON,
WALLOWA-WHITMAN NATIONAL FOREST, OREGON

By Patrice La Vigne

Instead of blazes, we follow paw prints. Some are solidified in the soil like concrete, while others are so fresh it sends a chill up my spine. Most people who adventure in the Wallowas head up to the 9,000-footers—they don't come here, to the bottom of rough and rugged Joseph Canyon. That lack of humans is almost certainly why this basalt canyon doubles as an animal highway—we follow scat piles and bear, deer, and even mountain lion prints all the way to camp. When we get there, a surprised black bear lumbers up the hillside and out of sight. There may not be any people here, but no doubt we'll be sharing this riverine camp with a warm-blooded visitor or two.

> ## TRIP PLANNER
>
> **SEASON** April to November
>
> **PERMIT** None
>
> **CONTACT** Wallowa-Whitman National Forest, www.fs.usda.gov/wallowa-whitman

DISTANCE: 15.8 miles (lollipop-loop)

TIME: 2 days

DIFFICULTY: ★★★

THE PAYOFF: While more than 150,000 people visit 2.3-million-acre Wallowa-Whitman National Forest each year, fewer than 1 percent of them head into Joseph Canyon. Best part: It isn't even hard to get to. Find this wildlife mecca just off OR 3—no dirt roads required.

TRAILHEAD: Chico (45.7137, -117.2713); 21 miles north of Enterprise off OR 3

MILES AND DIRECTIONS

FROM THE CHICO TRAILHEAD:

1. Head 3.6 miles east on the **Chico Trail (#1658),** over Starvation Ridge and down to a junction at Swamp Creek.

2. Ford the creek (can be shin-deep) before picking up the **Swamp Creek Trail (#1678);** follow it 4.8 miles north to the confluence of Davis and Swamp Creeks.

3. Locate the unmarked **Davis Creek Trail (#1660)** on the embankment and take it 6.2 miles south to a fork.

4. Veer west onto the **Chico Trail** and retrace your steps 1.2 miles to the trailhead.

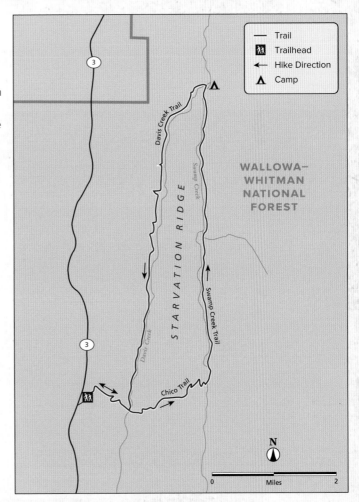

Legend:
— Trail
🧍 Trailhead
← Hike Direction
▲ Camp

WALLOWA-WHITMAN NATIONAL FOREST

STARVATION RIDGE

Davis Creek Trail
Swamp Creek
Swamp Creek Trail
Davis Creek
Chico Trail

N

0 — Miles — 2

ALL THE EXTRAS

DON'T MISS THIS CAMPSITE: CONFLUENCE OF SWAMP AND DAVIS CREEKS (MILE 8.4)

Bed down in a meadow so plush you can ditch the sleeping pad on the other side of Swamp Creek (rock-hop across). There are a bunch of flat spots that back up to ponderosa pines so you can have unobstructed tent-door views down the basalt canyon.

KEEP YOUR EYES PEELED: WILDLIFE

Explore the meadows at twilight for the best chance of viewing black bears, moose, deer (white-tailed and mule), and elk. Coyotes, mountain lions, mountain goats, and eagles are more elusive, but scan the canyon walls for these critters. Most of the animals here are most active come fall.

Black bear

21: GO GREEN
COLUMBIA RIVER GORGE, OREGON AND WASHINGTON

Pacific Northwesterners cherish this wilderness mecca, with its vibrant greenery, roaring waterfalls, and bird's-eye summit views. But many hikers have stayed away since the Eagle Creek fire tore up nearly 49,000 acres of the Gorge in 2017. Bad decision. Enjoy the best of the National Scenic Area—and avoid the fire damage—with these tips and trips from local expert **Ryan Ojerio**. By Ryan Wichelns

THE INSIDER

It's Ryan Ojerio's job to know the trails in the Columbia River Gorge. As the Southwest Washington Regional Manager for the Washington Trails Association, the Portland native has managed the maintenance and construction of local paths and led advocacy, outreach, and education in the area for the last decade.

1. BEST DAYHIKE

"If I could teleport somewhere, I'd choose Table Mountain," Ojerio says, which should tell you a bit about the views from the 3,417-foot summit—and how hard the peak is to get to. The 7.2-mile approach includes crossing various creeks, negotiating boulderfields, and, of course, climbing up and around Table's iconic south face: a sheer, 800-foot-tall plate of basalt. To do it, start from the Bonneville trailhead and hike .6 mile to meet up with the Pacific Crest Trail. Follow the PCT through a mix of dense rainforest and new growth timber to the summit spur near mile 6. There, ascend 1.2 miles up the spine—it gains 1,700 feet—to the crow's nest-like perch. Spot 12,280-foot Mt. Adams to the north and Mt. Hood's pyramid to the south before scanning over the Columbia River to spy the steel bridge connecting Cascade Locks and Stevenson. It marks where, between 1200 and 1600 AD, a major landslide sheared off the south slope of Table Mountain, sending it into the river and creating a natural land bridge (since washed away) that the native Klickitats referred to as the "Bridge of the Gods."

2. BEST PAYOFF

No matter where you end up in the Gorge, Beacon Rock is hard to miss. The 848-foot-tall volcanic plug—where Lewis and Clark first measured the tides of the river—stands like a stone sentinel over the Columbia. It's a popular, mile-long Stairmaster climb to the top, but you can lengthen the approach (and add solitude) with Ojerio's spin on the classic: Instead of starting at the Beacon Rock trailhead, begin farther south on the underrated River-to-Rock Trail. The mile-long path contours north from the Columbia to the Beacon Rock Trail, wending beneath 100-foot-tall Douglas firs and past Ridell Lake along the way. "It extends the hike and adds a little more diversity than just going straight up the rock," Ojerio says.

3. TOP OVERNIGHT

With most of the Oregon side of the Gorge off-limits between Angel's Rest and Starvation Falls because of fire damage, you'll need to venture higher to find trails long enough to service a multiday adventure. Think of it as a blessing because the views are bigger and the trails emptier. Ojerio's favorite trip: the 13.8-mile lollipop-loop tracing Mt. Hood's eastern skyline from Polallie Creek. Highlights include a flower-studded meadow campsite and a rocky ridge with wide-open scenery. From the trailhead (25 minutes south of Hood River) on OR 35, take the East Fork Trail to link up with the Elk Meadows Trail, which twists through stands of skyscraping pines en route to its grassy namesake at mile 6.3. Tent in the trees on the edge of a field of summer wildflowers like purple tundra aster in the shadow of 11,250-foot Mt. Hood before veering onto the Bluegrass Ridge Trail, where an old burn zone offers straight-shot views to the toothy skyline. Join back up with the Elk Meadows Trail at mile 11.5 and head back to your car.

4. BEAT THE RAIN

Escape to the eastern side of the Gorge when the forecast calls for rain. There, on the other side of the Cascades, rainforests and mountains give way to the high desert of Coyote Wall. Check it out on the 7.7-mile Labyrinth Loop, which leads past grassy plateaus, rock outcroppings, and mini canyons. "It's like a different planet," Ojerio says. From the Coyote Wall trailhead, take the Labyrinth Trail uphill through oaks to river views before looping back on the Atwood Road Trail and a series of dirt roads.

5. DAMAGE CONTROL

The Oregon side of the Columbia River was ravaged by September 2017's fire, but the Washington side remained largely untouched. That makes the latter your best bet for finding a riverside hike—and the best view across the river to the damage. Satisfy your curiosity on the 8.3-mile Cape Horn Loop, which offers plenty of cross-river views as it circles through stands of maple and oak and meadows of purple delphinium (blooming in May and June). When the viewshed opens, look across the Columbia to identify Angel's Rest, the popular Oregon overlook that's now a grave of charred tree trunks.

6. APRÈS

With 12 breweries dotting the Gorge, good beer and fare await. Ojerio likes Walking Man Brewing in Stevenson, Washington, for its chicken gyro and namesake IPA, and Thunder Island Brewing Co. in Cascade Locks, Oregon, for its outdoor patio.

TRIP PLANNER

SEASON April to October

PERMIT Required for overnight stay (free); self-issue at the trailhead kiosk. The Northwest Forest Pass is required for parking in some federal sites, and the Discover Pass is required in Washington state parks.

CONTACT Columbia River Gorge National Scenic Area, www.fs.usda.gov/crgnsa

---

Play the slots in Grand Staircase-Escalante National Monument
(page 110). Photo: iStockphoto

SOUTHWEST

22: CANYON CONFIDENTIAL
GRAND GULCH, CEDAR MESA SPECIAL RECREATION MANAGEMENT AREA, UTAH

By Greg Child

I t's a sunburned September day in southeast Utah, and I'm following ten parched hikers through a jumble of burnished boulders and sparsely spaced cottonwood trees on the floor of a sinuous canyon called Grand Gulch. Amber-tinted sunbeams filter into the 700-foot-deep chasm and light up our lanky, long-haired, bird-legged backpacking guide, Vaughn Hadenfeldt. He's hunting for potable water, but the only pools we've found so far are a speckled latte brown. "A flash flood ripped through here two weeks ago," he tells us, "and these pools still aren't settled. If we don't find one that is, we'll be pickin' grit out of our teeth all night."

Flash floods tear through this spot a couple of times a year here in Grand Gulch Primitive Area, a 37,580-acre maze of protected canyons 30 crow miles from Bluff, Utah. Most hikers enter the 52-mile Grand Gulch from the top of the canyon, via a handful of trailheads off UT 261, but our group, a mix of lawyers, medicos, a retired sociology professor, and an environmental engineer, started walking at the mouth of Grand Gulch. This is the farthest point from those trailheads and the least visited section. We were just halfway through our journey.

We got to the mouth via a five-day, 65-mile raft trip down the lazy San Juan River, a journey worth doing in its own right. This morning, we beached our rafts (river guides would take the boats downstream and out) and hoisted our packs to follow Vaughn, who owns a guide company called Far Out Expeditions. Over the next five days, we'd hike north 40 miles to Collins Canyon through the Grand's winding chasms, where at almost every turn lie the homes, tools, and art of the ancient Anasazi, or Ancestral Puebloans, as archaeologists now call them. This canyon is thought to have been the most densely populated area in the pre-European United States.

I'm here because—like the majority of my hiking partners—I've become an archaeology junkie. After three decades of scaling Himalayan peaks, I've traded frozen summits for canyon secrets. And I've quickly learned that—when it comes to timeworn redrock terrain filled with ancient petroglyphs, cliff dwellings, and artifacts—Grand Gulch is the Southwest's Everest.

VAUGHN PREDICTED WE'D FIND GOOD WATER IN SHANGRI-LA CANYON, and 20 minutes later, we catch up to him pumping clear liquid out of a natural cistern into a nylon bladder. The spring isn't on maps, and it'd be easy to miss if you didn't know where to look. We gather around the waterhole and guzzle long, cool, slaking gulps. Vaughn smiles. He doesn't carry maps, yet every nook of the gulch is imprinted on his mind like waypoints in a GPS.

A thunderhead rumbles as we begin setting up camp on a level bench a half mile upstream from the waterhole. Though the storm cell whips up dust devils that spin through a posse of hoodoos on the canyon rim, we get only a tiny spray of cold raindrops, as if from a squirt gun. Even so, we make our camp high: The trees in the streambed wear necklaces of brush around their trunks, signs of the recent flash flood. I ask Hadenfeldt if he ever has mixed feelings about taking clients to these occasionally dangerous and always remote and fragile locations.

"I've seen these canyons flood in minutes flat, but I always watch the weather and only do trips when conditions are good," he says. "And I'm not worried about leaving a few boot prints. I enforce strong ethics. No one grabs even a twig as a souvenir. No campfires. We pack out toilet paper. I worry more that if young people stop going to places like this, there'll be no appreciation for wild lands and their history and no next generation to protect them." Our conversation ends before he can elaborate, when the thunderhead passes and a rainbow forms across the canyon. Everyone gazes in silence, rapt in one of those ah-ha moments when you know with absolute certainty that you are in the right place at exactly the right time.

WE'RE 5 MILES INTO OUR SECOND DAY OF HIKING when Vaughn leads us to another ah-ha phenomenon: a circular stone kiva dug into a sandy bench beneath a cliff. Incredibly, two ladder rails protrude through a hatch in the log-and-adobe roof. I have the unnerving sense that the natives who built it are nearby, somewhere, watching us. It looks like a family walked away from here just yesterday.

I approach with the intention of going inside, but Vaughn vetoes all entry. The incredibly well-preserved structure is too delicate. "Plus," Vaughn adds, "it's a ceremonial chamber, and under the floor, beneath centuries of blown sand, there's a hollow shaft called a *sipapu*, representing the place where humankind emerged from an underworld. You don't want to fall through the floor into the underworld." Convinced, we tiptoe around the site, seeing potsherds, corncobs, and quartz flakes from tool knapping. "It's OK to pick them up and look, or take photos, but put everything back where you find it. Don't take anything out of context," Vaughn tells us.

Frankly, it amazes me that anything remains here at all, for the modern history of Grand Gulch is one of plunder. Four cowboy brothers who ranched around Mancos, Colorado, in the 1880s—the Wetherill boys—popularized the Ancestral Puebloan world when they discovered the ruins of Mesa Verde, the now-famous national park that attracts a half million visitors annually. The trove of artifacts they found there spurred them on a quest into Four Corners' prehistory, and by the 1890s they were horsepacking along Grand Gulch, digging up artifacts and "mummies," as they called them. It was an era before archaeological discipline, when digs resembled hasty robberies and the booty was displayed in traveling road shows or sold to museums and collectors. By the time the 1906 Antiquities Act stopped the excavating free-for-all, thousands of artifacts and hundreds of disinterred corpses had been carted out.

In the early evening of our second day, we make camp by Shaw Arch, 11 miles from the river. The path, alternating between sandy streambeds and dusty game trails, leads under the span, opening magically onto a shaded and breezy grove and a spring. Burgundy handprints daubed on the walls at head height and corn-grinding slicks atop boulders show that we're not the first—by a long shot—to find this a good stopping point.

Vaughn dumps his pack, fetches water, and begins preparing hors d'oeuvres. "You know, there's some controversy about this arch," he muses while slicing cheese. "It's named on maps for Merlin Shaw, a Mormon bishop and Boy Scout leader who died in 1963. Shaw's admirers incorrectly persuaded the USGS that he'd discovered it, but locals have always called it Wetherill, or Grand Arch." Vaughn petitioned the USGS to change the name, but Shaw Arch stuck. "Somewhere in these cottonwoods I've seen a log with an 1894 Richard Wetherill signature on it," he says. "I doubt he missed seeing the arch."

The next two days pass in similar fashion, with easy mileage (6 to 10 miles per day) through otherworldly geography. Side trips take us to more perfect ruins. At midday, when the temperature reaches 100°F and the air feels like hot syrup, we hug the shady canyon flanks. All I can think about is replenishing my water bottles.

Water, or lack of it, probably forced the ancient canyon dwellers out of here. Tree ring analysis of logs from ruins indicates a terrible drought from AD 1276 to 1299. The pressure on communities must have been extreme: A pot of water could have been worth more than life itself. Indeed, the archaeological record of the final phase of habitation in this canyon suggests warfare and even hints at cannibalism. By 1300, the canyons were empty, the inhabitants having marched south to the Rio Grande. Luckily, with Vaughn's expertise, we find water in tiny springs and smooth, brine shrimp–filled potholes.

On our fifth and final day, I wake to another clear, cobalt sky framed by orange canyon walls. We haven't seen another soul, and the only hint of modernity is a set of footprints in the sand. I slurp down a cup of acrid instant coffee, shoulder my pack, and fall into line with the group. Just past The Narrows, where Grand Gulch constricts to a 20-foot-wide slot, we veer west into Collins Canyon. We slog uphill for the last 2 miles on an old cattle trail that, at times, is literally chiseled into the canyon wall. A cliff dwelling's dark and empty doorways look like ghost eyes peering down on us. The wall is covered with images of spear shafts and warriors that seem to guard the remainder of Grand Gulch, which winds ahead to the top of Cedar Mesa. And there's the famous line of musical notes India-inked on a cliff; researchers think Richard Wetherill's wife, Marietta, penned them 110 years ago to mimic a canyon wren's song.

Near the lip of the canyon, we file through a cave littered with saddle grease tins from the cowpoke era, then hit a 4WD road. Vaughn's wife, Marcia, waits at the trailhead with the Far Out Expeditions van. She greets every sweat-stained body with a hug and aims us at a cooler packed with soda and Moosehead lager.

We sit on our packs with sighs of relief and knock back a few while looking out at the white caprock dotted with pockets of pinyon and juniper. The depths of Grand Gulch vanish beneath the trees like a labyrinth of crevasses beneath a glacier. And I realize that nature's best gifts are those that lie beneath the surface.

TRIP PLANNER

SEASON March to June and September to November

PERMIT Required for overnight stay ($8 per person); obtain from the Kane Gulch Ranger Station

GUIDE If you wish to go deeper into Grand Gulch or approach from the mouth, inquire with Far Out Expeditions (faroutexpeditions.net). Prices vary.

CONTACT Cedar Mesa Special Recreation Management Area, bit.do/cedar-mesa-blm

DO IT

DISTANCE: 23.8 miles (point to point)

TIME: 2 to 3 days

DIFFICULTY: ★★★★

THE PAYOFF: Explore a redrock wonderland brimming with ruins from the Ancestral Puebloans. Like any trek, this one promises to be quieter the farther you venture into the canyon, but consider this a great beginner's option with easier navigation and water than the paddle-and-hike described on the previous page.

TRAILHEAD: Kane Gulch (37.5249, -109.8961); 50 miles northwest of Bluff on UT 261

SHUTTLE CAR Bullet Canyon (37.4308, -109.9495); 42 miles northwest of Bluff on South Road

MILES AND DIRECTIONS

FROM THE KANE GULCH TRAILHEAD:

1. Create an L-shaped route: Follow the faint **Grand Gulch Trail** west into Kane Gulch, a can't-miss, orange funnel that corkscrews 3.8 miles to where it merges with Grand Gulch, near 37.5122, -109.9379.

2. Continue contouring generally southwest through the redrock canyon on a user trail, passing natural arches and 1,000-year-old ruins and pictographs, roughly 12 miles to where Grand Gulch meets Bullet Canyon near 37.4457, -110.0422. (Many springs litter this route; call ahead to make sure they're reliable.)

3. Where Grand Gulch jackknifes, veer east into **Bullet Canyon** on-trail and follow the spindly chasm some 8 miles to where another faint social path climbs out of the canyon to the parking lot on South Road.

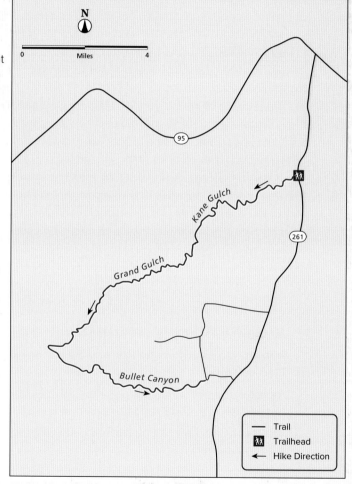

N

0 — Miles — 4

95

261

Kane Gulch

Grand Gulch

Bullet Canyon

— Trail

Trailhead

← Hike Direction

23. SECOND IS THE BEST
BUSH MOUNTAIN,
GUADALUPE MOUNTAINS NATIONAL PARK, TEXAS

Thank goodness for 8,740-foot Guadalupe Peak: Hikers flock to the state's high point, leaving nearby 8,615-foot Bush Mountain's see-forever slopes much quieter. With its views over the white Salt Flats, golden Patterson Hills, and evergreen-studded Dog Canyon, the penultimate peak juts out of the Chihuahuan Desert like a limestone shiv. We bet you won't even miss those 125 feet.

Photo: Ray Chiarello

TRIP PLANNER

SEASON October to May

PERMIT Required for overnight stay (free); obtain at the Pine Springs or Dog Canyon Visitor Centers

CONTACT Guadalupe Mountains National Park, www.nps.com/gumo

DISTANCE: 13 miles (out and back)

TIME: 2 days

DIFFICULTY: ★★

THE PAYOFF: Savor a West Texas view when you tackle the state's second-tallest peak.

TRAILHEAD: Pine Spring (31.8967, -104.8281); 112 miles east of El Paso off Pine Canyon Drive

MILES AND DIRECTIONS

FROM THE PINE SPRING TRAILHEAD:

1. Pick your way across Spring Canyon on a short user path to an intersection 0.2 mile away.
2. Turn west onto the **Tejas Trail,** which gradually ascends 3.2 miles (gaining some 2,000 feet of elevation) to a junction near the ridgeline.
3. Veer west onto the **Bush Mountain Trail** and take the airy catwalk 3.1 miles to the summit on the broad peak's western escarpment.
4. Retrace your steps to the trailhead.

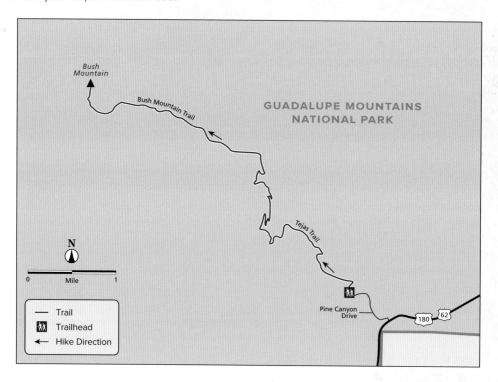

DON'T MISS THIS CAMPSITE: BUSH MOUNTAIN (MILE 6.2)

Nab one of five sites on the southern shoulder of the 8,615-foot peak. Each is set apart in a flat area, shaded by pines, and only a quick, 0.3-mile jaunt to the true summit. Be sure to make a trip to the western escarpment for sunset. ***Note:*** BYO water.

24: BLAST FROM THE PAST
YAPASHI PUEBLO,
BANDELIER NATIONAL MONUMENT, NEW MEXICO

For more than 400 years, Bandelier was the home of an Ancestral Puebloan civilization. Nearly 700 years later, it's a national monument filled with ancient artifacts—from potsherds to multistoried buildings—and more than 70 miles of trail. Ladders allow access to frontcountry ruins in Frijoles Canyon, but backcountry archaeological sites remain comparatively untouched. Take advantage of a tour to Yapashi Pueblo, the largest unrestored pueblo in Bandelier.

Adapted from text by Paul Chisholm

DISTANCE: 16 miles (lollipop-loop)

TIME: 2 days

DIFFICULTY: ★★✦

THE PAYOFF: Find rarely visited, ancient ruins on a lonely, desert mesa trek.

TRAILHEAD: Frijoles Canyon (35.7784, -106.2705); 14 miles south of Los Alamos off Entrance Road

MILES AND DIRECTIONS

FROM THE FRIJOLES CANYON TRAILHEAD:

1. Head west on the **Frijoles Rim Trail,** which traces the canyon and overlooks ancient, ladder-accessible structures, before descending to Alamo Creek, one of the route's few seasonal water sources, near mile 6.2.

2. Veer southeast on the **Stone Lions Trail,** ascending the mesa and traversing past Yapashi Pueblo, to a three-way junction at mile 10.1. (Budget time to explore Yapashi Pueblo, where oblong boulders rest in a 650-foot-diameter circle, the remains of the Cochiti Puebloans' 385-room village. Surveys indicate that it was four stories tall.)

3. Loop 4.6 miles back to the main drag on the **Mid-Alamo Trail.**

4. Retrace your steps 1.3 miles on the **Frijoles Rim Trail** to the trailhead.

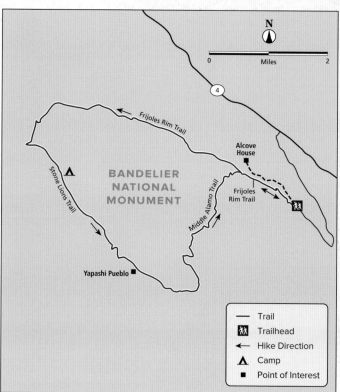

TRIP PLANNER

SEASON March to October

PERMIT Required for overnight stay (free); obtain from the visitor center

CONTACT Bandelier National Monument, www.nps.gov/band

ALL THE EXTRAS

DON'T MISS THIS CAMPSITE: ALAMO MESA (MILE 7.2)

While dispersed camping in the canyon bottoms is subject to unpredictable closures, tenting is always allowed on the mesas and ridge tops in Bandelier. Think of that as a good thing, because you'd never know about the big-sky plateau's camping prospects if you settled for a waterside spot. Tank up at Alamo (a gallon per person) and continue about a mile to the mesa separating Alamo and Capulin Canyons. Find a spot that's backed up against pinyons for wind protection and look up. The Milky Way never looked so good.

KEEP YOUR EYES PEELED: FLORA

Prickly pears, cane cholla, and yucca choke the mesa tops, while aspens thrive in the pocket oases, like Lummis Canyon (mile 12.5 on this route). Four varieties of sage grow in Bandelier, though sagebrush is by far the most prevalent. Make like a Native American and steep its gray-green leafy parts in hot water to treat the common cold. Your body can't break down the leaves' volatile oils, instead excreting them through sweat and expelling them through your lungs' capillary blood vessels—in other words, causing "wet, functional" coughs that soothe the lungs.

FUN FACT: GEOLOGY

Bandelier's pinkish cliffs are made of tuff, or consolidated volcanic ash. Tuff is very light and soft—which is why the Ancestral Puebloans only needed hand tools to carve and build apartment-style homes along the canyons and cliff faces.

EXTRA CREDIT: ADD A HIKE

You pass Yapashi Pueblo on this particular route, but don't stop there. See a cave full of pictographs on a 7.6-mile out-and-back from the junction at Yapashi Pueblo near mile 9 on this itinerary. Head downcanyon on trail to sluice through Capulin Canyon, where a short, 0.1-mile spur leads across a dry tributary into Painted Cave. There, see red markings across the mouth of the tan-colored cave that were made by Ancestral Puebloans using a mineral rich with iron. Pictographs that range from 100 to 700 years old depict wolves, elk, and even a church with a tall steeple (evidence of contact with the Spanish). Speculate at will—the site remains an active shrine to the people of the Cochiti Pueblo, who don't reveal ancestral secrets—but do not enter.

25: DESERT OASIS
MAZATZAL WILDERNESS, ARIZONA

Think backpacking in Arizona is all about how much water you can carry? Not in the Mazatzal Wilderness, a high-desert preserve straddling the Tonto and Coconino National Forests. Here springs and creeks knit together steep canyons, Sonoran Desert shrublands, and pine-fir forests—where javelina, black bears, and river otters wander. For perfect weather, join them in the fall with these tips and tricks from local expert **Chad Hummer**. By Elisabeth Kwak-Hefferan.

THE INSIDER

As a longtime Arizona Trail Steward, Chad Hummer roamed the Mazatzal Wilderness's roughest terrain, checking route conditions and water availability for the Arizona Trail Association. But the born-and-raised desert dweller was already hooked on the Mazatzal's magic: "I love hiking in places with shade and water—a precious commodity out here."

1. SECRET FOLIAGE HIKE

All year, Hummer looks forward to October in the Mazatzal—fall brings relief from both searing summer temperatures and monsoon rains, giving way to dry, hiker-friendly weather (expect highs in the mid-70s). Even better: Starting in mid-October, the wilderness pops with bright oranges, yellows, and scarlets as hardwoods show off their fall colors. Hummer's favorite leaf-peeping trek traces Sycamore Creek under a canopy of golden cottonwoods. From the Mormon Grove trailhead, take the Saddle Mountain Trail (#91) through a pinyon-juniper canyon 3 miles to the abandoned Story Mine. A few shafts dot the canyon walls (don't enter them), but the real attraction is the medley of shady, seasonal pools. Spend the night, then return the way you came.

2. BEST MULTIDAY TRIP

Circumnavigate 7,903-foot Mazatzal Peak on a 22-mile, three-day loop featuring water-falls, shady campsites, and reliable springs. You'll score views of the Verde River and the 200-mile-long cliff face of the Mogollon Rim. From the Barnhardt trailhead, take the Y Bar Trail (#44) southwest, gradually ascending blocky Mazatzal Peak (experienced scram-blers can go for the Class 3 summit, but loose rock and thick brush make it challenging). Around mile 5.5, scout a secluded social site under the pines. Next day, turn north on the Arizona Trail for vistas extending to the Verde River and Horseshoe Reservoir. Camp at Horse Camp Seep near a year-round spring before closing the loop: Backtrack to the Barnhardt Trail and descend steeply along a canyon wall dotted with cascades.

3. TOP SWIMMING HOLE

With its gushing waterfalls, staircase travertine deposits, and clear springs ("they're 30 feet deep, and you can still see the bottom," Hummer says), Fossil Creek draws the hordes—so much so that in spring and summer, the Forest Service bans camping and requires advance reservations just to park. But starting in October, the crowds fade and restrictions loosen, opening up one of Arizona's primo escapes to backpackers. From the Fossil Springs trailhead, descend 1,600 feet on the 4-mile Trail #18 to reach the string of swimming holes on Fossil Creek. Splash away, then head at least 1.4 miles west to scout a cottonwood-shaded site at least 100 feet from the creek; camping is allowed west of Fos-sil Creek Bridge.

4. BEST BASECAMP

Pitch a tent under the pines at the Peeley trailhead, then spend a few days exploring the three trails that spiral out from there (high-clearance vehicle required; 4WD after rains). "There are awesome views overlooking the Mogollon Rim to the north and the valley below, and the higher elevation (6,000-plus feet) makes it nice and cool at night," Hum-mer says. Grab an established site with a fire ring (BYO water), then pick a direction for your next day's adventure: You can trace a ridgeline on the Mazatzal Divide Trail, follow a lush waterway on the Deer Creek Trail, or check out an old mine on the Cornucopia Trail.

TRIP PLANNER

SEASON September to May

PERMIT Required for overnight stay (free); self-issue at trailhead kiosks

CONTACT Tonto National Forest, www.fs.usda.gov/tonto

26: SPRING FLING
WINDING STAIR MOUNTAIN, OUACHITA NATIONAL FOREST, OKLAHOMA

By Erica Zazo

Snow blankets many of the country's wilds in early spring, but here in the Ouachitas, I trek through a different kind of white: trillium. I navigate around moss-covered boulders and past pockets of springtime blooms en route to Winding Stair Mountain, where I hit sensory overload. Ribbons of purple geranium and yellow violet decorate forested hills under a cloudless sky. Not bad for the first overnight of the season.

TRIP PLANNER

SEASON Year-round

PERMIT Required for overnight stay ($3 per party per day); self-issue at trailhead kiosk

CONTACT Ouachita National Forest, www.fs.usda.gov/ouachita

DISTANCE: 12.8 miles (lollipop-loop)

TIME: 2 days

DIFFICULTY: ★★

THE PAYOFF: So few hike the Ouachita National Recreation Trail that the path's governing body doesn't even keep stats—that spells utter solitude for springtime petal-peepers in the South.

TRAILHEAD: Cedar Lake North Shore (34.7785, -94.6924); 18 miles north of Big Cedar on Cedar Lake Road

MILES AND DIRECTIONS

FROM THE CEDAR LAKE NORTH SHORE TRAILHEAD:

1. Pick up the **Horsethief Springs Trail** and head 2.1 miles south.

2. Take its west fork (or head east for a shorter first day) and continue to a T-junction at mile 5.3.

3. Hike 1.4 miles east across Winding Stair Mountain—more a gunsight-like ridge than a peak—on the **Ouachita National Recreation Trail** to a fork (pass Horsethief Springs near mile 6.6).

4. Hook up with the **Horsethief Springs Trail** again and descend off the ridge, continuing north to close the loop near mile 10.7.

5. Retrace your steps 2.1 miles to the trailhead.

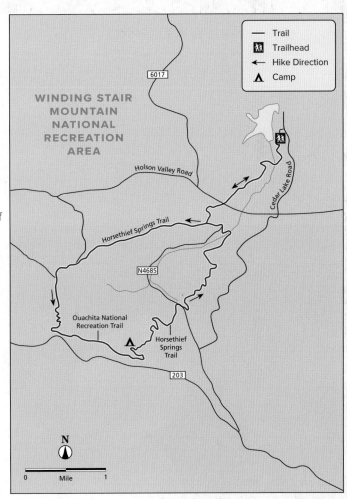

ALL THE EXTRAS

DON'T MISS THIS CAMPSITE: LIMESTONE BLUFF (MILE 7)

To camp near the midway point, park it in this pine-protected social site just west of the switchbacks off Winding Stair Mountain on the back end of the loop. It's not visible from the trail, so take it slow on the downclimb—otherwise you'll miss this pocket of Ouachita goodness and end up at the Cedar Creek sites with the other overnighters. Seasonal streams run near the trail, but top up 0.4 mile back at Horsethief Springs, the most reliable water on the route.

KEEP YOUR EYES PEELED: FLORA

Scan for blooms like green trillium, purple wild geranium, and yellow violets growing trailside in early spring. By summer, sunflowers like asters and black-eyed Susans hit their prime.

FUN FACT: NAMING RIGHTS

In the post-Civil War 1800s, outlaws including Jesse James and the Daltons would hide out near the natural spring on Winding Stair Mountain and ambush passing travelers—hence "Horsethief Springs."

White trillium

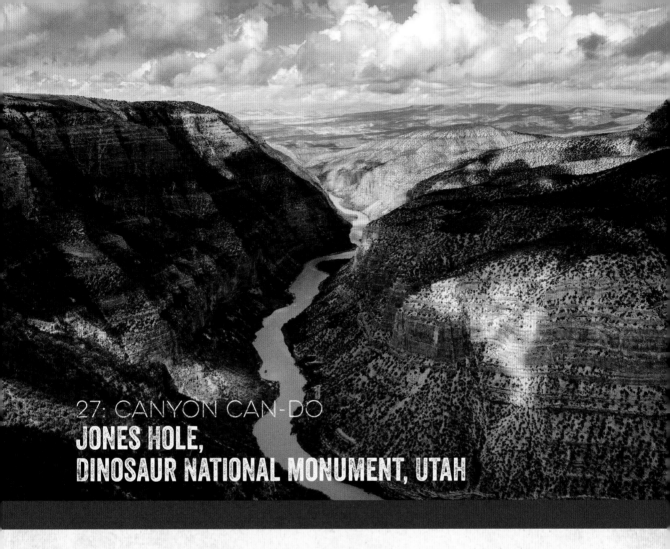

27: CANYON CAN-DO
JONES HOLE,
DINOSAUR NATIONAL MONUMENT, UTAH

Lack of water for drinking and cooking bumps many canyon-country trips out of the beginner category: If you don't have advanced water-scouting skills, you're stuck hauling in a heavy load of your own supply. Not here, where a stupid-short approach leads to a bona fide oasis, where two creeks meet 1,000 feet beneath sunset-hued cliffs. Early Native Americans must have liked it, too—petroglyphs and pictographs on the rocks date to the Fremont people, who lived here more than a millennium ago.

TRIP PLANNER

SEASON Year-round

PERMIT Required for overnight stay (free); obtain from the Quarry Visitor Center

CONTACT Dinosaur National Monument, www.nps.gov/dino

Adapted from text by Sarah L. Stewart.

DISTANCE: 3 miles (out and back)

TIME: 2 days

DIFFICULTY: ★

THE PAYOFF: Discover swimming holes, waterfalls, petroglyphs, and an idyllic campsite—less than 2 miles deep into canyon-riddled Dinosaur National Monument.

TRAILHEAD: Jones Hole Fish Hatchery (40.5842, -109.0552); 47 miles northeast of the Quarry Visitor Center on Jones Hole Road

MILES AND DIRECTIONS

FROM THE JONES HOLE FISH HATCHERY:

1. Trek 1.5 miles south on the pancake-flat **Jones Hole Trail** to Ely Creek.
2. Retrace your steps to the trailhead.

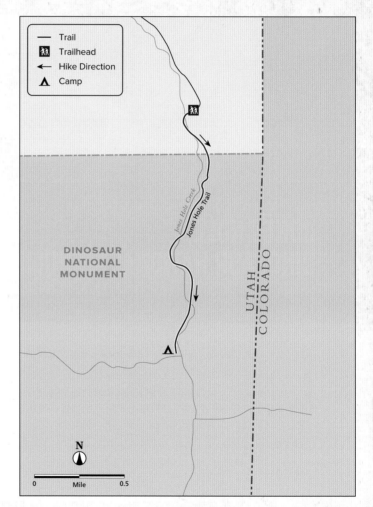

ALL THE EXTRAS

DON'T MISS THIS CAMPSITE: ELY CREEK (MILE 1.5)

Nab this spot for its central location: The best swimming hole is 0.4 mile west, and the Green River and Whirlpool Canyon (where dinosaur fossils have been uncovered) are 1.5 miles south. Set up your tent (there's room for two) on the far side of the bridge over Ely Creek.

KEEP YOUR EYES PEELED: ROCK ART

See thousand-year-old Fremont artwork just past the first bridge (mile 1.2), under the rock overhang. There you can identify well-preserved pictographs of humans, bighorn sheep, and repeating triangles, as well as a petroglyph of an intricate sun.

GEAR TIP: PACK A ROD

Find brown and rainbow trout in Jones Hole Creek, and, if you make it to Whirlpool Canyon, cast a line for foot-long roundtail chub (catch-and-release only).

EXTRA CREDIT: ADD A HIKE

Sure, you can cool down in Jones Hole Creek at any point on the hike, but break from the main trail just before camp to find a camp, but break from the main trail at mile 1.5 to find a secluded pool inside a side canyon. Before you cross Ely Creek, veer 0.4 mile west on a user trail to find a 12-foot waterfall that spills into a basin ideal for swimming and soaking. The microclimate here is so cool, a few Douglas firs even grow in the cove.

Fremont artwork

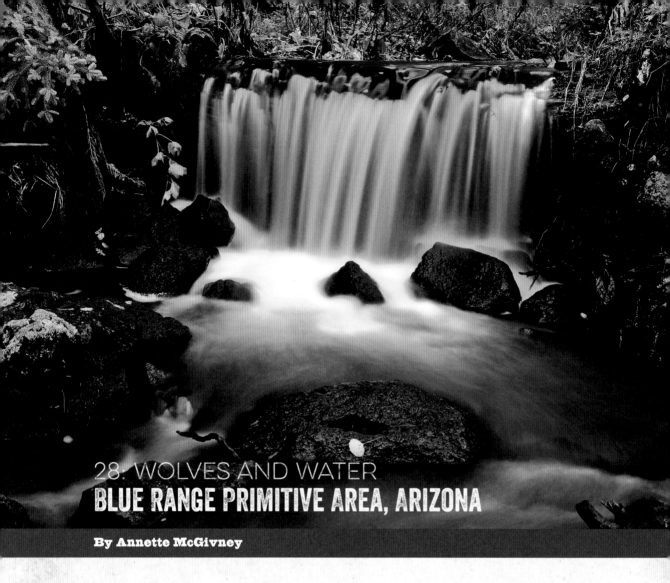

28: WOLVES AND WATER
BLUE RANGE PRIMITIVE AREA, ARIZONA

By Annette McGivney

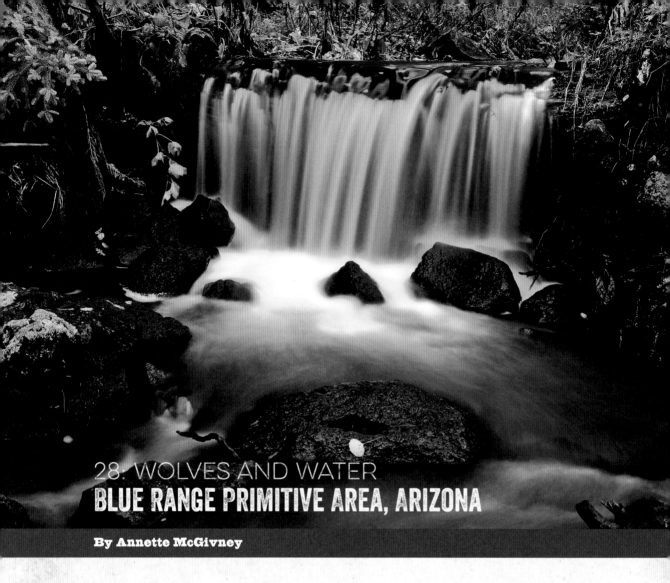

I had a different kind of campsite in mind for tonight, one smack in the middle of a sunny alpine meadow, encircled by golden-leafed aspens, bustling with elk in rut and within earshot of the howling wolves that roam these mountains. There are plenty of places like that here in Arizona's Blue Range. Instead, I find myself setting down my pack in a dark, forested boneyard at the bottom of Grant Creek Canyon, the only flat spot for miles. All manner of gnawed ungulate body parts from at least half a dozen elk or deer are strewn about. Not only am I within likely earshot of wolves, but it appears I am also in the middle of their mess hall.

Even though most hikers head to the picture-postcard-perfect White Mountains next door, I have always been drawn to the Blue Range. It has clear mountain streams and year-round alpine pools, making it one of the desert's best-kept secrets. After nearly a decade of backpacking trips in the 174,000-acre wilderness on the Arizona-New Mexico state

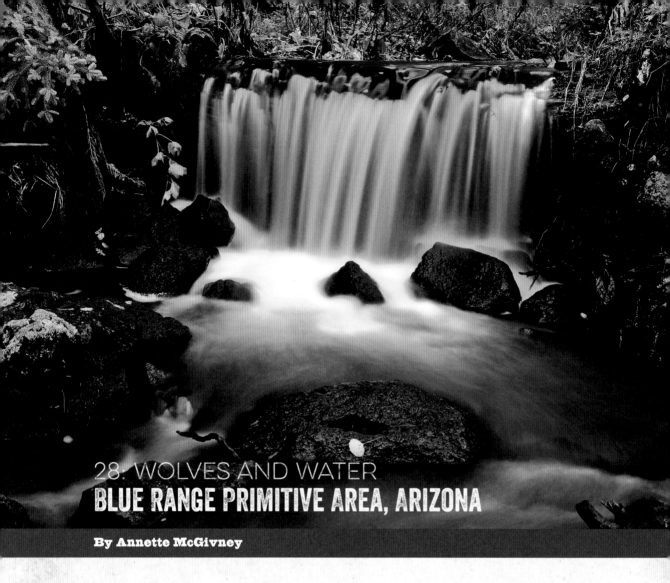

Photo: Scott Lefler

line—hiking from the 9,000-foot-high aspen and fir-forested peaks soggy with snowmelt down to the oak-covered foothills and cactus-studded canyon bottoms—I thought I knew these mountains. But I had no idea how much the endangered Mexican gray wolf (reintroduced in 1998) had reclaimed this land.

If Aldo Leopold were here today, he'd be pleased to see how well the one hundred-plus wolves are doing and how "primitive" the Blue Range Primitive Area (a wilderness he helped establish) remains. In 1908, while patrolling the Blue Range during the early years of his Forest Service career, Leopold had a wolf encounter that planted the seed for a conservation ethic that helped inspire our nation's early environmental movement.

In Leopold's famous environmental treatise, *A Sand County Almanac*, he recalls the day when he and his coworkers were sitting on a canyon bluff and spotted a pack of wolves. Exterminating wolves, grizzlies, and other "vermin" was part of their job, so they proceeded to pull out their rifles and fill the pack with lead. Leopold shot the alpha female.

"We reached the old wolf in time to watch a fierce green fire dying in her eyes," he wrote. "I realized then, and have known ever since, that there was something new to me in those eyes—something known only to her and the mountain. I was young then and full of trigger-itch; I thought that because fewer wolves meant more deer, then no wolves would mean a hunter's paradise. But after seeing the green fire die, I sensed that neither the wolf nor the mountain agreed with such a view." It took decades—and thousands of deer starved through overpopulation—for the federal government to agree with Leopold's assertion that wolves were essential to maintaining the ecology of wildlands.

There have been rumors of reintroduced wolves killed by area ranchers, but it would be hard for any animal not to thrive in these mountains. There is a force of nature here that emanates from the gurgling of every stream, every canyon bottom, every forested peak, every pile of bones. As Leopold found when he looked into the wolf's eyes, there's a wild energy hereabouts that's more powerful than anything human. I feel it as I crouch over my stove boiling water for dinner. *Or is it the presence of wolves that is sending a chill down my spine?*

A sound unlike any I've ever heard rises from the bluff behind me. It's not the hoot of an owl, but neither does it sound like a classic wolf howl. Then again, perhaps it is the "deep, chesty bawl . . . of wild defiant sorrow" that Leopold heard in the Blue Range. There is still much I have to learn from these mountains. As Leopold said, "Only the mountain has lived long enough to listen objectively to the howl of a wolf."

TRIP PLANNER

SEASON March to May and September to November

PERMIT None

CONTACT Apache-Sitgreaves National Forests, www.fs.usda.gov/asnf

DISTANCE: 11.4 miles (lollipop-loop)

TIME: 2 days

DIFFICULTY: ★★⟋

THE PAYOFF: An abundance of wolves and water—rarities in the desert—make this alpine tour a treat for hardy hikers.

TRAILHEAD: Hannagan Meadow (33.6358, -109.3221); 23 miles southwest of Alpine off US 191

MILES AND DIRECTIONS

FROM THE HANNAGAN MEADOW TRAILHEAD:

1. Follow a user trail 0.1 mile east to a junction.

2. Split south onto the **Steeple Trail (#73)** and take it 1.2 miles through stands of conifers and across small meadows to another intersection.

3. Head east onto the **Upper Grant Creek Trail (#65),** which follows its namesake 3.9 miles through a narrow canyon studded with Douglas firs and aspens. (Keep your eyes peeled for elk, mule deer, and black bears.)

4. At the head of the canyon near mile 5.2, veer southwest onto the **Long Cienega Trail (#305)** to close the loop. This path meanders 3.4 miles through upland meadows trimmed with firs and aspens to another intersection.

5. Continue 2.7 miles north on the **Steeple Trail (#73),** passing the turnoff to Upper Grant Canyon, to the original junction.

6. Retrace your steps 0.1 mile to the trailhead.

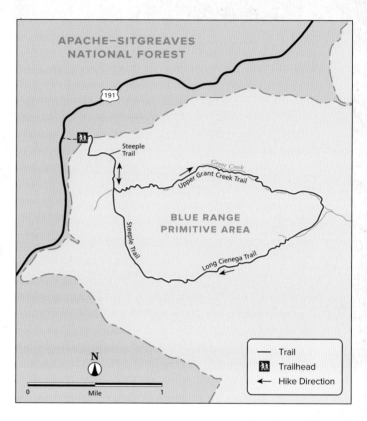

APACHE–SITGREAVES NATIONAL FOREST

Steeple Trail

Grant Creek

Upper Grant Creek Trail

BLUE RANGE PRIMITIVE AREA

Steeple Trail

Long Cienega Trail

N

——	Trail
🚶	Trailhead
←	Hike Direction

0 — Mile — 1

29: COLOR COUNTRY
PRAIRIE DOG TOWN FORK,
PALO DURO CANYON STATE PARK, TEXAS

Throw down in a rare native grassland with unbroken views of the copper-colored Prairie Dog Town Fork of the Red River and the banded, 800-foot-high cliffs, and you may think you got away with something. Consider it strategy: To protect archaeological sites (Comanche and Kiowa tribes lived here until the 1870s), backpacking in this 27,000-acre state park is restricted to the southeastern corner. Most folks stay in the north end of the area, but instead of following them, head over to the park's roadless southern boundary, where you'll find this slice of paradise. Tip your cap to the deer and aoudad sheep who keep the grass to shin height, so you can savor the 360-degree panorama without leaving your tent.

TRIP PLANNER

SEASON March to May and September to November

PERMIT Required for overnight stay ($12 per party per night); obtain from park headquarters

CONTACT Palo Duro Canyon State Park, bit.do/palo-duro-canyon-sp

---

Photo: Rob Greebon

DISTANCE: 6.4 miles (out and back)

TIME: 2 days

DIFFICULTY: ★★✦

THE PAYOFF: Land a private backcountry campsite and escape the frontcountry crowds at this popular park when you venture off-trail.

TRAILHEAD: Equestrian Camp (34.9314, -101.6369); 30 miles southeast of Amarillo on Park Road 5

MILES AND DIRECTIONS

FROM EQUESTRIAN CAMP:

1. Follow the Prairie Dog Town Fork of the Red River 1.7 miles southeast on the **Equestrian Trail** to its terminus.

2. Continue cross-country, paralleling the river southeast for 1.5 more miles to find an established campsite overlooking the river.

3. Retrace your steps to the trailhead.

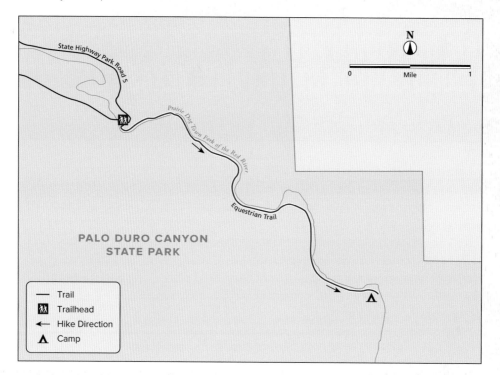

PALO DURO CANYON
STATE PARK

Legend:
— Trail
🚶 Trailhead
← Hike Direction
⛺ Camp

Adapted from text by Kelly Bastone.

ALL THE EXTRAS

DON'T MISS THIS CAMPSITE: BLUFF OVER PRAIRIE DOG TOWN FORK (MILE 3.2)

Find an impacted site north of the fence line that overlooks the river. From your high vantage, you can pinpoint all the colors in the rock walls: the ash layer from the Yellowstone eruption and the Tecovas layer that ranges from purple to gold. Though the park protects the exact location of the rock art, you can stage dayhikes around camp to poke around for a depiction of a chief wearing a red warbonnet.

KEEP YOUR EYES PEELED: WILDLIFE

White-tailed and mule deer may wander through your camp—as well as bobcats. The medium-size cats are generally reclusive, but they favor the same things you do: rocky outcrops and overwhelming solitude.

EXTRA CREDIT: STRETCH IT OUT

We know: Palo Duro is out there. If you're not keen on immediately hiking after your big drive (or vice versa), consider bookending your off-trail overnight at the Juniper Campground, a new tenting area a mile west of Equestrian Camp off the main park road near 34.9368, -101.6482. Formerly a day-use area, the eighteen-site Juniper Campground opened in summer 2016—so new that it doesn't appear on most park maps. The sites ($26 per party per night) remain blissfully private for now and offer views of 3,400-foot-tall Fortress Cliff.

Bobcat

30: DESERT MIRAGE
PYRAMID PEAK, GREAT BASIN NATIONAL PARK, NEVADA

No doubt this out-of-the-way national park isn't at the top of your bucket list. But with 12,000-foot peaks that rise more than a mile above the sagebrush plains, it should be. Leverage its anonymity into an unforgettable trip among the bristlecone pines, rocky moraines, and alpine lakes with staggering desert views and you'll know why this park earned national park status. Best part? Only 3 percent of Yosemite's annual visitors. That's no mirage.

TRIP PLANNER

SEASON June to October

PERMIT None

CONTACT Great Basin National Park, www.nps.gov/grba

Adapted from text by Ali Herman.

DISTANCE: 12.7 miles (loop)

TIME: 2 days

DIFFICULTY: ★★★

THE PAYOFF: Climb out of desert heat to breezy solitude in this underrated national park.

TRAILHEAD: Baker Creek (38.9766, -114.2456); 8 miles west of Baker on Baker Creek Road

MILES AND DIRECTIONS

FROM THE BAKER CREEK TRAILHEAD:

1. Begin a gradual, 5.5-mile climb on the aspen-shaded **Baker Creek Trail** to Baker Lake, a small pool nestled near treeline in an amphitheater of sheer, glacier-carved stone below its 12,298-foot namesake.

2. Head south on a user trail, following large cairns through wide meadows, to link up with the **Snake-Baker Pass Trail,** which ascends a drainage filled with monkeyflower (blooming in midsummer) to 9,871-foot Snake Pass near mile 7.5. (From here, you can bag Pyramid Peak on a 1-mile, round-trip detour that gains 600 feet.)

3. Downclimb 2.4 miles on the main trail to an intersection.

4. Close the circuit on the **South Fork Baker Creek Trail,** which leads 2.8 miles back to the trailhead.

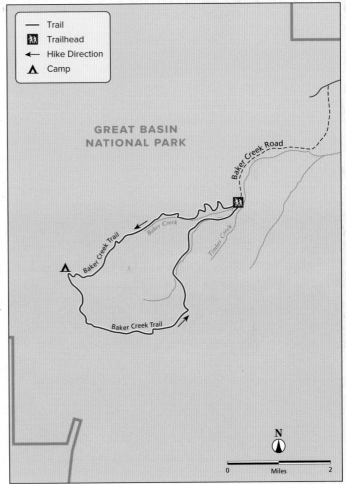

GREAT BASIN NATIONAL PARK

Legend:
— Trail
Trailhead
← Hike Direction
▲ Camp

N

0 — Miles — 2

ALL THE EXTRAS

DON'T MISS THIS CAMPSITE: BAKER LAKE (MILE 5.5)

Camp on the northwest side of the tarn, backed up against the sheer ramparts of Baker Peak. The viewshed opens southeast toward symmetrical, 11,926-foot Pyramid Peak, which can be snowcapped in shoulder season or mantled with purple lupine and penstemon in summer.

EXTRA CREDIT: ADD A DAY TRIP

High on the wind-scoured crest of the Snake Range, find a grove of gnarled bristlecone pines that's older than the Bible. From Snake Pass (mile 7.5 on this itinerary), head 2 miles south along the ridge (off-trail, but easy to negotiate) to the eastern flank of Mount Washington, where the squat trunks, burnished a golden brown by eons of ice pellets, stand in haunting silhouettes spread across a canvas of gray limestone gravel.

Monkeyflowers

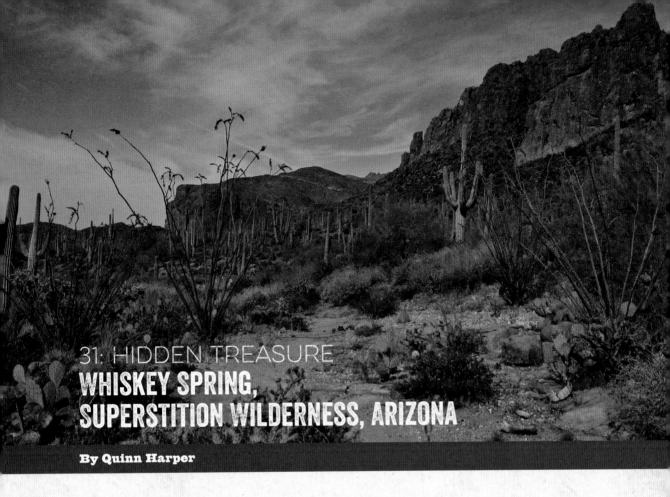

31: HIDDEN TREASURE
WHISKEY SPRING,
SUPERSTITION WILDERNESS, ARIZONA

By Quinn Harper

Legend has it that there's a fortune in gold hidden somewhere in these desert peaks of the Superstitions. A German man supposedly found it in the nineteenth century and kept its whereabouts a secret before he passed away. But so far, all I've found is merciless catclaw. I've spent the better part of the day scampering up barely there trails and sidestepping ornery rattlesnakes. But, after a 1,200-foot climb deposits me on Red Tanks Divide, the high point of this loop, the desert opens up in all directions, naked stone and towering saguaro glowing in the afternoon sun. I think I've found the prize.

TRIP PLANNER

SEASON September to May

PERMIT None

CONTACT Tonto National Forest, www.fs.usda.gov/tonto

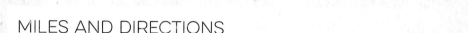
DISTANCE: 19.2 miles (lollipop-loop)

TIME: 2 days

DIFFICULTY: ★★★

THE PAYOFF: Venture beyond the Flatiron and Weavers Needle to the unmanicured desertscape around Red Tanks Divide for a quiet—but close to home—overnight adventure.

TRAILHEAD: Peralta (33.3971, -111.3481); 34 miles east of Mesa on Peralta Road

MILES AND DIRECTIONS

FROM THE PERALTA TRAILHEAD:

1. Take the **Dutchman's Trail (#104)** for 2.7 miles to a fork.
2. Continue along the valley floor, following the **Coffee Flat Trail (#108)** to mile 7.1.
3. Veer north up Randolph Canyon on the **Red Tanks Trail (#107),** cresting the divide and cutting through Upper La Barge Box Canyon to mile 13.
4. Turn south onto the **Whiskey Spring Trail (#238)** and head 3.6 miles back to the original fork, splitting Miners Canyon near mile 15.
5. Retrace your steps 2.7 miles on the **Dutchman's Trail** to the trailhead.

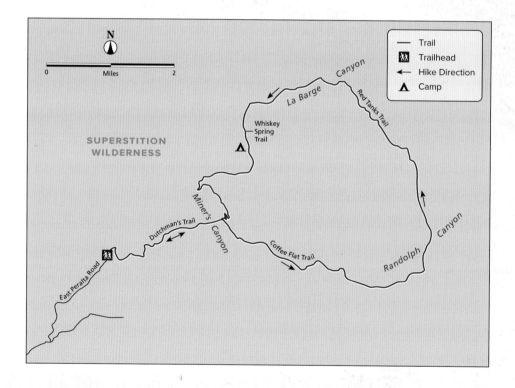

ALL THE EXTRAS

DON'T MISS THIS CAMPSITE: WHISKEY SPRING (MILE 13.7)

Select a shaded spot beneath the cottonwoods, which turn yellow by November. You can count on Whiskey Spring to flow in fall after the summer monsoons, but it's iffy in springtime (call ahead to check). If you want a shorter first day, flip the route clockwise to hit this oasis near mile 5.5 overall.

KEEP YOUR EYES PEELED: TREASURE

Legend has it that there is an ore mine somewhere in the craggy heart of the Superstitions that, at one point, produced gold from the desert's innards by the drum. The man who protected its whereabouts—a German by the name of Jacob Waltz—died more than a century ago, and still no one has located the Lost Dutchman's Mine. Scan for flickers of gold in the soil, and perhaps you will be the one to finally unearth Arizona's grandest fortune.

EXTRA CREDIT: ADD A HIKE

If Whiskey Spring is dry and there are no potholes of rainwater (called *tinajas*) in Red Tanks Canyon (as in late spring), you have two options: You can haul in water or you can tack on a 4-mile round-trip detour to a reliable spring. Water is heavy (a gallon weighs 8 pounds), so save your back with option two. La Barge Spring flows year-round, and it's just 2 miles beyond the Whiskey Spring Trail junction (step 3 on the itinerary described on page 94) on the Red Tanks Trail. Plan to pack in a gallon for the first day's hike, then top off enough for camp and day two's hike at La Barge.

32: THE HIGH LIFE
HIGHLINE TRAIL, HIGH UINTAS WILDERNESS, UTAH

By Steve Howe

I love wildlife, but this is getting ridiculous," Pete laughs, after a coyote wail scares the bull moose we've been watching just outside of camp. He has a point. We'd only hiked a half mile from the trailhead near Hacking Lake on a warm August day when we stopped to ogle a herd of thirty-five mountain goats. Minutes later, a weasel darted upon our track with a mouse hanging in its mouth. Another half mile, and Pete stumbled upon two spotted elk calves lounging near timberline. Then, two more goat herds on the 5-mile climb to 11,700-foot Gabbro Pass, from which we flush one hundred elk on the far side. After just 10 miles of hiking, we've had about one animal encounter per mile. And that's just counting the obvious ones. We surely missed more, with 100-mile vistas hogging our attention nearly every step of the way.

Views of every kind—distant horizons, nearby wildlife, isolated lake basins—are better on ridgeline hikes. And the king of the hill is the Highline Trail, which runs 78 east–west miles through the 456,705-acre High Uintas Wilderness of northeast Utah. The often-bouldery track crosses nine major passes and seldom dips below 10,500 feet. It's the perfect aerie to spy the wilderness's twenty-six summits above 13,000 feet, an estimated 1,000 lakes and ponds, thirty-six major streams, and megafauna galore. My partner Pete, an Appalachian Trail thru-hiker from North Carolina, brought a fly rod, and I've packed my camera, the tools of our stop-and-play hobbies. This is not a recipe for ticking off miles, but with these surroundings, we'd be fools to rush it.

You'd think all of this unobstructed beauty would attract a crowd, but fewer than fifty people a year thru-hike the ridge-hugging track—it's overshadowed on a regional menu that includes the Tetons, Sawtooths, Wind Rivers, and Colorado's Fourteeners. The Uintas' long, brick-red ridgelines of billion-year-old quartzite, gradually being swallowed by their own talus, have a powerful majesty that nineteenth-century explorer Ferdinand Hayden singled out among all the mountain ranges he'd seen. Compared to others, he wrote, the Uintas stands alone for its "contrast so pleasing to the eye."

Of course, treeless alpine grandeur doesn't come without some risk. The next night, we camp at Fox Lake in a bowl not far below 12,710-foot Anderson Pass, at mile 33, the trail's highest point. Clouds appear and gusts swirl. We get ready to run for it, but fortunately no lightning appears.

We drop packs atop Anderson Pass the next morning to side hike to Kings Peak, Utah's 13,528-foot high point. There's no summit register, just another world's-end vista of lake-dotted tundra, spiked pine forests, and mazes of snow-banked ridgeline. On lesser treks, this would be the highlight moment. Here, such views are routine.

Descending from the peak into Painter Basin, we skirt the banks of Yellowstone Creek in a huge bowl filled with stunted pines and rushing blue water, our horizon ringed by tiered ridges. The sun sizzles our skin while the breeze simultaneously cools it. We can't help but take another long pause, this time to yak, snack, and scratch ourselves lazily in a state of high-road aboriginalism.

The next morning, in Oweep Basin at mile 52, thick frost makes the bouldery trail around Mount Lovenia a slick-footed struggle. Atop the broad saddle of Red Knob Pass, beneath the talus slopes of Tokewanna Peak, we gawk at the shattered tooth of 12,516-foot Mount Beulah rearing across the gorge. Our next destination, Dead Horse Lake, shines like a milky turquoise mirror at the head of the valley. Immediately beneath us, a large elk herd grazes on an alpine shelf. Three small calves play on a snowbank, spinning and bucking like rodeo bulls. We watch for an hour, then descend to camp. Feeding trout spread rings across the calm water, and Pete heads off with his rod. I scout the wealth of five-star sunset vantage points. Like every camp so far, this one seems finer than the last.

At mile 62, we reach a junction and a choice: Take the official Highline Trail and drop into forest to quickly reach the trailhead (mile 73.4), or extend our vista trek by detouring on the Head of Rock Creek Trail.

We loop north another 5 miles to stay in the alpine zone. When faced with a quandary, always take the high road.

TRIP PLANNER

SEASON June to October

PERMIT None

COMMERCIAL SHUTTLE Inquire with Wilkins River Bus Lines (wilkinsbuslines.com). Prices vary.

CONTACT Ashley National Forest, www.fs.usda.gov/ashley

DISTANCE: 78 miles (point to point)

TIME: 7 to 10 days

DIFFICULTY: ★★★★↙

THE PAYOFF: Watch your step on the seldom-visited Highline Trail; the nonstop views and rampant wildlife are distractingly spectacular.

TRAILHEAD: Leidy Peak (40.7772, -109.8152); 35 miles northwest of Vernal on FR 043

SHUTTLE CAR Highline (40.7230, -110.8639); 32 miles east of Kamas on FR 456

MILES AND DIRECTIONS

FROM THE LEIDY PEAK TRAILHEAD:

1. Hop on the **Highline Trail** and take it 78 miles west across the spine of the Uinta Mountains to the Mirror Lake Byway, passing through pine forests, camping in high-alpine meadows, and crossing eight major passes.

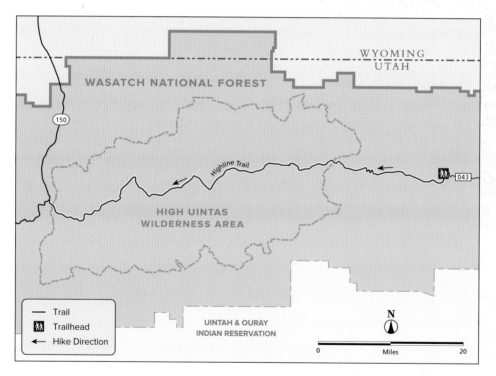

33: SACRED GROUND
CHARON'S GARDEN, WICHITA MOUNTAINS WILDLIFE REFUGE, OKLAHOMA

When North America's once millions-strong bison herd teetered on the brink of extinction at the turn of the twentieth century, the Bronx Zoo sent fifteen of the animals by train to this refuge in an effort to save the species. More than one hundred years later, about 650 of the beasts graze in its mixed-grass prairie, which was spared the plow thanks to the patchwork of granite outcroppings littering the area. Best part? You can camp smack in the middle of prime bison-spotting territory at the refuge's western edge—where your chances of glimpsing some of the preserve's 600-member elk herd are equally high.

TRIP PLANNER

SEASON September to May

PERMIT Required for overnight stay ($2 per person); reserve online or obtain from the refuge visitor center

CONTACT Wichita Mountains Wildlife Refuge, bit.do/wichita-mountains

DISTANCE: 4.8 miles (out and back)

TIME: 2 days

DIFFICULTY: ★✈

THE PAYOFF: Only ten overnight campers are allowed in this 5,000-acre backcountry at a time, which means the fringe where timber and prairie converge is all yours—if you're willing to share with the wildlife.

TRAILHEAD: Sunset (34.7315, -98.7242); 24 miles northwest of Lawton off OK 49

⟪ —— ⟫

MILES AND DIRECTIONS

FROM THE SUNSET TRAILHEAD:

1. Follow the **Charon's Garden Trail** 2.4 miles across a dry drainage and south through a boulder field that would seem more at home at the foot of the Rockies than in southwestern Oklahoma.

2. Turn around at Treasure Lake, retracing your steps to the trailhead.

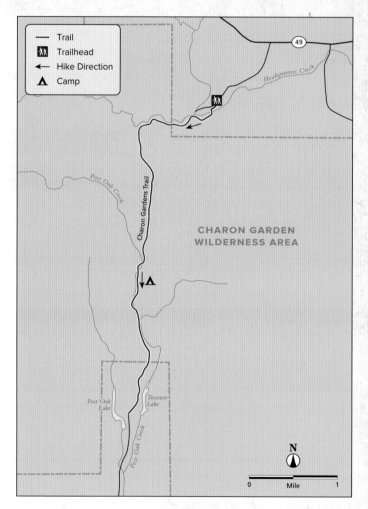

Adapted from text by Sarah L. Stewart.

ALL THE EXTRAS

DON'T MISS THIS CAMPSITE: HEADQUARTERS CREEK VALLEY (MILE 0.5)

Pitch your tent in a rock-strewn meadow where the bison often roam. In addition to the 2,000-pound behemoths, nab a view of 2,770-foot Elk Mountain, a slabby granite dome that hogs the horizon to the southeast. Next day, pick a route to the big kids' jungle-gym for roped climbing before continuing on to explore the rest of the Charon's Garden Trail.

KEEP YOUR EYES PEELED: WILDLIFE

Bison and Rocky Mountain elk have good company: Bobcats, white-tailed deer, river otters, mountain lions, and even longhorn cattle share this refuge. There are 240 bird species, too, including burrowing owls and bald eagles.

GEAR TIP: PACK IN WATER

While there are a few streams on this route, they are unreliable. Call ahead to check if they're running, or plan on carrying in all drinking and cooking water (one gallon per person per day in mild conditions). Good news: Camp is ultraconvenient to the trailhead, so you only need to camel the load a half mile.

Bison

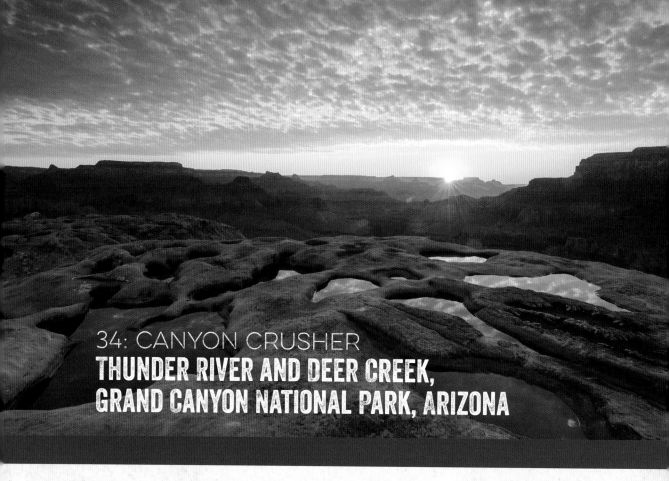

34: CANYON CRUSHER
THUNDER RIVER AND DEER CREEK, GRAND CANYON NATIONAL PARK, ARIZONA

Here's a secret: You need not wait in a life-list line to cash in on Grand Canyon's life-list scenery. Truth be told, simply avoiding the corridor trails guarantees you a slice of quietude in the country's second-most visited national park. But solitude gluttons should aim higher: Consider the North Rim the backdoor to the Big Ditch's sheer red cliffs, soaring desert pinnacles, and utter scope. The permits are easier, the campsites are emptier, and the terrain is spicier. See for yourself on the Thunder River–Deer Creek Loop, where more than 14,000 feet of elevation change, blazing sunshine, and a series of faint trails (OK, no trails) mean you'll be telling your grandchildren about this sufferfest. And, thanks to the Eden-like waterfalls and 20-mile views of redrock cliffs, temples, and buttes, we guarantee you won't regret a single sunbaked mile.

TRIP PLANNER

SEASON May to November, but be wary of scorching temps in midsummer

PERMIT Required for overnight stay ($10 per party plus $8 per person per day); download the application online and mail it in up to four months before departure

CONTACT Grand Canyon National Park, www.nps.gov/grca

DISTANCE: 26 miles (lollipop-loop)

TIME: 3 to 5 days

DIFFICULTY: ★★★★↙

THE PAYOFF: Explore the Mars-like Esplanade and three lush canyons from the North Rim.

TRAILHEAD: Bill Hall (36.4347, -112.4298); 45 miles south of Fredonia off Ryan Road

⇇ ——————————————————————————————— ⇉

MILES AND DIRECTIONS

FROM THE BILL HALL TRAILHEAD:

1. Descend more than 2,000 feet into the Grand Canyon on the **Bill Hall Trail,** navigating across the otherworldly Esplanade to a junction near mile 7.

2. Tackle the loop portion of the lollipop by heading another 3,000 feet into the canyon on the **Thunder River Trail,** which splits east before paralleling Tapeats Creek to the Colorado River near mile 12.

3. Trek 4 challenging miles west, alternating between faint user trails and trailless canyon walls and embankments, as you trace the Colorado River to Deer Creek. **Note:** There are sections of extreme exposure on this section.

4. Veer north on the **Deer Creek Trail,** climbing 2,000 feet over 3 miles to the loop's apex.

5. Retrace your steps 7 miles through the Esplanade and back out of the canyon to the trailhead via the **Bill Hall Trail.**

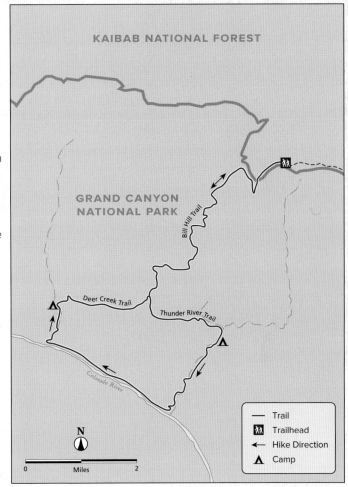

KAIBAB NATIONAL FOREST

GRAND CANYON NATIONAL PARK

Bill Hill Trail

Deer Creek Trail

Thunder River Trail

Colorado River

N

0 — Miles — 2

—— Trail
🚶 Trailhead
← Hike Direction
⛺ Camp

ALL THE EXTRAS

DON'T MISS THIS CAMPSITE: UPPER TAPEATS CREEK (MILE 10)

Camp in a cool riparian zone near Tapeats Creek where sandbars make for flat, comfy tent sites (and invite barefoot lounging) and lush cottonwoods provide privacy. There are a handful of established sites, but claim one of the waterside spots so you can soak ankles and knees sore from the crushing descent without leaving your digs.

DON'T MISS THIS CAMPSITE: DEER CREEK (MILE 16)

The secluded camp is nice, but the natural soaking basins and slick flumes are better. Deer Creek doubles as a water park here, which you'll appreciate after the challenging off-trail section along the Colorado River. From camp, grab a daypack and pick a path of least resistance roughly half a mile along the skinny rim above gushing Deer Creek and down a slope of loose scree to discover 200-foot-tall Deer Creek Falls, a fireworks blast of a cascade that pours over a bright-red rock wall dotted with hanging gardens.

EXTRA CREDIT: STRETCH IT OUT

If gonzo daily objectives aren't your thing, break up the mileage of this trip better by spending a night or two on the Esplanade. Dispersed camping is permitted on the 20-mile-long sandstone shelf, which you traverse on either end of the loop, so you can throw down among the hoodoo-like formations, mushroom-shaped rocks, and dark recesses. Be sure to pack in all water if you go this route (unless there's been recent rain, in which case you can drink from the potholes); there's no more until you hit Thunder River. Either way, budget extra time for impromptu exploring in the otherworldly landscape of the Esplanade—it's a North Rim gem.

35. AUTUMN OASIS
AREA B,
LOST MAPLES STATE NATURAL AREA, TEXAS

By Judy Paul

Can Creek cuts a vein through the woodlands, twisting through the vermilion bigtooth maples and out of sight to the horizon. It's the only feature that gives the expanse of color any definition. Elsewhere in the country, hikers are putting away their boots and packs for the winter, but here in Lost Maples, I'm about to set up a picture-perfect campsite on an outcrop 400 feet above the fall scenery. Tomorrow, I'll tour the woods, limestone canyons, and crystalline streams that set this area apart from other Texas wilds, and, since it's just a few hours from Austin, I can take my time. Just like the seasons.

DISTANCE: 6.6 miles (lollipop-loop)

TIME: 2 days

DIFFICULTY: ★

THE PAYOFF: Backpack where most folks dayhike and you'll get this park's marquee creeks, hardwoods, and bluffs with a side of solitude when night falls.

TRAILHEAD: East-West (29.8149, -99.5758); 6 miles north of Vanderpool off Ranch Road 187

MILES AND DIRECTIONS

FROM THE EAST-WEST TRAILHEAD:

1. Hike 0.4 mile north on the **East-West Trail** to a fork.

2. Stay right to complete the loop counterclockwise (for a longer first day, go clockwise), following the **East Trail** to a junction at mile 1.1.

3. Head 0.8 mile north toward Area B.

4. Retrace your steps to the junction between the East and West Trails at mile 2.7.

5. Peel off onto the **West Trail,** which curls 3.5 miles around to the East-West Trail.

6. Close the lollipop-loop by retracing your steps 0.4 mile on the **East-West Trail** to the trailhead.

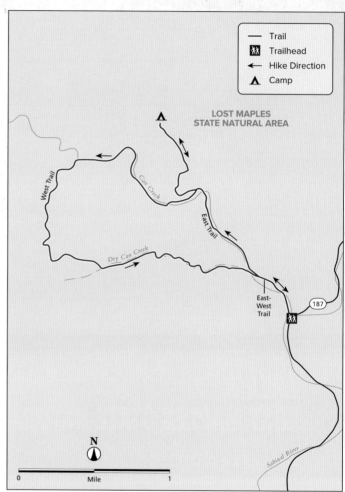

TRIP PLANNER

SEASON September to May

PERMIT None

CONTACT Lost Maples State Natural Area, bit.do/lost-maples-sna

ALL THE EXTRAS

DON'T MISS THIS CAMPSITE: AREA B (MILE 1.9)

Pitch your tent beneath the oaks in Campsite B. The steep, 400-foot climb to the top of the hillock is enough to deter most hikers (who instead opt for the pond area), so expect solitude. There are a handful of established spots ($10; online reservation recommended). Don't forget to top off your water at Can Creek before making the climb; it's dry up here. Keep an eye out for red-tailed hawks overhead.

KEEP YOUR EYES PEELED: FOLIAGE

The park's namesake bigtooth maples turn in November. Expect a killer bird's-eye vantage from the overlook in Area B, but check the Lost Maples Foliage Report for current information on where and when at bit.do/lost-maples-foliage-report.

EXTRA CREDIT: ADD A DAY TRIP

From basecamp at Area B, hike about a mile east on the East Trail to the Grotto, where maidenhair ferns cover limestone canyon walls. Continue about 0.5 mile to aptly named Monkey Rock, which rises above a tributary of the Sabinal River.

Fall colors in Area B

36: MIND OVER MUSCLE
THE MAZE,
CANYONLANDS NATIONAL PARK, UTAH

There's a reason people talk about The Maze in hushed tones. Once you enter the most remote section of Canyonlands' labyrinth of rain-channeled redrock, you're truly out of pocket. The scarcity of water, the shoulder-width slots, the walls that stretch toward the heavens—add in the fact that most of The Maze's features are unnamed, and many are even unmapped—it's not surprising you're unlikely to find anyone else in its interior. But that's the point.

TRIP PLANNER

SEASON March to May and September to November

PERMIT Required for overnight stay ($30 per party); reserve online or try for a walk-in

WATER TAXI Tex's Riverways; book a round-trip water-taxi ride from Potash Boat Ramp at texsriverways.com

CONTACT Canyonlands National Park, www.nps.gov/cany

Photo: Bruce Tremper

DISTANCE: 18.8 miles (lollipop-loop)

TIME: 2 to 3 days

DIFFICULTY: ★★★★✦

THE PAYOFF: Plunge headlong into terrain others avoid to experience a lifetime of desert highlights—slickrock canyons, ancient ruins and pictographs, meandering creeks, and red sandstone arches and hoodoos.

TRAILHEAD: Spanish Bottom (38.1609, -109.9285); a water taxi will drop you off at the trailhead

MILES AND DIRECTIONS

FROM SPANISH BOTTOM:

1. Find the obvious footpath and negotiate the singletrack 1.4 miles west over crumbly redrock, ascending 1,200 feet, to the spires of the Doll House.

2. Veer north onto a dirt "road," which wends 4 miles through the desertscape to Chimney Rock Campground and the apex of the loop.

3. Create an 8-mile, on- and off-trail loop: Connect the **Petes Mesa** and **Plug Trails** roughly 5 miles counterclockwise before veering south down an unnamed slot (near 38.2059, -109.9923) that spits you out back at Chimney Rock.

4. Retrace your steps 5.4 miles to the launch at Spanish Bottom.

DON'T MISS THIS CAMPSITE: CHIMNEY ROCK CAMPGROUND (MILE 5.4)

Find a piece of real estate in the shadow of the area's spindly namesake to make a basecamp. Next day, when you tackle the 8-mile loop described above, head out with a lighter pack, leaving your shelter and sleeping bag behind. (Warning: Only experienced desert travelers and navigators should attempt this trip. If you check both of those boxes, bring a GPS unit in addition to your map and compass. When you're tracking off-trail, you'll appreciate the ability to leave a virtual breadcrumb trail.)

GEAR TIP: PACK IN WATER

Unless there's been very recent rain, you can bet the Maze is dry. Pack in at least one gallon per person per day (in mild conditions) for drinking and cooking. You can stow the latter at camp for the dayhike along the Petes Mesa and Plug Trails.

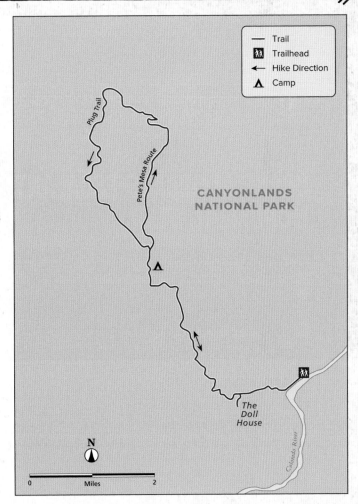

Photo: Austin Connelly

INSIDER'S GUIDE

37: CANYON COUNTRY
GRAND STAIRCASE-ESCALANTE NATIONAL MONUMENT, UTAH

If it's true desert wilderness you seek—snaking slots, deep redrock chasms, and secret swimming oases—then you can't do better than this now 1-million-acre park sprawling across southern Utah. Plan a slickrock adventure with these tips and tricks from local expert **Rick Green.** By Elisabeth Kwak-Hefferan

THE INSIDER
Rick Green may be king of the desert rats: As the eighteen-year owner of the outfitter Excursions of Escalante, he racks up some 200 canyon days every year. Totaled, that's more than eight solid years of exploring Escalante's hidden corners.

1. EASY-ACCESS DAYHIKE
Even though Big Horn Canyon is just 10 miles outside the town of Escalante, it remains surprisingly quiet: "Everyone's in a hurry to go way the heck out to Coyote Gulch, and they drive right by the canyons near town," Green says. The few who do explore the twisty, redrock canyon's sandstone towers and narrows enter on the north end, but Green prefers the "top-secret entrance." From the unmarked trailhead (just past a corral about 5 miles down Hole-in-the-Rock Road), follow Harris Wash 2 miles to join Big Horn Canyon to the north. Enter Big Horn and take the first fork on your right to snake through

a rust-colored slot canyon and reach an open sandstone basin swirled with reds and oranges. Continue exploring up the main fork of Big Horn Canyon as the walls stretch 150 feet above you, then retrace your steps for a 6- to 8-mile hike (depending on how far up you go).

2. BEST MULTIDAY TRIP

Looking for the classic Escalante experience—but not in the mood to share? Head for the under-the-radar Upper Paria River area on Green's favorite 33-mile, four-day shuttle hike down a deep (500 feet in spots), sculpted sandstone canyon packed with opportunities for exploring side gorges. "It's wide like the Grand Canyon in some places, there are giant ponderosa pines and cottonwoods to camp under, and if you have a keen eye, there's rock art the length of this hike," Green says. From the pullout off Cottonwood Canyon Road (37.5110, -112.0339), descend along the Paria Wash to the Sheep Creek confluence at about mile 10. Day two, hike 5 miles to Deer Creek and set up camp, then explore Deer Creek and West Oak Creek Canyons just downstream. Day three takes you 8 miles to Hogeye Canyon, another worthy side trip (and your last reliable water). Finish with a 10-mile hike to your shuttle car on Cottonwood Canyon Road (37.2278, -111.9289). Target May or early fall for the best conditions and pack a 50-foot hand-line for navigating the scrambly bits in some side canyons (free permit required; pick up at Cannonville Visitor Center).

3. TOP BASECAMP

The sandy, cottonwood-shaded campsite at the confluence of the Escalante River and Death Hollow tops Green's list for its nearby swimming holes (1.5 miles up Death Hollow Canyon), soaring canyon walls, and abundant rock art. But now it's better than ever, thanks to extensive volunteer work over the past couple of years that has cleared the canyon of its overgrowth of invasive tamarisk and Russian olive. To get there, follow the Escalante River 7 miles upstream from the Escalante River trailhead, passing a natural rock bridge and panels of pictographs and petroglyphs on the south-facing canyon walls, to heavenly camping at the mouth of Death Hollow (free self-issue permit required).

4. SECRET CAR CAMPGROUND

Calf Creek Campground, between Boulder and Escalante on U.S. 12, draws campers like flies to honey for its rich red canyon walls, desert spring, and proximity to 126-foot-tall Calf Creek Falls. But just down the road, Deer Creek Campground offers similar highlights "with 2 percent of the people," Green says. From your tent, hike down Deer Creek Canyon for rock art and trout fishing—but no waterfalls. Best bet: Take a dip in Calf Creek Falls, then hightail it to Deer Creek ($10 per night).

5. SLOT CANYONS

Visiting Escalante without wiggling through a few tight spots is like going to Yellowstone and skipping the geysers. For beginners, Green recommends the 5-miler connecting

Peek-a-Boo and Spooky Gulches: "They give everyone a chance to climb and squeeze through classic, twisting slots." From the Dry Fork trailhead, spider through Peek-a-Boo, then hike 0.5 mile east across the desert to join narrower Spooky (no permit needed for day trips).

6. POST-TRIP REFUELING

"Easy choice: Escalante Outfitters," Green says. The guide company-cum-gear-shop cum restaurant in Escalante serves up tasty pizza (try the ham-and-goat-cheese Big Horn) and local microbrews, including their own, Vagabond Ale. "The maps and cool vibe there make it the place to hang out."

TRIP PLANNER

SEASON March to May and September to November

PERMIT Required for overnight stay (free); obtain at any ranger or visitor center

CONTACT Grand Staircase-Escalante National Monument, bit.do/grand-staircase-blm

---

Calf Creek Falls

STAY HYDRATED

Like wine to the gods, water is the nectar of athletes. "Losing just 1 percent of weight from water loss can impair performance," says Colleen Cooke, a sports nutritionist at the Boulder Center for Sports Medicine. Countless hikers and mountaineers have turned to her for advice on nutrition. Their number-one question: How do I stay hydrated? Here's what she recommends.

DRINK EARLY. While you sleep, you lose as much as 1.5 pounds of fluid through sweat and respiration. Before breaking camp, replenish with 16 to 24 ounces of water, a sports drink, or noncaffeinated tea.

SIP OFTEN. According to Cooke, some hikers walk for three hours, sip a few ounces on a rest break, and pay for it at the end of the day. Instead, drink 4 to 6 ounces of liquid every 20 minutes; it'll help you feel strong, even on the last hill. Hydration bladders encourage drinking more than water bottles.

ADD ELECTROLYTES. "Sweat is made up of sodium and potassium, which need to be replaced," says Cooke. If they're not, you'll likely feel sluggish. Sip a sports drink (powdered versions work well in the field) or munch on salty snacks.

EAT CARBS. "Every gram of carbohydrate you eat pulls three grams of water into your digestive system, which helps keep you hydrated," explains Cooke. Cooke recommends a carb-protein-fat ratio of 60-20-20 for backpackers on multiday trips.

WATCH FOR SYMPTOMS. Headaches, dizziness, and difficulty concentrating can signal dehydration. The fix: Rest, eat, and drink. Anxiety, a weak or rapid pulse, and clammy or hot and dry skin point to serious dehydration. Set up camp: A long rest, a good meal, and lots of water are your best bets for feeling stronger in the morning.

Explore the best of the Rockies in southern Colorado's oxygen-starved
San Juan Mountains (page 158). Photo: Glenn Randall

MOUNTAIN
WEST

38: HELL HATH NO FURY
HELLS CANYON NATIONAL RECREATION AREA, IDAHO/OREGON

By Michael Lanza

Pfft . . . pfft.

The sound barely registers inside the warm cocoon of my sleeping bag. It's different—softer—than the anesthetic patter of rain that lulled me to sleep hours ago. Working slowly, like a cranky old PC, my brain powers up to identify the source: snow. In April.

I crack an eyelid to check for daylight. The tent is intensely dark, like the recesses of a cave. I shut down for a few more hours of deep unconsciousness, the gentle brushing of snowflakes on my nylon roof as effective a narcotic as any.

At daylight, I step outside on urgent business and discover a landscape that has changed radically overnight. Visibility is 50 feet, and 3 inches of wet stuff blankets the ground. Perfect, fat flakes flutter down from a ceiling so close it's almost claustrophobic. There's no wind, no sound. I've been in many whiteouts, but stepping so abruptly into a space so blank gives me a disorienting rush of vertigo. After a few moments, my eyes and equilibrium adjust, and I begin to relax—and appreciate the emptiness. My little white bubble is as peaceful as the world gets.

When I hit the trail an hour later, the clouds lift enough to reveal the looming cliffs, deep side canyons, and steep, sage- and grass-covered slopes of Hells Canyon, all

DO IT

DISTANCE: 50 miles (lollipop-loop)

TIME: 4 to 6 days

DIFFICULTY: ★★★★★

THE PAYOFF: This remote chasm boasts big views, craggy mountains, abundant wildlife, and—especially on the west side—staggering solitude.

TRAILHEAD: Freezeout (45.3750, -116.7615); 44 miles east of Joseph on FR 4230

MILES AND DIRECTIONS

FROM THE FREEZEOUT TRAILHEAD:

1. On the **Saddle Creek Trail,** ascend Freezeout Saddle and drop off to the east to a junction and the start of the loop near mile 3.

2. Head 19.3 miles north on the **High Trail** to a T-junction.

3. Fall off the ridge to the west toward Wisnor Place and another trail intersection.

4. Take the **Temperance Creek Trail** northeast to the teal-colored Snake River at mile 27.4.

5. Parallel the water nearly 14 miles on the **Oregon Snake River Trail** to where Saddle Creek courses into Hells Canyon.

6. Turn west onto the **Saddle Creek Trail,** climbing out of the canyon and back to the original junction near mile 47.

7. Retrace your steps over Freezeout Saddle back to the trailhead.

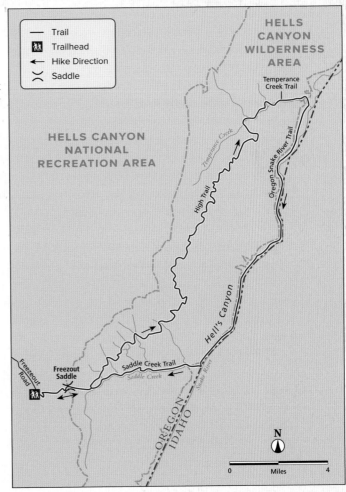

HELLS CANYON WILDERNESS AREA

Temperance Creek Trail

HELLS CANYON NATIONAL RECREATION AREA

High Trail

Temperance Creek

Oregon Snake River Trail

Hell's Canyon

Freezeout Road

Freezeout Saddle

Saddle Creek Trail

Saddle Creek

Snake River

OREGON / IDAHO

Trail
Trailhead
Hike Direction
Saddle

N

0   Miles   4

whitewashed by the storm. I chuckle to myself at the fickle notion of seasons. Here in North America's deepest river gorge, weather ignores the calendar. I've seen snow on the 4th of July and sunbathed the first week of March. The canyon is big enough to make its own weather, but its climate is mostly a function of elevation change, something the canyon has in greater measure than many US mountain ranges.

This is a place defined by extremes—of scale, solitude, grandeur. Perhaps more than any wild land I've known, this canyon fills me with a sense of having dropped out of time, of diving, wide-eyed, into Alice's rabbit hole. The biggest disconnect? That a place so unblemished and diverse could attract so few visitors.

Which is exactly why I've returned for a four-day, 50-mile spring hike, during which I'll loop from the top of Hells Canyon down to the Snake River and back up again, sampling every part of the canyon's geography.

AND WHAT A GEOGRAPHY IT IS. "Hells," as some locals call it, is a 70-mile-long chasm dividing western Idaho from northeastern Oregon. Over eons, the Snake River and its tributaries have carved a vast, complex topography of side canyons and draws branching from the main gorge like the roots of an old cottonwood.

On the Oregon side, where I started yesterday, the rim rises 5,500 feet above the river. The relief on the Idaho side is even more dramatic. More than 8,000 feet separate the river from the top of the Seven Devils Mountains, making Hells deeper than the Grand Canyon by more than half a mile. The canyon is arid—nearly a desert—and largely treeless, except at higher elevations, where snowfall nurtures conifer forests. But the conditions don't stop the canyon and its surrounding peaks from being one of the richest wildlife refuges in the Lower 48, home to more than 350 species, including life-listers like bighorn sheep, black bears, bald eagles, and mountain lions, plus river otters and scads of rattlers. Congress designated the 652,000-acre Hells Canyon National Recreation Area in 1975; today the area includes 214,000 acres of wilderness.

The loop leads me on a wild tour of the seasons—sometimes multiple in a single day. I began yesterday afternoon in "summer," marching nearly 2,000 feet uphill on the Saddle Creek Trail. After fifty switchbacks on a sunbaked slope, I'd sweated through my T-shirt like a linebacker at an NFL training camp. At 5,448-foot Freezeout Saddle, I stepped abruptly into autumn—a chill wind and patches of snow. Even the view raised goosebumps. Snow-capped mountains rose in two directions—the Seven Devils to the east, Oregon's Wallowas to the west. The great gash of Hells fell away so far below I couldn't see the bottom. Then it was forward into spring, as I descended 1,500 feet of switchbacks beneath a warm drizzle and a vibrant rainbow.

Today, sunrise brought my wintry surprise. The black, pinnacled cliffs of Summit Ridge, towering hundreds of feet overhead, display a thin, new cape of white. A light snow falls as I hike the High Trail, a path set on a broad, miles-long bench at 4,200 feet. It cuts through open groves of trees, past waterfalls, and across broad, grass-covered ridges.

The unpredictable weather hints at the immensity of Hells Canyon, but it doesn't tell the full story. With each passing hour, my eyes adjust to the breadth and depth of scenery in the way a theatergoer's ears tune in to Shakespearean dialogue. Like a great mountain range turned inside-out, the canyon's contours leap and fall endlessly, from the creek-scoured ravine I step across to the multiple layers of distant ridges and tributary canyons. Land features seem to swell to tremendous size, then fade slowly to relative obscurity against a vast backdrop, a phenomenon of perception I've experienced only here and in the Grand Canyon.

Late in the morning on my second day, five elk dart uphill away from me, moving with an effortless speed that belies the slope's severe angle. Within seconds, they've disappeared into the sparse pine forest. In the canyon's middle elevations, the elk seem as numerous as birds. On previous trips, I've watched as many as one hundred of these majestic animals flow uphill in such a dense cluster it gave the illusion of the ground moving.

BY MID-AFTERNOON, THE STORM PASSES. My load light, I lope nearly 2,000 feet down numerous switchbacks to the valley of Temperance Creek—and back into spring. I strip to short sleeves and make camp in an overgrown meadow called Wisnor Place, then poke around a dilapidated cabin and some long-abandoned farm equipment rusting in the tall grass. Tiny, mouse-infested shacks like this one are scattered around the canyon, stark reminders of the remote, marginal lives of the settlers who farmed and ranched here from the late 1800s until the Depression.

A mile below Wisnor Place, knee-deep Temperance Creek ducks between 400-foot cliffs on its descent to the Snake River. Except for one spot where it climbs steeply to a great overlook of this side canyon, the Temperance Creek Trail hugs the water so closely it requires you to ford it some twenty-one times in 3 miles. I change to hiking sandals and splash downstream.

When I reach the Snake on my third morning, it feels like July in St. Louis. At 1,300 feet, I'm two seasons and four-fifths of a vertical mile removed from the snowy highlands where I started. Under a desert sun, I follow the Oregon Snake River Trail south. The nonstop views of the meandering ribbon of water beneath cliffs and grassy, nearly treeless ridges leave no doubt why 68 miles of the Snake River are designated as wild and scenic. There

TRIP PLANNER

SEASON March to November

PERMIT None

CONTACT Wallowa-Whitman National Forest, www.fs.usda.gov/wallowa-whitman

are sandy beaches, broad flats covered with bunchgrasses and prickly pear cactus, and a remarkably well-built path clinging to cliffs 400 feet above the roiling whitewater.

On my last night, I pitch my tent near the mouth of Saddle Creek on a perfectly flat lawn at the edge of an abandoned orchard. A ranching family tended cherry, apricot, apple, pear, and peach trees here from about 1915 to 1938, I'll later learn from an 87-year-old woman who remembers playing among the neat rows. My only neighbors now are wagon wheels and a plow slowly sinking into the earth (though a group of wild turkeys will awaken me at dawn with their boisterous foraging). Evening paints the rock bands and grassy hillsides across the river in a warm, golden light.

Looking at the old farm equipment, I think about what life must have been like here a century ago—and conjure an image at once daunting and appealing. Then I realize that this spot almost certainly feels lonelier and more remote today than it did then. In four days, I've seen just one other person, a woman running a rustic lodge at Temperance Creek. On other visits, I've seen no one at all. For a backpacker, that kind of solitude is always a glorious thing, but it's truly rare when you find it in a landscape so transcendent. That's the story of Hells Canyon, the rare American wilderness whose beauty far eclipses its renown.

Bighorn sheep

39: NUMBERS GAME
MOOSE BASIN, GRAND TETON NATIONAL PARK, WYOMING

Park use statistics": Where others imagine boring spreadsheets, you should see a golden opportunity for peace and quiet. That's how you waltz into one of the most visited national parks with a walk-in permit that grants you access to an area dominated by glacier-gouged canyons and wildflower-studded drainages—and so seldom visited by humans that the park describes grizzly sightings as "frequent." The stats show that John D. Rockefeller, Jr. Memorial Parkway, on the park's northern border, issues a fraction of the backcountry permits that Grand Teton does. But the parkway's lone trail, the Glade Creek Trail, connects to a network of under-the-radar canyons inside the Tetons' boundaries. The canyons never fill, and, in fact, rarely do they see foot traffic at all. When you're standing amid chest-high wildflowers with an unimpeded view south to 13,770-foot Grand Teton and the other Cathedral Peaks, you may wonder why—but you won't be upset about it.

TRIP PLANNER

SEASON July to October

PERMIT Required for overnight stay ($25 per party); obtain at any ranger station

CONTACT Grand Teton National Park, www.nps.gov/grte

Photo: Justin Sharick

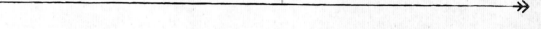
DISTANCE: 34.2 miles (lollipop-loop)

TIME: 3 to 4 days

DIFFICULTY: ★★★⸠

THE PAYOFF: Venture to the northern boundary of Grand Teton to discover a quiet canyon loop that only the bears and wolves know about.

TRAILHEAD: Glade Creek (44.0899, -110.7243); 42 miles north of Moose on Ashton-Flagg Ranch Road

MILES AND DIRECTIONS

FROM THE GLADE CREEK TRAILHEAD:

1. Hike 5.3 miles south on the **Glade Creek Trail** to a junction near the west bank of Jackson Lake, the apex of the loop.

2. Do it counterclockwise for better views: Proceed west on the **Berry Creek Trail,** which meanders 1.8 miles through a lodgepole forest dotted with meadows (prime megafauna habitat) to another intersection.

3. Veer south onto the 1.6-mile cutoff trail to connect with Owl Canyon.

4. Follow the chasm southwest on the **Owl Canyon Trail** to crest 9,718-foot Moose Basin Divide for big views of Mount Moran near mile 16.7.

5. Exit via the steeper, rockier **Webb Canyon Trail,** which descends to Jackson Lake and swings north to reconnect with the initial junction.

6. Retrace your steps 5.3 miles on the **Glade Creek Trail** to the trailhead.

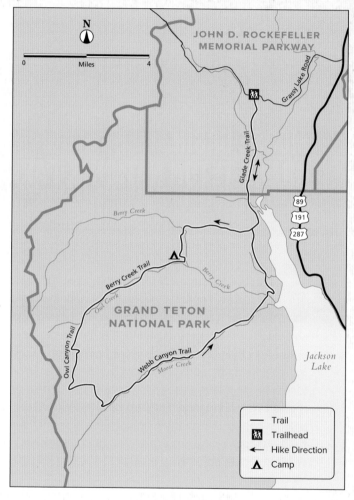

Adapted from text by Elisabeth Kwak-Hefferan.

ALL THE EXTRAS

DON'T MISS THIS CAMPSITE: CONFLUENCE OF BERRY AND OWL CREEKS (MILE 8.7)

Find a trailside bench above the confluence of the creeks where the area is thick with evergreens. Keep an eye out for bears (both kinds) lumbering through the fringes at twilight; practice bear safety, of course. From camp, you're in prime position to tackle the long, gradual climb up Moose Basin Divide on day two.

KEEP YOUR EYES PEELED: FLORA

Time your trip for midsummer and the alpine meadows and drainages will look like something out of a Monet painting, with indigo bluebells, yellow asters, violet monkshood, fuchsia fireweed, blue lupine, and snowy columbines and bistort.

FUN FACT: GEOLOGY

Glimpse obvious, zebra-like striations of light rock smushed against dark rock on the north walls of both Owl and Webb Canyons. A contact point between the southern Teton Range's granite and the northern Teton Range's limestone, the Forellen Fault extends from Ranger Peak to Survey Peak—straight through this loop.

Arnica blooms near Jackson Lake

40: PEAK SEASON
SNOWMASS AND WILLOW LAKES, MAROON BELLS-SNOWMASS WILDERNESS, COLORADO

By Maren Kasselik

When I unzip my tent door at dawn, two things are abundantly clear: For one, high-country air is good for my lungs *and* my soul. For another, it's obvious why the Four Pass Loop is a perennial life-list trip. But you won't find this private view of the striated, brick-red Maroon Bells on that busy route. I'm camped beside an alpine lake just north of that track, below the pyramidal giants on the last day of a quiet, three-day adventure—a three-pass loop that shares only 3.8 miles with its popular alternative. It's led me to deserted campsites and atop a Fourteener, 14,099-foot Snowmass Mountain. I'd trade the extra 12,000-foot pass for that any day.

TRIP PLANNER

SEASON July to October

PERMIT Required for overnight stay (free); self-issue at trailhead kiosk

CONTACT White River National Forest, www.fs.usda.gov/whiteriver

---

DISTANCE: 23.6 miles (loop)

TIME: 3 days

DIFFICULTY: ★★★★

THE PAYOFF: Go on a high-alpine tour through Colorado's Elk Mountains, stopping over at two relatively quiet lakes en route.

TRAILHEAD: Snowmass Creek (39.1992, -107.0014); 38 miles south of Glenwood Springs on Snowmass Creek Road

MILES AND DIRECTIONS

FROM THE SNOWMASS CREEK TRAILHEAD:

1. Follow the **Snowmass Creek Trail** generally south for 6.3 miles to a beaver dam. **Note:** Some topos refer to this trail as the northern segment of the **Crater Lake Trail (#1975).**

2. Cross the gentle, knee-deep water or shimmy across logs to the western shore of the beaver dam, then pick up the singletrack again; reach Snowmass Lake at mile 8.3.

3. Follow signs for Buckskin Pass, staying on the same pack trail as it curls 4.3 miles east over the 12,462-foot saddle to a junction.

4. Veer north on the **Willow Lake Trail (#1978),** which climbs over another 12,000-foot pass and drops down to its namesake near mile 15.3.

5. Retrace your steps 0.6 mile to a junction.

6. Go 7.7 miles north on the **East Snowmass Trail (#1977)** (cross East Snowmass Pass at mile 16.9 and dip back below treeline at mile 18.8) to close the loop and return to the trailhead.

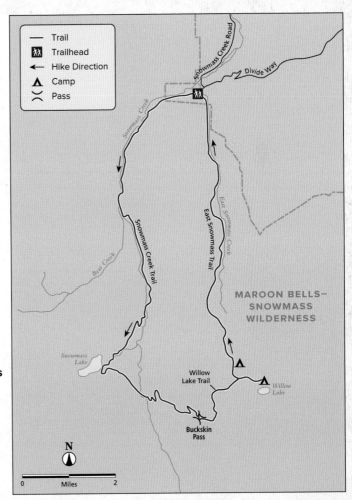

Legend:
— Trail
🚶 Trailhead
← Hike Direction
▲ Camp
⌣ Pass

ALL THE EXTRAS

DON'T MISS THIS CAMPSITE: SNOWMASS LAKE (MILE 8.3)

For primo sunrise alpenglow on 14,099-foot Snowmass Mountain's silvery slopes, set up camp at one of the two established sites on the lake's eastern shore. You'll catch the behemoth's reflection on the lake outside your tent door and be tucked away from the slew of wooded sites east of the lake.

DON'T MISS THIS CAMPSITE: WILLOW LAKE (MILE 15.3)

Spend night two on a ledge overlooking blue-green Willow Lake, 100 feet below. Set up your tent near rust-colored the fire pit amid a grove of pines, which open south to the water.

EXTRA CREDIT: ADD A HIKE

Nab one of the state's spiciest nontechnical Fourteeners—14,099-foot Snowmass Mountain—on a 5-mile out-and-back from Snowmass Lake. First, track 0.9 mile on a faint user trail around the southern shore to the scree field. From here, it's 1.6 miles up steep talus (gaining 3,000 feet) to the Elks' knife-edge ridge. A final 50-foot, Class 4 push leads to the true summit of Colorado's fifth-most remote Fourteener. After the crux, scan the ridgeline to see 14,131-foot Capitol Peak to the northwest and the iconic Maroon Bells to the southeast.

Snowmass Mountain's knife edge

41. MOUNTAINS MAJESTY
TWIN LAKES,
SAWTOOTH NATIONAL RECREATION AREA, IDAHO

Crystal-clear lakes cupped by granite peaks, an enormous crag called El Capitan—you might think you're in Yosemite except for the lack of crowds. This circuit around 10,280-foot Parks Peak in the Sawtooth National Recreation Area benefits from its non-national park designation and relative remoteness. Best part? You don't even need to be mountaineer-fit to cash in: The route racks up just 3,100 feet of elevation gain in 18.5 spectacularly pretty miles.

TRIP PLANNER

SEASON July to October

PERMIT Required for overnight stay (free); self-issue at trailhead kiosk

CONTACT Sawtooth National Forest, www.fs.usda.gov/sawtooth

DISTANCE: 18.5 miles (loop)

TIME: 2 or 3 days

DIFFICULTY: ★★⌐

THE PAYOFF: Explore a granitic playground of peaks, lakes, meadows, and wildlife in an underrated national recreation area.

TRAILHEAD: Tin Cup (43.9842, -114.8716); 20 miles south of Stanley on FR 362

MILES AND DIRECTIONS

FROM THE TIN CUP TRAILHEAD:

1. Trek 7.8 miles west on **Trail 095,** passing Pettit, Alice, and Twin Lakes to 9,390-foot Snowyside Pass, true to its name until late July.

2. Drop north off the saddle on **Trail 092,** which switchbacks 2.5 miles down to a junction on the north shore of Toxaway Lake, where big brookies swim.

3. Continue northeast down the canyon of Yellow Belly Creek on **Trail 096** to an intersection near mile 16.3.

4. Veer south on **Trail 041** over the ridge to drop back down to the Tin Cup trailhead.

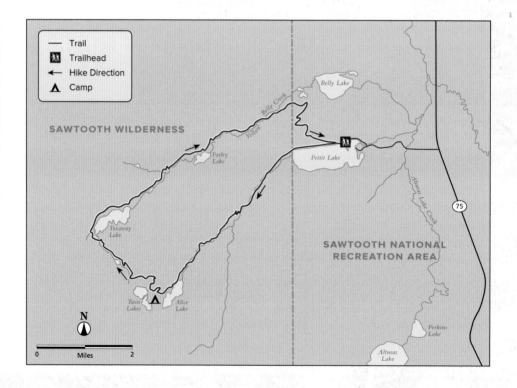

Adapted from text by Dougald MacDonald.

ALL THE EXTRAS

DON'T MISS THIS CAMPSITE: TWIN LAKES (MILE 6.7)

Not that this place sees many people in the first place, but those who do visit typically execute dayhikes to Alice or Toxaway Lakes. Your strategy: Camp between at this duo of turquoise pools. The Caribbean-blue water and granite reefs might even suggest snorkeling—if you can withstand the water longer than 30 seconds.

GEAR TIP: PACK LAYERS

You'll want a swimsuit or a pair of quick-dry shorts—and a Michelin Man-style puffy. The diurnal temperature swings in the Sawtooths are the stuff of legends. Also, don't forget trekking poles—you'll want them for challenging creek crossings, especially during afternoon runoff.

EXTRA CREDIT: ADD A HIKE

If the weather is good atop Snowyside Pass, scramble 0.8 mile up the east ridge of 10,651-foot Snowyside Peak. From the high point, the alpine tarns littered across the pocked granite, both on this route and west into Boise National Forest, look like teal gems on a coronet. The Sawtooth Range extends north and south like a gunsight.

Pica

42: VANISHING ACT
YELLOWSTONE NATIONAL PARK, WYOMING/MONTANA

By Michael Behar

Last night I pitched my tent at 8,500 feet atop the Buffalo Plateau, in a mile-wide meadow laced with spring-fed brooks. From the campsite, overlooking the remote northeast corner of Yellowstone National Park, I have the option of descending back to the base of the plateau and making a horseshoe end run around its north side. But a ranger in the backcountry office had told me about an off-trail shortcut through a lodgepole burn that would save 4 miles. Of course, like most cross-country bushwhacks, it was debatable if the "shortcut" would actually save time. I knew it would require acrobatic scrambling over and under fallen timber. But who can pass up the allure of such a little-used route?

It's late June and I'm in Yellowstone on a six-day, 40-plus-mile hike with my wife, Ashley, and three friends: Jake and Wendy, who are buddies from Seattle, and Hope, an old friend from San Francisco. None of us has backpacked in the park before, and the Buffalo Plateau is an unlikely location for first-timers. With a week to amble through the iconic park, most Yellowstone rookies hit one of the classics—Bechler Meadows, the Lamar Valley, or the Gallatin Range. These are each life-list treks, to be sure, but to hike them you have to wait until late summer—when passes aren't snowbound and river crossings aren't life-threatening—and you must be willing to share the deservedly popular routes with other hikers. None of that would do.

I, perhaps selfishly, wanted what every Yellowstone backpacker wants: a wildlife-packed, people-free, accessible trek. With help from Dagan Klein in the backcountry office, I found my prize on the Buffalo Plateau with a point-to-point route that promised it all, plus a chance to explore the dramatic Black Canyon of the Yellowstone.

One reason the area has remained under the radar screen: Most photos of the Buffalo Plateau, taken in late summer, show ochre grasslands that suggest heat and dust. But we departed the Hellroaring Creek trailhead after a season of above-average snowfall had saturated the park. On the morning we started hiking, the sun shined brightly on a landscape transformed by the moisture, like all of Yellowstone had been treated with Miracle-Gro. Had I been drugged and blindfolded and then told I'd been delivered to the Mayo coast in western Ireland, I'd have had no trouble believing it.

Our plan was to follow the Buffalo Plateau Trail north, then link up with Hellroaring Creek and, turning west, end with a tour down the Black Canyon. After the first mile, we reached a suspension bridge that crosses the Yellowstone River, swollen with snowmelt, running milky and full. From the bridge, we faced a 6-mile, 2,500-foot climb to our first camp on the plateau. The ascent was steep but not arduous; valley updrafts kept the air cool, in the mid-60s. Radiant meadows glowed a dozen shades of green, and the trail, hidden beneath lush spring growth, varied from barely visible to entirely vanished.

We climbed through a minefield of glistening dung patties so fresh that bison must have moseyed by only an hour earlier. They also left behind fist-size clumps of fur that clung like Velcro to low-slung shrubs. By the time we set up camp in the high meadow, without having seen another backpacker all day, I knew we'd come to the right place.

EVEN SO, I'M PREPARED FOR THE WORST when we embark on that shortcut in the morning. It's the only section of our route that passes through backcountry torched during the 1988 Yellowstone fires. And though the going is tough—we must balance on fallen and charred trunks, which frequently collapse underfoot—the reward is well worth the effort: The rejuvenated landscape amazes us. Thousands of lodgepole saplings have sprouted like a deep-wilderness Christmas tree farm. Wildflowers run amok—lupine, Indian paintbrush, bluebells, shooting stars, and forget-me-nots—in undulating rainbow bands. Sparrows nest in deadwood hollows, and the mounds of pocket gophers furrow the chocolate-hued topsoil. The ground itself bursts with water as brooks upwell through electric-green moss, like champagne bubbling to the surface.

The shortcut deposits us just beyond the park boundary. Wild chives fringe a shallow spring-fed pond, and I sample a handful before rejoining the established trail. After crossing a muddy woodland, the path emerges on an exposed ridge that rises 1,000 feet above Hellroaring Creek, which flows so furiously that it vibrates the earth. We continue 3.2 miles to our second camp, an airy bench at the confluence of Hellroaring and Horse Creeks, where we stoke the flames of a campfire and munch on squares of artisan dark chocolate that Ashley had secretly packed. After a 10-plus-mile day, it's a moment to savor: The fire warms our faces, stars blaze overhead, and lightning flickers on the horizon.

The next morning, our route veers south along Hellroaring Creek, its banks flush with huckleberries just beginning to ripen. We've walked less than 500 yards when we glimpse a black bear at the base of a pine, pacing nervously. Suddenly, a beagle-size cub scurries up the trunk. We can hear its raspy, eerily human cries. The sow follows effortlessly into the treetop. But when we stick around snapping photos, mama scampers back down. Upsetting a bear that's protecting a newborn ranks right up there with the all-time stupidest back-country tricks, so we divert onto a slippery embankment that rejoins the trail downriver. Later, we recognize what's left of an elk. Its remains are stripped clean except for inedible sinew; stamped in the mud nearby is the unmistakable paw print of a gray wolf.

THE TERRAIN CHANGES ABRUPTLY ON OUR THIRD DAY. The forest thins, undergrowth recedes, and fragrant sage and juniper appear amid craggy outcrops of orange rock. It's a classic high-desert landscape, and the last place I'd expect to encounter a grizzly. But at dusk that's exactly what comes galumphing toward our campsite. After a frozen second, we realize that it doesn't see us. The bellowing river and stiff breeze muddle its senses. Instant, unbridled hollering solves that problem. It perks its ears and then does an about-face, disappearing behind a furrow in the hillside. After the adrenaline clears my system, I'm reminded of the exceptional solitude we've found. It's no exaggeration to say we've seen more bears (three) than other backpackers (zero).

On our fourth day of hiking, we link up with the Yellowstone River Trail and follow it to the mouth of the Black Canyon. It's also the day that the weather—consistently sunny and pleasantly warm until now—gnashes its teeth. When we intersect the Yellowstone River,

TRIP PLANNER

SEASON May to October

PERMIT Required for overnight stay ($3 per person per night); apply ahead of time (costs an extra $25) or try for a walk-in at any of the ranger stations

CONTACT Yellowstone National Park, www.nps.gov/yell

the sky resembles wet concrete, and thunder reverberates in menacing claps. Thankfully, 8 miles of easy walking brings us to our fourth campsite, situated beside the Yellowstone River near Crevice Lake.

We pitch our tents on a sandy shelf just a few feet above the river, where there's a secluded beach. We'll stay two nights here and use the layover to explore the Black Canyon of the Yellowstone before completing the final 4.2 miles to the Blacktail Deer Creek trailhead, where we left a shuttle car, on day six. At camp, Wendy wades into the strong current for a dip and plunges up to her neck in the frigid water. She doesn't stay long. I opt to douse myself with water hauled ashore in a cooking pot. I'm still drying off with a Lilliputian camp towel when the storm strikes. I dive into my tent, where the spattering rain sounds like buckshot.

It's 8 miles from Crevice Lake through the Black Canyon to the terminus of the Yellowstone River Trail in Gardiner, Montana. We decide to dayhike halfway. Without a full pack, I feel weightless as we enter the chasm and descend through an increasingly desertlike landscape marked by prickly pear cactus and sagebrush lizards. The temperature pushes 80°F, which triggers tremendous snowmelt. A mile from camp, 15-foot-high Knowles Falls, on the Yellowstone River, fire hoses over the drop. Farther west, the canyon narrows to the width of a freeway, funneling water into frothy rapids that catapult RV-size hunks of forest detritus downstream.

Walking silently, I scan the river valley for movement, hoping to spot more animals—bears or elk or bison. But if there's one thing about Yellowstone—especially when it comes to wildlife—it's that you should be careful what you wish for. At that moment, I unwittingly straddle a 5-foot-long prairie rattlesnake coiled on the trail. It clacks its tail, then bluff-strikes at my legs, at which point I shatter the Olympic long jump record.

When I breathe again, we've reached our lunch spot, a black-sand beach that wouldn't look out of place ringing the shore of a Tahitian isle. The setting reminds me just how much we've seen in less than a week. We've fast-tracked nearly every Rocky Mountain ecosystem—subalpine meadows, montane forest, riparian valleys, and a desert biome. And for the final act, we're treated to a slice of the park's volcanic soul. With one night to go, I only have one concern about my first trek in Yellowstone: Where will I go on the second?

DO IT

DISTANCE: 36 miles (point to point)

TIME: 3 to 5 days

DIFFICULTY: ★★★★

THE PAYOFF: Disappear into Yellowstone's secret northern fringe, where you'll find a rejuvenated landscape and total solitude (except for the bison and grizzlies).

TRAILHEAD: Hellroaring Creek (44.9490, -110.4509); 4 miles northwest of Tower Junction off Grand Loop Road

SHUTTLE CAR Blacktail Deer Creek (44.9555, -110.5938); 11 miles west of Tower Junction off Grand Loop Road

MILES AND DIRECTIONS

FROM THE HELLROARING CREEK TRAILHEAD:

1. Join the **Hellroaring Creek Trail** for 1.5 miles as it crosses over the Yellowstone River.

2. Veer northeast onto the **Buffalo Plateau Trail,** which ascends a wind-scoured plateau into Montana en route to a three-way intersection near mile 6.7.

3. Turn northwest onto the user trail toward **Campsite 2B1** at mile 7.4.

4. Trek 2.1 miles off-trail, heading northwest through open meadows to sweep east around an unnamed 8,716-foot peak to hit the **Poacher Trail,** just outside the park boundary.

5. Follow the Poacher Trail as it doglegs west, plummeting a quick 900 feet to Coyote Creek.

6. Head north on the **Coyote Creek Trail,** following the drainage north around 8,272-foot Bull Mountain to reconnect with the **Hellroaring Creek Trail** near mile 15.3. (Camp in a vast creekside meadow near the patrol cabin—where the author saw the black bear and cub.)

7. Continue south on the water-hugging Hellroaring Creek Trail to a T-junction near the Yellowstone River at mile 23.7.

8. You could veer south to stay on the Hellroaring Creek Trail, which meanders less than a mile to the Buffalo Plateau Trail junction (from step 2, above), and close a roughly 26-mile circuit. But to add in the Black Canyon of the Yellowstone (worth it), turn northwest onto the **Yellowstone River Trail** and follow the path nearly 8 miles to camp at Crevice Lake. From there, stage dayhikes into the chasm and to the black-sand beaches described in the story.

9. Double back 0.5 mile upriver to a trail junction.

10. Peel south onto the **Blacktail Deer Creek Trail,** which climbs out to the trailhead and your shuttle car on Grand Loop Road. No spare car? Hitch—or walk—8 miles east to the Hellroaring Creek trailhead.

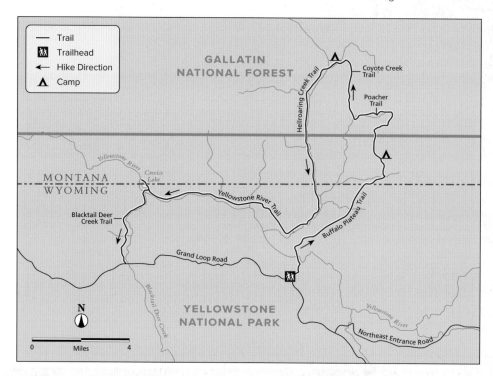

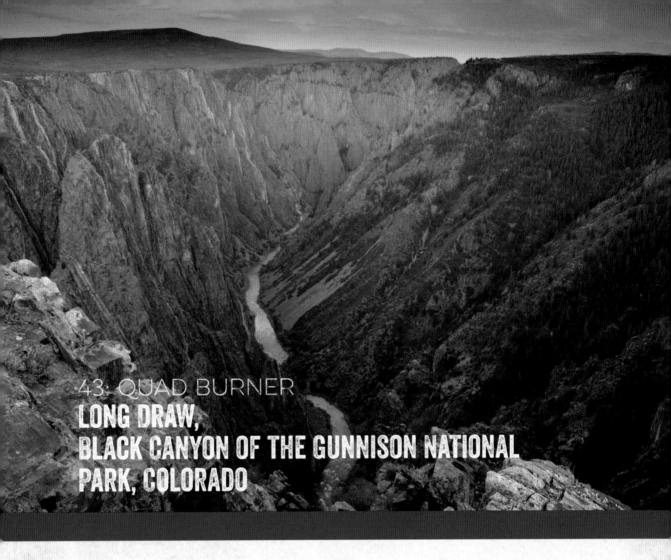

Photo: iStockphoto

43: QUAD BURNER
LONG DRAW,
BLACK CANYON OF THE GUNNISON NATIONAL PARK, COLORADO

Think you've seen deep, sheer, and narrow? Not until you go rim-to-river in this mind-bendingly steep gash. The 48-mile-long Black Canyon swoops to a depth of 2,722 feet and stretches just 40 feet across at its narrowest point. Venturing down is more controlled fall than hike, but you'll get in-your-face views of Colorado's tallest cliff, gold-medal trout fishing, and a bottom-up perspective few ever see.

TRIP PLANNER

SEASON May to October

PERMIT Required for overnight stay (free); obtain from the North Rim Ranger Station

CONTACT Black Canyon of the Gunnison National Park, www.nps.gov/blca

DISTANCE: 1.4 miles (out and back)

TIME: 2 days

DIFFICULTY: ★★★★

THE PAYOFF: Take a little-known route beneath the rim of this gaping chasm to riverside solitude at Long Draw's single tent site.

TRAILHEAD: Long Draw (38.5785, -107.6919); 12 miles southwest of Crawford on G74 Road.

MILES AND DIRECTIONS

FROM THE LONG DRAW TRAILHEAD:

1. Plunge into elevator shaft-steep Long Draw, a tentacle-like side canyon that splinters north from Black Canyon, on the **Long Draw Trail.** The scrubby singletrack drops 1,700 feet in elevation in just 0.7 mile to its terminus at the campsite.

2. Retrace your steps to the trailhead.

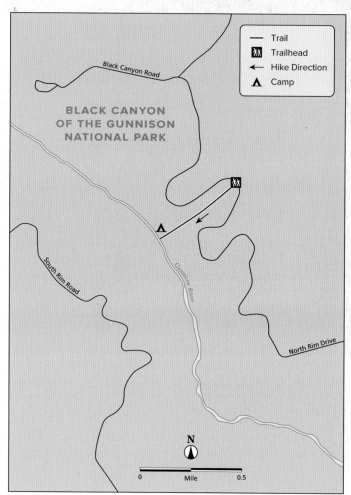

Adapted from text by Elisabeth Kwak-Hefferan.

ALL THE EXTRAS

DON'T MISS THIS CAMPSITE: LONG DRAW (MILE 1.6)

Any of the park's steep routes will deliver you to riverside solitude, but Long Draw's single site guarantees you'll be alone with the plentiful trout and rushing river. That's the math, anyway: Since there is only one site here, the Long Draw Trail might as well be your personal yellow-brick road to backcountry quietude. From your back-country digs, head 0.2 mile to the river to scan downcanyon when the low-hanging sun transforms your personal cathedral a deep-red hue.

KEEP YOUR EYES PEELED: WILDLIFE

Spy bighorn sheep scaling the rocks and mule deer browsing in vegetated areas. Listen for yellow-bellied marmots squeaking amid the talus (and occasionally sun-bathing on flat rocks) and coyotes yipping at night.

GEAR TIP: PACK PANTS

The Long Draw gully is less a trail than a recommendation, so prepare for hand-over-hand climbing and belly-sucking squeezes between tight, truck-size boulders. Pants will help deflect the unavoidable scrapes—and the park's legendary, 8-foot-tall poison ivy thickets.

Marmot

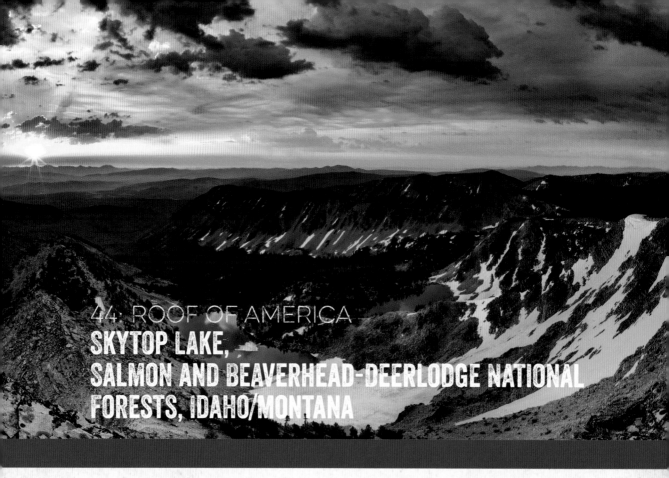

44: ROOF OF AMERICA
SKYTOP LAKE, SALMON AND BEAVERHEAD-DEERLODGE NATIONAL FORESTS, IDAHO/MONTANA

The Continental Divide Trail, as its name implies, is supposed to follow America's backbone. Of course, that's easier said than done, and in many places even thru-hikers will leave the official CDT to traverse the actual Divide. That's especially true in the Beaverheads, where granite peaks penetrate the sky and glacier-gouged drainages spill into stark canyons. It's the recipe for a perfect view—but the official CDT is routed 2,000 feet below the goodness. In this case, consider the alternate route mandatory.

TRIP PLANNER

SEASON July to October

PERMIT None

CONTACT Beaverhead-Deerlodge National Forest, www.fs.usda.gov/bdnf

Photo: Leland Howard

DISTANCE: 15.8 miles (point to point)

TIME: 2 days

DIFFICULTY: ★★★★

THE PAYOFF: Take a little-known detour off the official Continental Divide Trail to savor one of the grandest views along America's backbone.

TRAILHEAD: Continental Divide (45.1430, -113.5687); 67 miles west of Dillon, Montana, off Bloody Dick Road

SHUTTLE CAR Continental Divide (45.2443, -113.4779); 55 miles west of Dillon, Montana, on Berry Creek Road

MILES AND DIRECTIONS

FROM THE CONTINENTAL DIVIDE TRAILHEAD ON GOLDSTONE PASS:

1. Pick up the true **Continental Divide Trail** and follow it 3.1 miles northbound along the ridgeline that separates Idaho and Montana. (The Salmon National Forest falls off to the west and the Beaverhead-Deerlodge National Forest to the east.)

2. Instead of following the official CDT east off the divide (where it eventually traces the Jahnke Creek drainage east), stay high: Pick a path of least resistance along America's spine to mile 6 or so.

3. Above Skytop Lake, peel east off the Divide. Expect Class 3+ climbing as you negotiate the scree to the Pioneer Lake basin near mile 7.2.

4. Find the official **Pioneer Creek Trail,** which wends 3.9 miles down the wooded drainage to reconnect with the CDT at mile 11.1.

5. Proceed northeast on the CDT (now a rutted Jeep track) 1.5 miles to where it splits north on singletrack.

6. Instead of continuing northbound all the way to Canada, keep following the track 3.2 miles to your shuttle car at Van Houten Lake.

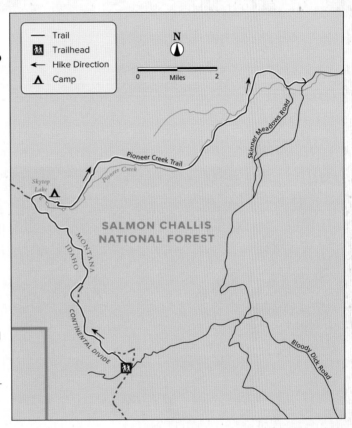

Legend:
- — Trail
- 🚶 Trailhead
- ← Hike Direction
- ▲ Camp

N

0 — Miles — 2

Skinner Meadows Road

Pioneer Creek Trail

Skytop Lake

Pioneer Creek

SALMON CHALLIS NATIONAL FOREST

MONTANA / IDAHO

CONTINENTAL DIVIDE

Bloody Dick Road

ALL THE EXTRAS

DON'T MISS THIS CAMPSITE: HIGHUP LAKE (MILE 6.5)

After you drop off the Divide, navigate around Skytop Lake to the pool where it drains just below: Highup. If weather cooperates, make camp among the conifers on the east bank of Highup and brace yourself for tangerine-hued morning alpenglow off the rock faces above. If the winds are whipping, drop even lower to Pioneer Lake, which is more protected.

EXTRA CREDIT: TAKE A BREAK

If conditions allow, plan to linger on the Continental Divide above Skytop Lake. The spin-around view stretches west across the lush Lemhi River Valley and east to the pinnacles and ridges of the Beaverheads. North and south, the Divide stretches outward like a gunsight, outrunning your vision until it melts into the horizon.

Photo: iStockphoto

Indian paintbrush

45: PICTURE PERFECT
NORTH TWIN LAKES,
MEDICINE BOW NATIONAL FOREST, WYOMING

You could throw a dart at a map of the Snowy Range and end up with a quiet alpine lake that's less than a few miles from the nearest trailhead and totally vacant. That's good news for any backpacker, but particularly solitude gluttons. Case in point: the North Twin Lakes. The side-by-side tarns are less than 2 miles from an easy-access trailhead and more often frequented by mule deer and elk than hikers. Use the perfectly situated lakes to stage a bigger trip into the Medicine Bows—or simply stay put. When perfection is this close at hand, there's no need to push it.

TRIP PLANNER

SEASON July to October

PERMIT None

CONTACT Medicine Bow National Forest, www.fs.usda.gov/mbr

DISTANCE: 3.2 miles (out and back)

TIME: 2 days

DIFFICULTY: ★

THE PAYOFF: Earn high-alpine glory—including trout galore—on a stupid-short trip into the Medicine Bows' northern sub-range.

TRAILHEAD: Sheep Lake (41.3725, -106.2454); 36 miles west of Laramie on Brooklyn Lake Road

MILES AND DIRECTIONS

FROM THE SHEEP LAKE TRAILHEAD:

1. Take the **Sheep Lake Trail** 1.6 miles north through stands of spruce and past unnamed pools to the North Twin Lakes.

2. Retrace your steps to the trailhead.

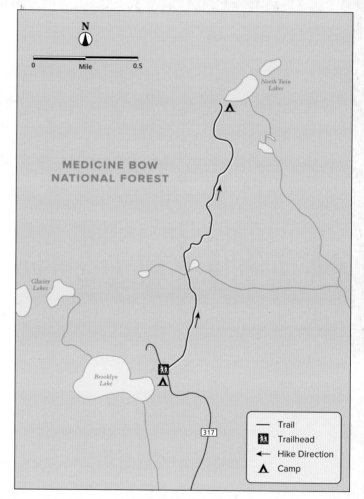

N

0   Mile   0.5

North Twin Lakes

MEDICINE BOW NATIONAL FOREST

Glacier Lakes

Brooklyn Lake

317

——	Trail
🚶	Trailhead
←	Hike Direction
⛺	Camp

ALL THE EXTRAS

DON'T MISS THIS CAMPSITE: NORTH TWIN LAKES (MILE 1.6)

The sweat-to-reward ratio may be no more skewed than at the North Twin Lakes, where an hour of hiking lands you at an alpine paradise. A dispersed camping policy means you can throw down wherever suits, but pick a spot beside the nearest of the lakes if you plan to catch your dinner (cutties swim in the lake closer to the trail, while the farther one is fishless).

KEEP YOUR EYES PEELED: WILDLIFE

More than 15,000 elk roam the southern Wyoming mountains, including the Snowies—where they are easily spotted on treeless, alpine expanses (like North Twin Lakes) throughout the summer and fall. Your best chance of a sighting is in the morning and evening, when elk graze tundra grasses and wildflowers (midday, they generally hide out among the trees). Their cream-colored rumps often give them away; so do the males' huge antlers, which can grow up to an inch per day during their summer growth spurt.

GEAR TIP: PACK A ROD

The fishing in the Snowies is renowned: Plan for hours of shore-casting into any number of the trout-filled tarns on this route. Expect to reel in both cutties and brookies that top a foot in length.

EXTRA CREDIT: MAKE IT LONGER

Turn this route into a 12-mile loop that serves up constant views and threads together the range's best fishing lakes (but climbs fewer than 1,500 vertical feet) by continuing past North Twin Lakes. Connect the Sheep Lake, North Gap Lake, and Lost Lake Trails around the west side of the Snowies and back over to the east side to close the circuit. There's great camping on the plateau above Crescent Lake and near the Telephone Lakes.

46: FULL CIRCLE
ROCKY MOUNTAIN NATIONAL PARK, COLORADO

By Dougald MacDonald

Avocado or peanut butter? I linger over the choice of bagel toppings, feeling no rush to smear, pack, and sprint for the summit of Longs Peak. On the opposite (northeast) side of the mountain, hundreds of storm-wary climbers undoubtedly left the standard trailhead before dawn, hoping to beat the inevitable midday lightning strikes. Not so for this lazy climber. I'm propped on a boulder by my tent, relishing the solitude. From my camp in the lonely southern side of the park, it's just 1.5 miles to the summit, and I know I can top out by noon, even with a late start. Might as well slather another bagel with avocado and refill my French press.

I've climbed more than a dozen routes up Longs, but never from the south. Few people do—they're scared off by the bushwhack approach and a 1,600-foot crawl up a scree-filled gully. But while researching a book about the 14,259-foot peak, I'd lucked into an infinitely more interesting way to reach the south face, one pioneered by two speed-hiking, Depression-era guides.

Hull Cook and Clerin Zumwalt worked at the old Boulderfield Shelter Cabin, a two-story stone hut at 12,750 feet, in the early 1930s. Every summer morning, they'd wake at 4 a.m., lead two summit climbs, and pocket $1 each. The routine was fun but grueling; it left the two little time to explore the rest of the 265,770-acre park. Until, that is, they schemed the ultimate mountain fix: a 47-mile loop across the Continental Divide and back around, ending with a rare ascent of Longs from the south. The caveat? They only had one day.

Like Cook and Zumwalt, I'd spent most of my twenty-five "Rocky" years climbing Longs and other peaks. Now ready to see the park's remoter edges, I decided to retrace Cook and "Zumie's" route—but not like those fast-and-lighters. Shouldering a 35-pound pack, I would savor every step of the journey, averaging a leisurely 7 miles per day. The grand finale: an ascent of Longs via Keplinger's Couloir.

COOK AND ZUMIE WOUND DOWN FROM THE BOULDERFIELD, the high camp on Longs's mega-popular Keyhole Route. They crested 12,324-foot Flattop Mountain and the Continental Divide, and followed the 13-mile Tonahutu Creek drainage to the village of Grand Lake. After a quick lunch, they headed home along East Inlet Creek, recrossing the Divide via 12,061-foot Boulder-Grand Pass, scrambling up Longs, and descending back to the Boulderfield 24 hours after they started. I planned to take seven days to complete their loop, camping at four designated trailside sites and in one off-trail zone, resupplying in Grand Lake, and climbing Keplinger's Couloir before descending Longs via the Keyhole Route.

From the Bear Lake trailhead, I grunted up 4.4 miles of switchbacks to Flattop's summit and made my first Continental Divide crossing by noon. The Divide winds 40 miles through the heart of the park, crossing eighteen named 12,000- and 13,000-foot peaks (but avoiding Longs, which lies 2 miles to the east). It parts watersheds—sending snowmelt to the Gulf of California via the Colorado River, and to the Gulf of Mexico via the Big Thompson. It also shapes most people's park experience. Rocky's 4.5 million annual visitors crowd onto trails and campgrounds in the valleys east of the Divide and north of Longs Peak, but hiker traffic drops exponentially to the west of that mountainous line.

I headed northwest down the gentle tundra slopes of Bighorn Flats on the Tonahutu Creek Trail, likely following the same paths once used by the Utes and Arapahos to migrate and hunt. Two huge elk grazed among wind-stunted willows. After 4 miles above treeline, I descended along Tonahutu Creek into the wetter, wilder west side of the park. While the landscape east of the Divide resembles the High Plains (dry, with short-grass meadows, powerful winds, and ponderosa pines), there it suggested Montana: dense spruce-fir forests, white-flowered kinnikinnick, pine martens, and moose. Only a single maintained trail—the one I followed over Flattop—crosses the Divide anywhere inside the park.

My first day was one of the hardest on this loop—I wouldn't reach a higher elevation until Longs Peak—and in late afternoon I was happy to soak my feet in the icy creek at Renegade campsite. At this point, 15 miles into their hike, Cook and Zumwalt had barely gotten started, and chances are the superfit youths were still feeling peppy. Zumwalt summited Longs fifty-three times in 1932, still a single-year record. And Cook once draped an injured mountaineer over his back and carried him more than 500 vertical feet up Longs's east face to the summit.

I woke up ready for a 6-mile stroll along rushing Tonahutu Creek. The trail descended through spruce and fir that gave way to lodgepole pines ravaged by mountain pine beetles. Pausing frequently for photos in 2-mile-long Big Meadows, I set up camp just past the final meadow, where friends had told me I might spot moose feeding along the creek. They were right: At dusk, an enormous bull strode into the grass and stood almost motionless for 10 minutes.

From Big Meadows, I cruised 3 downhill miles to the boardwalk-lined storefronts of Grand Lake. Cook and Zumie had already put in more than 25 miles by the time they arrived here. "We were getting a little bit gaunt," Cook recalled in an interview sixty years later. The two men beelined to a café, where they made an awful discovery. "Zum thought I had money, and I thought Zum had money," Cook said. "Between the two of us, we scraped together 37 cents—enough for one piece of pie." They had 15 miles and 8,000 vertical feet to go.

I had a haul ahead of me, too, but carved out time for a late breakfast, plus a ceremonial slice of cherry pie at the Fat Cat Café. After stocking up on fresh spinach and tomatoes at Mountain Food Market, I cooled off in the clear water of Colorado's largest natural lake and walked around the north shore to pick up the East Inlet Trail.

It was my first time in East Inlet Valley, and it quickly joined my favorite spots in the park. The trail led past a succession of sparkling lakes—Lone Pine, Verna, Spirit, Fourth—that pulled me upward with a continuous promise of new vistas. Over 7 miles, my rock climber's eye roamed the steep walls of Aiguille de Fleur and the Cleaver, tracing imaginary routes up the granite faces. Although I passed other hikers, the trails were virtually empty.

By the time I reached the Lake Verna campsite, I was ready for my planned rest day. In the morning, I hiked a couple of miles to Fifth Lake, a sapphire tarn below a curving, 2-mile-wide rampart of 1,000-foot cliffs and airy needles at the head of the valley. Back at camp, I lolled on the boulders by Lake Verna; at sunset, a cow elk surprised me when she splashed through the shallows.

Though no trail exists, the next day's route over 12,061-foot Boulder-Grand Pass was the easiest way across the Divide. From Fourth Lake on, the path is only a rumor, but the pass looms directly east-northeast. I shot a compass bearing and bushwhacked uphill. Before long, the trees thinned and the way became obvious. From the pass, I could see Longs hulking at the north side of broad Wild Basin. By the time I hit Thunder Lake, nearly 1,500 feet below the pass, a cold wind ripped spray from whitecaps. I headed to bed before dark.

If they were feeling gaunt in Grand Lake, Cook and Zumwalt must have been wasted by the time they traversed 11,600-foot North Ridge to reach the south face of Longs. A single slice of pie delivers 500 calories, about enough to power one hiker for an hour in this terrain. That may explain why they opted to bivouac—despite not having sleeping bags—before climbing the peak the following morning.

With a permit for Hunters Creek, I followed the same approach, albeit with a 32°F mummy and fat sleeping pad. On the Lion Lakes Trail, I spent an hour photographing columbine in the wet hollows around Lion Lakes 1 and 2, both perched on benches below 13,310-foot Mount Alice. Following Cook and Zumie's route over North Ridge to a campsite, I pitched my tent in a place few people camp, below a route few ever climb.

ON MY FINAL MORNING, I wrap up my breakfast, finish the last of my coffee, and break camp. Because this route is a loop, I don't have the luxury of taking only the essentials, so I leave shouldering a full pack. It proposes to be a grunt: 2,750 vertical feet from my camp, up Keplinger's Couloir to the summit. But I'm in no rush.

With each foot placement, the views grow more spectacular—the spine of the Divide winding through the Indian Peaks Wilderness; Pikes Peak and Mount Evans shimmering in the distance. At about 13,600 feet, I bump into the vertical Palisades cliffs and veer left over rock-strewn slabs to join the Keyhole Route just below the Homestretch—the granite ramp that leads 300 vertical feet to the summit. Already, thunderheads are building, so I snapshot the view from the top and join the first people I've seen in more than 24 hours for the descent.

After popping through the Keyhole to Longs's north side, I wind down to the Boulder-field. It's 8 miles of downhill hiking to my car, and I pause to refill bottles and fuel up on gorp. Three generations before me, Hull Cook and Clerin Zumwalt ended their loop here in time for breakfast. After a week on the same route, I'm amazed at their feat, but can't help indulging in a little one-upmanship: Yes, the whippets made history, but they didn't slow down to savor the best-kept secrets on the most-secret side of the Rockies' iconic park.

←— DO IT —→

DISTANCE: 47 miles (loop)

TIME: 4 to 7 days

DIFFICULTY: ★★★★★

THE PAYOFF: Explore the quieter side of Colorado's park on a historically inspired route that summits 14,259-foot Longs Peak on a forgotten climber's route.

TRAILHEAD: Bear Lake (40.3119, -105.6456); 13 miles west of Estes Park on Bear Lake Road

TRIP PLANNER

SEASON July to October

PERMIT Required for overnight stay ($26 per party); reserve online or gun for a walk-in at the Headquarters Wilderness Office

CONTACT Rocky Mountain National Park, www.nps.gov/romo

MILES AND DIRECTIONS

FROM THE BEAR LAKE TRAILHEAD:

1. Follow the **Flattop Mountain Trail** 4.4 miles to the Continental Divide.
2. Pick up the **Tonahutu Creek Trail** and take it 15.6 miles down the west side of the Divide to the town of Grand Lake.
3. Road-walk 1.7 miles clockwise around Grand Lake on Summerland Park and West Portal Roads.
4. Find the **East Inlet Trail** and take it 6.6 miles to its terminus at Lake Verna.
5. Pick a path of least resistance northeast up 12,061-foot Boulder-Grand Pass.
6. Downclimb off the Continental Divide on the **Thunder Lake Trail** to the path's namesake near mile 33.5.
7. Veer east off-trail to connect with the **Lion Lake Trail,** less than a mile away.
8. Continue up toward Mount Alice on the Lion Lake Trail to its terminus beneath North Ridge.
9. Bushwhack up North Ridge (use game trails) and into the cirque below Longs's south face, where Keplinger's Couloir offers a stout, 1,600-foot climb to the Notch, between Longs and Mount Meeker.
10. Some Class 3+ moves bring you to the base of the Palisades cliffs, where you should traverse left until you connect with the main drag.
11. Follow what's likely to be a conga line to the true summit of Longs Peak near mile 38.
12. Head off the summit on the **Keyhole Route** before linking up with the **North Longs Peak** and **Glacier Gorge Trails,** which deposit you back at Bear Lake trailhead.

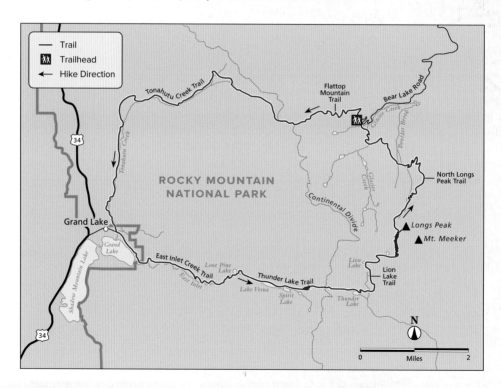

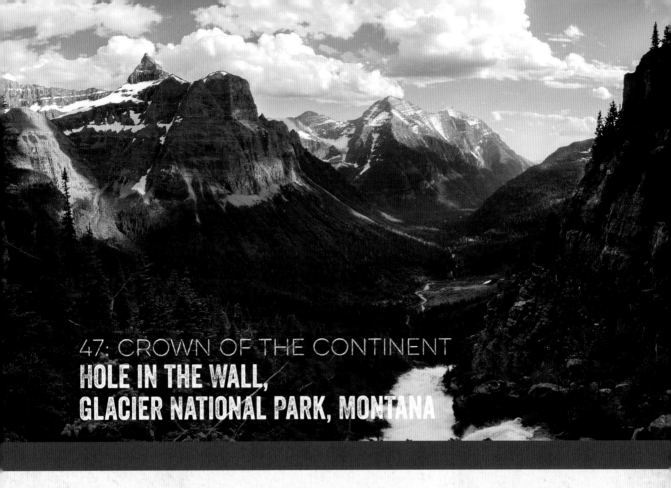

47: CROWN OF THE CONTINENT
HOLE IN THE WALL, GLACIER NATIONAL PARK, MONTANA

There is no single hallmark of Glacier's twisted topography. It has 10,500-foot peaks that cut into the horizon like granite cleavers. It has roiling rivers that surge over vertical rock faces like fireworks blasts. It has glacial lakes the color of a summer sky and vast meadows packed with purple blooms. Wildlife sightings only add to the drama, with grizzlies, black bears, and mountain goats roaming its slopes. And here's a secret: You can score it all at Hole in the Wall, a hanging valley in the national park's northern reaches, where the sum is somehow even greater than the parts—and what they add up to is one of America's most beautiful campsites.

TRIP PLANNER

SEASON July to September

PERMIT Required for overnight stay ($7 per person per night); obtain a walk-in from any visitor center or ranger station or you can reserve online for an extra $40

CONTACT Glacier National Park, www.nps.gov/glac

DISTANCE: 32 miles (out and back)

TIME: 3 to 4 days

DIFFICULTY: ★★★⟋

THE PAYOFF: Take a tour through Glacier's high-relief wilderness and spend a night in a hanging valley with huge views—all with a surprisingly easy-to-get permit.

TRAILHEAD: Bowman Lake (48.8305, -114.2024); 34 miles north of West Glacier on Bowman Lake Road

MILES AND DIRECTIONS

FROM THE BOWMAN LAKE TRAILHEAD:

1. Trek northeast on the **Bowman Lake Trail,** tracing its namesake and following its drainage to 6,255-foot Brown Pass at mile 13.8.

2. Hang a left on the **Boulder Pass Trail,** which hugs sheer cliffs for 1.6 miles to another intersection.

3. Take the short, 0.6-mile spur into Hole in the Wall.

4. Retrace your steps to the trailhead.

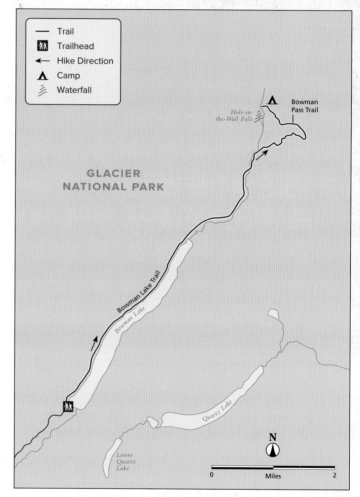

Adapted from text by Elisabeth Kwak-Hefferan.

ALL THE EXTRAS

DON'T MISS THIS CAMPSITE: HOLE IN THE WALL (MILE 16)

Perched in a hanging valley atop 1,200-foot cliffs, the three sites at Hole in the Wall offer a grandstand view down the Bowman Valley. A who's who of chiseled peaks, like 8,528-foot Boulder Peak and its chewing gum-blue glaciers, recede in wave after wave of bare rock, while the view behind isn't bad, either: Ribbons of water, including 800-foot-tall Hole in the Wall Falls, crash over the cliffs into the amphitheater.

EXTRA CREDIT: MAKE IT LONGER

If you have access to a second vehicle (or don't mind rolling the dice with hitching a ride), you can do this hike as a 39-mile horseshoe, with no backtracking. From Hole in the Wall, take the spur back out and continue west on the Boulder Pass Trail, ultimately dropping down to Kintla Lake.

Rocky Mountain goat

48: PEAKBAGGER'S DELIGHT
GORE RANGE,
EAGLES NEST WILDERNESS, COLORADO

Pitch-anywhere lakeshores and obscure summits are hard to find outside Denver— call it the one downside of living in the country's multisport capital. But there's a workaround: the Gore Range. Devoid of 14,000-foot peaks—and, quite frankly, trails—the area simply doesn't attract crowds, and for that reason it doesn't require a rigorous permit system. So you may feel like you're cheating when you're tracing its 50-mile-long rampart of Thirteeners, taking your pick of pointy peaks, glacially carved valleys, and aquamarine lakes. It's the way hiking in Colorado should be.

TRIP PLANNER

SEASON July to October

PERMIT None

CONTACT White River National Forest, www.fs.usda.gov/whiteriver

Photo: Jay Rush

DISTANCE: 16 miles (loop)

TIME: 3 days

DIFFICULTY: ★★★★↙

THE PAYOFF: Find the best of Summit County on this alpine traverse just behind the ski resorts.

TRAILHEAD: Gore Creek (39.6277, -106.2748); 5 miles east of Vail on Vail Pass/Ten Mile Canyon Trail (paved)

MILES AND DIRECTIONS

FROM THE GORE CREEK TRAILHEAD:

1. Follow the water 4.1 miles upstream on the **Gore Creek Trail** to a Y-junction.

2. Veer north onto the **Gore Lake Trail,** which ascends 1.9 miles to its namesake. (The trail is well marked, but the going is slow, not just for the 1,300 feet of elevation gain, but also for the midsummer explosion of monkshood, larkspur, and Indian paintbrush lining the path.)

3. Stage an off-trail assault to Deluge Lake, bagging Hail and Snow Peaks en route: First, retrace your steps 0.2 mile on the Gore Lake Trail to where it swings south.

4. Head off-trail, following game paths north into Snow Creek Valley.

5. Scramble the southeast ridge of 12,904-foot Hail Peak to gain it via a west-facing gully near mile 8.7.

6. Roller-coaster across the Class 2 ridge—which trends counterclockwise—to Snow Pass and tackle the straightforward scramble up 13,024-foot Snow Peak near mile 11.

7. Pick a path of least resistance down to Deluge Lake, where manicured—if a little overgrown—singletrack awaits.

8. Exit via the 4-mile **Deluge Lake Trail,** which lands you back at the trailhead.

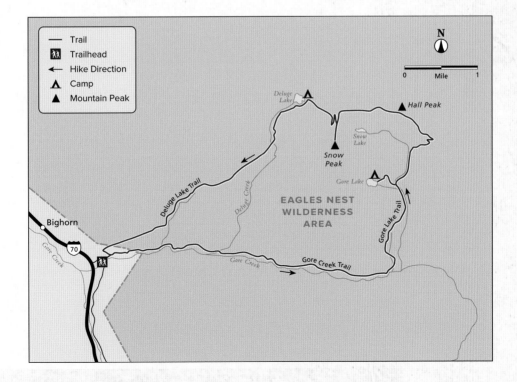

ALL THE EXTRAS

DON'T MISS THIS CAMPSITE: GORE LAKE (MILE 6)

This quiet bowl nestles beneath a crowd of craggy peaks, but the rocky turret of 13,024-foot Snow Peak—tomorrow's quarry—dominates the skyline to the northwest. Set up camp in a lakeside meadow on the east shore, and don't forget to set a morning alarm: You won't want to miss the sunrise having its way with the high rises across the water.

DON'T MISS THIS CAMPSITE: DELUGE LAKE (MILE 12)

Some 500 feet higher than Gore Lake, this tarn lacks the tree coverage, but if you hit it on good conditions, there may be no finer picture of alpine glory. The turquoise lake, which backs up against the spine of the Gore Range, does a good impression of an infinity pool, dropping off abruptly to the valley below. From here, you can bag aesthetic 13,180-foot Mount Valhalla via its south ridge on a 2-mile out-and-back, which, let's face it, if you're camping here is probably on the agenda already.

KEEP YOUR EYES PEELED: WILDLIFE

See the wilderness's namesakes riding updrafts around the craggy summits, and watch for other animals unaccustomed to humans, like black bears lumbering through meadows and porcupines waddling across the trails. You may even spot the makers of the game trails this itinerary has you following on day two: herds of mountain goats roaming the highlands.

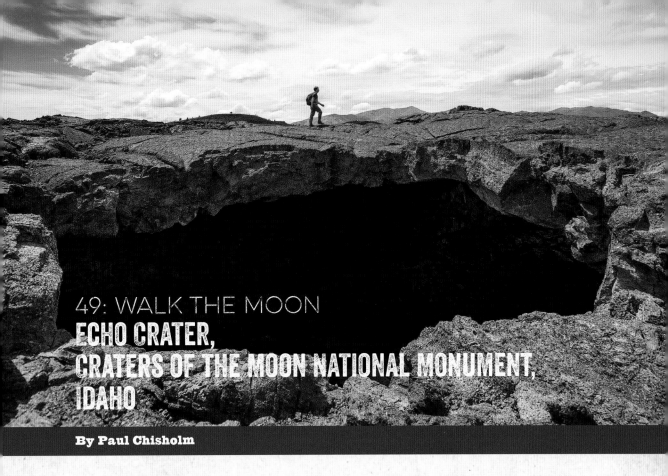

49: WALK THE MOON
ECHO CRATER, CRATERS OF THE MOON NATIONAL MONUMENT, IDAHO

By Paul Chisholm

Descending into the ancient volcano feels like being swallowed by a monster. I set up camp in the mouth of the beast, where 200-foot-tall cliffs steal the sunlight, leaving me with only overwhelming peace and quiet. But the tranquility in the crater bottom belies a violent past: Two thousand years ago, molten rock gushed from these cracks in the earth, while ferocious explosions from thousand-foot-high cinder cones sent car-size boulders hurtling through the air. I can still see evidence of this rocky past above ground, where cylindrical cavities mark the spots where trees were entombed in flowing lava before rotting away. Jagged chasms exist where ancient tunnels of lava formed and collapsed. A weekend of exploring these geologic wonders makes the mind reel—and ensures that I'll be back soon.

TRIP PLANNER

SEASON April to November

PERMIT Required for overnight stay (free); obtain from the visitor center

CONTACT Craters of the Moon National Monument, www.nps.gov/crmo

DISTANCE: 18.3 miles (lollipop-loop)

TIME: 3 days

DIFFICULTY: ★★★

THE PAYOFF: Fewer people camp in Craters of the Moon's backcountry in a year than do in a day in the marquee parks nearby, which means it is yours for the taking if you brush up on some basic navigation skills.

TRAILHEAD: Tree Molds (43.4282, -113.5488); 24 miles southwest of Arco off Loop Road

MILES AND DIRECTIONS

FROM THE TREE MOLDS TRAILHEAD:

1. Head 0.1 mile east along the walkway.

2. Turn southeast and follow the **Wilderness Trail** 1.7 miles past the Buffalo Caves (explore with a free permit) to a 0.1-mile-long side trail leading to a cluster of lava tree molds.

3. Continue about 1.6 miles on the main path toward Echo Crater.

4. Veer 0.4 mile off-trail into the crater (it's only accessible from the north end) to make camp.

5. With just a daypack, head back to the Wilderness Trail.

6. Continue 1.8 miles to the Sentinel, a 5,812-foot cinder cone.

7. Head east off-trail through the open sagebrush prairie, tracing a lava flow to a cluster of rock formations (marked with 8-foot-tall cairns) near mile 9.7. **Highlight:** the 25-foot-long Bridge of Tears, a tunnel that was named by an early explorer who hit his head on it.

8. Identify Echo Crater in the distance and use it as a point of reference to loop back northwest through the Little Prairie to your camp at mile 14.6.

9. Retrace your steps to the trailhead.

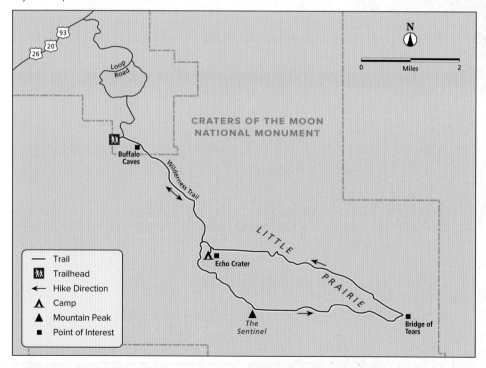

ALL THE EXTRAS

DON'T MISS THIS CAMPSITE: ECHO CRATER (MILE 3.8)

The crater's cliffs will shelter you from the winds that whip across the sagebrush steppe, while the rim provides an unmatched vantage point for catching the sunset over Idaho's Great Rift. Pitch your tent below the rare limber pines for shade and make it a basecamp. Since Echo Crater is near the apex of the lollipop-loop, it's ideally positioned for spending both nights (approximately miles 3.8 and 14.6, if you follow this route).

KEEP YOUR EYES PEELED: FLORA

There are four *kipukas*, or uplifts of land that were surrounded by lava flows, 1.5 miles northeast of Echo Crater. Since the flows protected them, their native plant community is largely preserved. Look for endemic whitish basalt milkvetch, purple Great Basin violet, and pink longleaf phlox (blooming April to June).

GEAR TIP: PACK IN WATER

Although USGS quadrangles show some blue squiggles, water is unreliable. Not convinced? The area's first nonnative explorers documented "innumerable little bright-red wrigglers" inhabiting the few puddles they found. Case closed: Pack it in (a gallon per person per day).

Indian tunnel

50: CROWN JEWEL
SAN JUAN MOUNTAINS, COLORADO

Even in a state revered for its wealth of mountains, Colorado's San Juans stand out as wilder, craggier, taller, and lonelier than the rest. Use these tips and tricks from local expert **Donna Ikenberry** to head above treeline to their oxygen-starved pinnacles and claim a piece for yourself. By Elisabeth Kwak-Hefferan

THE INSIDER

Photojournalist Donna Ikenberry became a master of peaks while authoring three editions of *Hiking Colorado's Weminuche and South San Juan Wilderness Areas*. "What I love about this place is that you never look down and see a city," she says. "There are no roads, nothing man-made. All you see are mountains."

1. WILD WEEK

A virtual Colorado highlight reel, Ikenberry's favorite multiday trip winds past meadows smothered with summer blossoms, ice-blue tarns, and a string of Thirteeners along the Rockies' spine. The 51.4-mile section of the Continental Divide Trail cuts across the South San Juan Wilderness from Cumbres Pass to Elwood Pass, rarely dropping below treeline. "Herds of elk and the occasional white-tailed ptarmigan make it extra-special," Ikenberry says. Leave a vehicle at Elwood Pass (no commercial shuttles available) and tackle the route in five days, camping at Trail Lake, Blue Lake, the Adams Fork Trail junction, and the Middle Fork Trail junction. The area is typically accessible July through October, depending on snow levels; Ikenberry recommends September for avoiding summer's frequent afternoon thunderstorms.

2. SECRET FLORA HIKE

You know the scene in *The Wizard of Oz* where Dorothy conks out in a field of poppies? That scene might as well be from the San Juan hillsides, where from mid-July to mid-August, columbine, aster, paintbrush, alpine forget-me-nots, and mountain harebells explode onto the scene. Ikenberry's favorite quick-access route to petal-peeping: the Stairsteps area on the Highline (also called Highland) Trail (#832), which passes through the tundra at 12,000 feet. Take the Hunters Lake Trail (#800) 1.1 miles to the Highline junction and continue to the flora-filled high country atop cliffy volcanic slopes near mile 2.5. Press on along the ridgeline to extend the hike by connecting to the Kitty Creek or Skyline Trails.

3. PEAKBAGGING ADVENTURE

After years of gazing at the remote summit of 13,821-foot Rio Grande Pyramid from afar, Ikenberry had to see the up-close view for herself. "When you're on other peaks, you'll look out and say, 'Oh, there's the Pyramid,'" she says. "After seeing it from all over the San Juans for years, I had to actually climb to the top and see the view from there." And what a view it is: The spiky Weminuche Wilderness fans out in all directions, while the spine of the Grenadier Range cuts through, ultimately extending to the Sawatch and La Garita Ranges. Reach the pinnacle on an 18.4-mile out-and-back on the Weminuche (#818) and Skyline Trails. Camp near mile 5.5 on Weminuche Pass before taking the summit spur at mile 8.3. The final 0.9-mile scramble gains 1,524 feet.

4. WILDLIFE VIEWING

The San Juans' expansive forests and clear streams attract A-list fauna like elk, moose, marmots, black bears, and mountain goats. For a quiet overnight with some of the best wildlife-spotting opps, head to the sites at Goose Lake: They're just far enough off the Continental Divide Trail to remain under the radar, so you won't have to share the primo cutthroat trout fishing or easy-access peakbagging side trips, either. Hike the Ivy Creek Trail (#805) 8.7 miles to the treeline lake and grab a site, then scan for wildlife both big (moose) and small (endangered boreal toads) in the shoreline shrubs. It's another 3.7 miles past Little Goose Lake and 13,148-foot South River Peak to link up to the CDT, where you might see marmots, pikas, and golden eagles.

5. STOCK UP

Durango's Bread bakery is Ikenberry's must-go for "the best cookies ever." For gear and maps, swing by Backcountry Experience (www.bcexp.com).

TRIP PLANNER

SEASON July to October

PERMIT Required for overnight stay (free); self-issue at trailhead kiosks

CONTACT San Juan National Forest, www.fs.usda.gov/sanjuan

Lacy waterfalls, hardwoods forests, and secret hideaways define the trips in this region. Photo: iStockphoto

MIDWEST

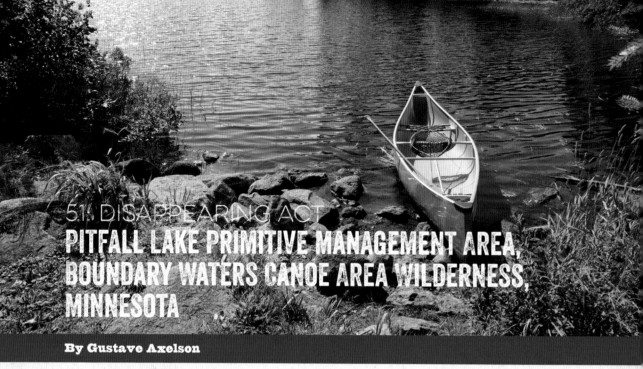

5.1: DISAPPEARING ACT
PITFALL LAKE PRIMITIVE MANAGEMENT AREA, BOUNDARY WATERS CANOE AREA WILDERNESS, MINNESOTA

By Gustave Axelson

An officious permit keeper in a green US Forest Service sweater stands between me and paradise. She peers down her nose and looks me up and down. "Not a lot of people go back there," she huffs. "It's just too hard." I wonder if she's measuring my ability by some inscrutable means, but then she scribbles on the authorization sheet, granting entry to the Pitfall Lake Primitive Management Area, deep within Minnesota's Boundary Waters Canoe Area Wilderness.

By definition, Boundary Waters is "an area where the earth and community of life are untrammeled by man." But the reality is, much of it is plenty trammeled. Established portage trails run between the lakes, and the Forest Service routinely maintains them. Camping is restricted to designated sites with a fire ring, a biffy (outhouse), and tent platforms. Given that 155,000 people visit the Boundary Waters annually (it's one of the nation's most popular federal wilderness areas), the impact-mitigating infrastructure makes sense. But it doesn't deliver the experience of true wilderness—going where it looks and feels like no human has ever gone. That's where the Primitive Management Areas (PMAs) come in. Pitfall Lake is a 6-square-mile restricted entry zone—no campsites, no portage trails—and now my party of four has the sole permit for the next five days.

"Good luck," the marm says with a faint smile. Then a parting shot: "Some people say it's Shangri-la, but you'll have to go through hell to get there."

THE 1.1-MILLION-ACRE BOUNDARY WATERS contains 12 PMA units totaling about 124,000 acres. Pull out a canoe country map, however, and you won't immediately see them. The PMAs are the places in between the developed regions; they're the empty spots, off the web of established portage trails and the shotgun blast of red triangles indicating maintained campsites. Since they're unmarked and difficult to access, PMAs see very few paddlers—fewer than one hundred groups per year combined.

"We only let one party into a PMA unit at a time, so you're really on your own," explains Steve Schug, assistant district ranger for recreation and wilderness in the Superior National Forest and Boundary Waters Canoe Area Wilderness. "The PMAs are set aside to offer the most outstanding opportunity to experience solitude. But there's no management, so it's just you and the land. Risks are higher. It can mean a lot of crawling through brush and hauling canoes over downed trees." (Editor's note: Since this story was published, Schug has retired.)

Schug says PMAs are a bit of a secret. "We don't market them. We don't go out and actively tell the public about them, because we don't want them to get busy," he says. "When we get questions about them, we emphasize that they're really only for experienced paddlers. People who know their map and compass skills and Leave No Trace principles. Most Boundary Waters visitors never go 10 feet beyond their campsite's pit toilet. But for those who wonder what's beyond the biffy, you can travel into a PMA and step on land that maybe hasn't seen people in fifty years."

OUR PARTY OF TWO CANOES—my friend Mike Kooi and I in one, photographer Layne Kennedy and Mike Prom of Voyageur Canoe Outfitters in the other—will travel about 40 hard miles over five days on an out-and-back to Pitfall Lake PMA. It takes a full day just to reach the unit's doorstep, 12 miles from entry point #55 at Saganaga Lake.

En route, we decide to camp on Ester Lake and enjoy a night of relative luxury before we go primitive. The tents go up easily on cleared and spacious tent pads. There's a bundle of firewood graciously left by the campsite's previous tenants. Prom lights a blaze in the fire ring and places fat steaks (packed frozen and now thawed in the bottom of a portage pack) on the USFS-provided cooking grate.

Wispy gray plumes rise from the other five campsites on our lake. A couple of loons appear on the water—followed by a couple of human onlookers in kayaks—and offer an evening yodel. I go for a swim, thoroughly enjoying our easy entry, like we're putting a toe in before jumping.

Prom calls me back with a plate of food in one hand and a Nalgene growler of India pale ale in the other.

"Steak and ale," he says cheerfully.

The next morning, we leave the relative comforts behind and learn what "primitive management area" actually means: war zone. Branches snap and curses fly as we bull overturned canoes through a tangle of brush and tree limbs. "Have we reached hell?" Kooi grins as he mops up a bloody forearm, courtesy of a black spruce that didn't yield the right-of-way. Earlier, we'd crossed Pitfall's threshold at Link Lake, then paddled a sinuous and overgrown arm to a short overland crossing to Gift Lake. Now we're negotiating a beaver dam, teeter-tottering on the flotsam of sunken logs with packs held over our heads. The logs sink 6 inches into the swamp under our weight.

Paddling on, we cross into the western expanse of the 32,000-acre Cavity Lake Fire, which burned halfway into Pitfall Lake PMA in 2006. The sun shines brightly here, since there's no forest canopy. We see rock ridges that were exposed when the duff burned away and boulders that were cracked open by the fire's intense heat. It's eerily silent; not even a songbird calls. Only our dipping paddles make any sound.

From Gift we paddle and portage onto Fish Lake, then consult the topo to find a route to our day's goal—Nawakwa Lake, just 4 miles from Ester. The shortest way tracks through a clump of bushy, green cedar trees. We land the canoes at the cedars and start humping our gear overland, only to meet up with a tangle of fallen trees. A flat, 30-yard portage takes more than an hour as we manhandle our canoes over and under the Pick-Up Sticks puzzle of timber. "This had better be worth it," Kooi says, looking at his scratched-up arms and legs.

We paddle the perimeter of Nawakwa Lake, scouting for outcrops. According to our permit, we must find a durable surface for our campsite, a place that won't show impact. "Your challenge is to blend into the wilderness," reads the sheet, in an eloquent departure from standard backcountry regs.

We see a bald granite face on the forested west shore where the fire didn't reach. It has plenty of room for our canoes and a cooking area, so I bushwhack into the woods to find a spot in the underbrush for our tent (shoreline camping is forbidden). When I return, treetop shadows are just beginning to slide across the lake, so we have another hour or so before sundown—prime fishing time. We launch the canoes and troll Rapalas and Daredevle spoons. For a while, we have zero success, but then we encounter a pair of whiskered, furry heads glaring at us. Otters are a dead giveaway to a fishing hole. We soon land two feisty, 24-inch northern pike and paddle back to camp with 8 pounds of fish for dinner. Prom lays out an assembly line of ingredients for fish tacos atop an over-turned canoe: tortillas, chopped cabbage, tomatoes, onions, and peppers. After dinner, we uncap IPAs and kick back in Crazy Creeks on the lakefront ledge, where we watch Jupiter outshine the stars in a darkening sky. The night is silent save for a beaver that stealthily cruises the shore to see the intruders.

"THIS DOESN'T FEEL LIKE THE BOUNDARY WATERS," Prom says over coffee the next morning. "It's like northern Canada. This isolation, being certain that we won't see another soul." Today, we'll take a day trip to an even more remote corner of the PMA. The map shows a squiggly blue line that connects Nawakwa to Trust Lake then Faith Lake—two apt names, since trust and faith are all we have. Who knows if the line is navigable?

We paddle 2 miles before we discover it's not. This is the kingdom of beavers. Chewed and stacked logs create an obstacle course for our canoes; we pry and wedge and scoot our boats over the underwater hurdles. A square, brown beaver head surfaces to see what we're up to, then silently submerges, leaving behind only bubbles. Sedge and willow squeeze us from both sides as we round each bend of the snaking channel. Soon the vegetation brushes our arms as we paddle, and we're ducking under deadfall. Then the bow hits a dam we can't climb over. We're about a quarter mile, maybe more, from Trust Lake. And we're not going any farther without stepping into hip-deep muck.

I climb a boulder for a better view, and I see a sedgy meadow. The Voyageurs—who shuttled pelts through this region 200 years ago—called these "savannahs," because they look like grassy fields and could be used to shortcut impassable waters on foot. It's still swampy, but it holds our weight. I see moose tracks in the sludge.

Trust turns out to be a shallow, turbid lake full of floating detritus. We paddle slowly, and Kooi, in the bow, asks, "What, exactly, are we doing here?" He's losing faith that there'll be any payoff. Maybe this is the reason nobody ever goes back here.

"Let's just see where it goes," I say half-heartedly. We land on Trust's south shore, lug the canoes over a spit of burned forest, and we see it.

Faith Lake is about 20 feet deep and Tanqueray clear. It sparkles in the sun. We fall silent, perhaps waiting for the next trick to be played on us in this forbidden zone. I eyeball the shore at the northeastern end. Yellow sand? We paddle over to find a sun-bleached moose antler, a signpost of pure solitude. Wolf tracks weave up and down the beach. We've reached the deepest point of the PMA accessible by canoe.

We remove our boots, and the sand massages our feet, tenderized by the epic portages. We wade out for a swim. Prom's eyes widen to saucer-size as he contemplates water where no one has cast a line in years or decades. Or ever? He launches a canoe and casually trolls a spoon, landing and releasing two pike pushing 40 inches—trophies that are twice the size of the fish we ate for dinner last night.

We lazily eat our lunch and then recline on the warm sand. I pull my hat over my face for a siesta. Now I can't say that the ranger in the permit office was wrong. This primitive area in the Boundary Waters is indeed rough. But who says there's no comfort in that?

TRIP PLANNER

SEASON June to November

PERMIT Required for overnight stay ($16 per party plus $6 reservation fee); obtain from the Gunflint Ranger Station in Grand Marais

CONTACT Superior National Forest, www.fs.usda.gov/superior

DO IT

DISTANCE: 40 miles (out and back)

TIME: 5 days

DIFFICULTY: ★★★★★

THE PAYOFF: Vanish in the quietest, wildest corner of the Boundary Waters when you net the permit for this primitive management area.

TRAILHEAD: Saganaga Lake #55 (48.1715, -90.8866); 55 miles northwest of Grand Marais off Gunflint Trail on Sag Lake Trail

MILES AND DIRECTIONS

FROM THE SAGANAGA LAKE ENTRY POINT #55:

1. Launch from End of the Trail Boat Access and paddle north up the narrow finger of **Saganaga Lake** toward Canada before bearing west around the peninsula to the far end of the pool near mile 11.2.

2. Portage roughly 0.5 mile south into **Ashdick Lake**.

3. Paddle the length of Ashdick (1.1 miles or so) to the short portage into **Ester Lake** at mile 13.

4. Now in the Pitfall Lake Primitive Management Area: Pick a path of least resistance across **Ester, Hanson, Link, Gift, Fish, Nawakwa, Trust,** and **Faith Lakes.**

5. Retrace your strokes to the put-in.

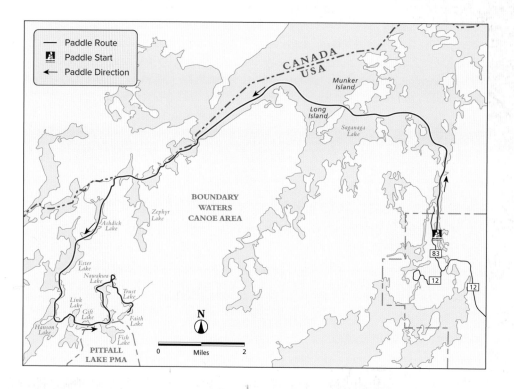

Photo: Taylor Reed

52: OUTSIDE THE LINES
INDIAN POINT,
GARDEN OF THE GODS WILDERNESS, ILLINOIS

Can't-miss plan for sussing out a stellar campsite: Go beyond the edges of where campers usually stay; evaluate sites on their merits, not on convenience; the higher you go, the better the views (usually); but don't waste so much energy that you sleep through a good sunrise. Such a strategy pays off in sites like this one in Garden of the Gods, a dayhike-oriented park that funnels what visitors it does receive into the car campgrounds on its fringes. You'll share the area's castellated bluffs and wide views with daytrippers in the afternoon, but when the sun melts into the prairie and paints the other-worldly rock sculptures unnatural shades of magenta, you'll have it to yourself.

TRIP PLANNER

SEASON April to November

PERMIT None

CONTACT Shawnee National Forest, www.fs.usda.gov/shawnee

DISTANCE: 11.6 miles (out and back)

TIME: 2 days

DIFFICULTY: ★

THE PAYOFF: Savor solitude in this out-of-place rocky playground when the sun goes down.

TRAILHEAD: Hitching Post Equestrian (37.5942, -88.4317); 14 miles southeast of Harrisburg on Gape Hollow Road

MILES AND DIRECTIONS

FROM THE HITCHING POST EQUESTRIAN TRAILHEAD:

1. Head 5.1 miles east on the **River to River Trail**—a 160-mile-long path that spans southern Illinois—passing through slender, eastern white pines rife with overlooks to a junction in the Garden of the Gods Recreation Area. (This section of the R2R merges with the **Karbers Trail.**)

2. Veer south onto the **Indian Point Trail,** which leads to a 300-foot-tall outcropping.

3. Retrace your steps to the trailhead.

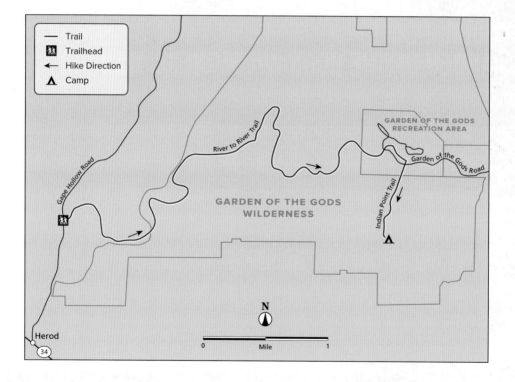

ALL THE EXTRAS

DON'T MISS THIS CAMPSITE: INDIAN POINT (MILE 5.8)

It's true: The overwhelming majority of overnight visitors to this park will claim a car campground or an RV hook-up. The park doesn't even advertise dispersed camping because it's just not a thing here. Consider that your good fortune. Weave between the rock towers and settle down at one of a handful of established tent sites along the route to Indian Point; nab one as close to the outcropping's edge as possible. There's a stellar spot tucked in a wooded area with wide-open eastern views over the tapestry of hardwoods—when the morning sun dispels the rock garden's evening cool, you'll know you found the right spot.

KEEP YOUR EYES PEELED: FOLIAGE

The River to River Trail passes several rocky overlooks on its route to Garden of the Gods. They may seem relatively workaday in midsummer, opening up to vast stretches of rolling greenery, but wait for October when the viewshed reveals a mosaic of yellow and orange hardwoods.

FUN FACT: GEOLOGY

Unlike most of the Midwest, which was scoured smooth by glaciers and ancient seas, the Garden of the Gods slipped by untouched, leaving behind a network of caves, cliffs, and hoodoo-like formations. The rocks here are colored with swirling red and brown designs, formed by the slow leaching of iron ores out of the limestone. Tack on the 0.5-mile Observation Trail to see the most interesting formations, like Camel Rock, Table Rock, and Devil's Smokestack.

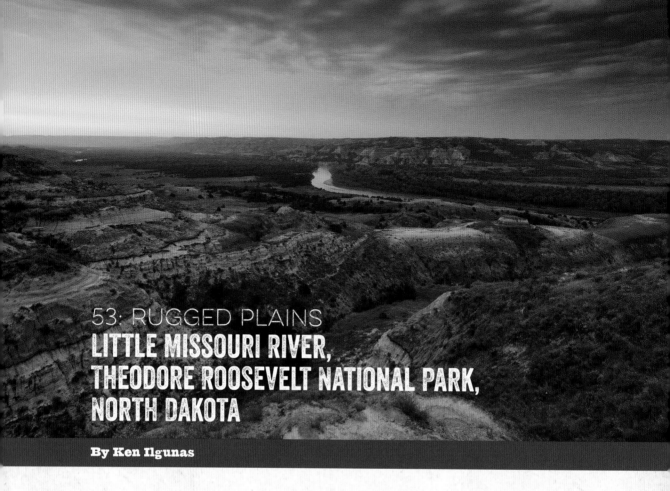

53: RUGGED PLAINS
LITTLE MISSOURI RIVER, THEODORE ROOSEVELT NATIONAL PARK, NORTH DAKOTA

By Ken Ilgunas

A lone bison munches on a thatch of thick prairie grass atop a butte. When I spot him, I'm walking along the rough and wild Achenbach Trail in the North Unit of Theodore Roosevelt National Park. If I was hiking with Teddy, who visited these badlands in his youth (where "the romance of my life began," he wrote later), he likely would have taken aim at the animal. His legacy of conservation, however, helped set aside this small-but-stunning composition of river, forest, and prairie where protected herds of pronghorn, elk, and bison thrive. Today, Teddy wouldn't be able to hunt them, but I bet he'd be glad for the tradeoff.

TRIP PLANNER

SEASON April to October, but river crossings are more manageable later in the season

PERMIT Required for overnight stay (free); obtain from the North Unit Visitor Center

CONTACT Theodore Roosevelt National Park, www.nps.gov/thro

DISTANCE: 17.6 miles (loop)

TIME: 2 days

DIFFICULTY: ★★↗

THE PAYOFF: The unmaintained Achenbach Trail delivers intrepid hikers into the heart of this national park's badlands, where few tent camp.

TRAILHEAD: Juniper Campground (47.5942, -103.3376); 55 miles north of Belfield off Scenic Drive

MILES AND DIRECTIONS

FROM JUNIPER CAMPGROUND:

1. Hike west across the Little Missouri on the **Achenbach Trail** to mile 0.7 or so.
2. Using the Achenbach merely as a handrail of sorts, hike west across the buttes and mud benches of the Achenback Hills to the Little Missouri River, near mile 8.
3. Instead of following the true Achenbach to higher ground, leave the trail and continue north along the Little Missouri River toward Sperati Point; parallel the wide river downstream to mile 10.6.
4. Pick up another branch of the unmaintained Achenbach and take it 4.8 miles east to Scenic Drive.
5. Follow the road 2.2 miles southeast to your vehicle.

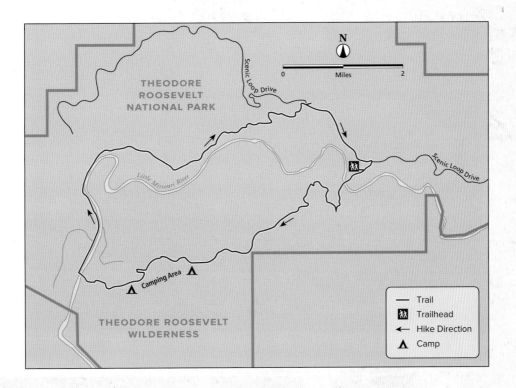

ALL THE EXTRAS

DON'T MISS THIS CAMPSITE: MUD BENCHES (MILES 5 TO 7.2)

You pass a handful of 200-foot-tall buttes in the few miles leading up to the second Little Missouri crossing; if weather allows, camp on one of these dried-mud benches that overlook the Little Missouri and badlands formations (ideal for stargazing and spying bison). Resupply water at Achenback Spring near mile 5.6.

GEAR TIP: BRING A MAP AND COMPASS

Yes, these are backpacking essentials for every hike, but they matter more on some trips than others. Make certain you know how to use both before setting out on this route. The unmaintained Achenbach does have trail markers, but many are tough to spot in the tall grasses (sometimes as high as 3 feet) or have been toppled by bison in need of backscratchers. Save yourself the frustration and chart your own path, using the Achenbach more as a rough and occasional guide. GPS is recommended.

American bison

Photo: iStockphoto

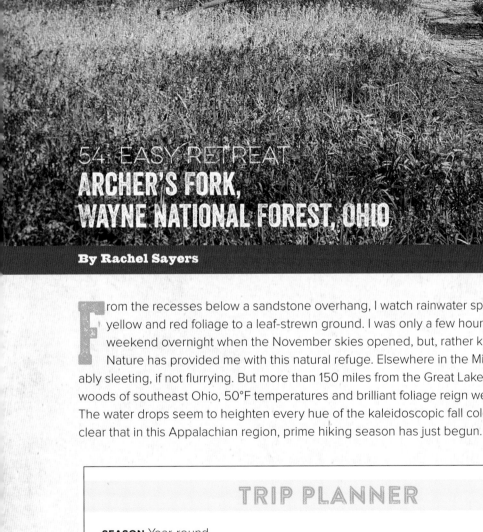

54 EASY RETREAT
ARCHER'S FORK,
WAYNE NATIONAL FOREST, OHIO

By Rachel Sayers

From the recesses below a sandstone overhang, I watch rainwater spill through the yellow and red foliage to a leaf-strewn ground. I was only a few hours into this quick weekend overnight when the November skies opened, but, rather kindly, Mother Nature has provided me with this natural refuge. Elsewhere in the Midwest, it's probably sleeting, if not flurrying. But more than 150 miles from the Great Lakes in the thick woods of southeast Ohio, 50°F temperatures and brilliant foliage reign well into late fall. The water drops seem to heighten every hue of the kaleidoscopic fall color—and make it clear that in this Appalachian region, prime hiking season has just begun.

TRIP PLANNER

SEASON Year-round

PERMIT None

CONTACT Wayne National Forest, www.fs.usda.gov/wayne

DO IT

DISTANCE: 11.5 miles (loop)

TIME: 2 days

DIFFICULTY: ★★✦

THE PAYOFF: Wander past cool rock formations in a quiet corner of the Appalachian Plateau where spring flowers arrive early and fall color lingers.

TRAILHEAD: Ludlow Catholic Cemetery (39.5240, -81.1810); 30 miles southeast of Caldwell on T-411

MILES AND DIRECTIONS

FROM LUDLOW CATHOLIC CEMETERY:

1. Head south on the **Natural Bridge Trail,** following the yellow blazes southwest along Archer's Fork to a typically ankle-deep crossing near mile 3.4.

2. Proceed across Upper Archers Fork Road and continue 1.7 miles east on the **North Country Trail** to a junction with the **Archers Fork Connector.**

3. Take the Connector northeast to an intersection at mile 7.4 near Jackson Run.

4. Cross the shallow stream and travel 4.1 miles generally counterclockwise on an unnamed-but-obvious footpath over various hills and across Irish Run back to the cemetery.

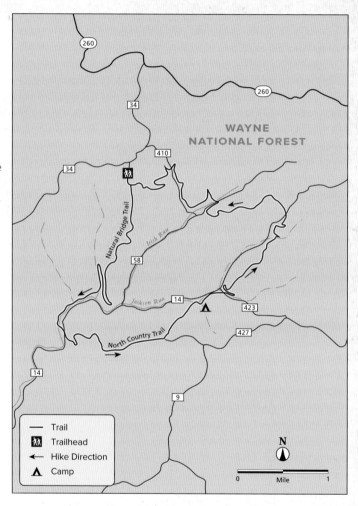

ALL THE EXTRAS

DON'T MISS THIS CAMPSITE: JACKSON RUN (MILE 5.7)

Situated in the junction of two trailside hollows, this campsite has it all: wind protection, water access, a 180-degree view of the river valley, and flat ground (rare on this trek). Bonus: deadfall chairs.

FUN FACT: GEOLOGY

When glaciers laid silt across most of Ohio 260 million years ago, they created the type of terrain that's ideal for farms and high school football fields. But the grinding blue ice missed this region. Here, gentle stream erosion carved lush ridgelines in the Appalachian Plateau, yielding undulating sandstone that eventually eroded into gorges, caves, cliffs, and arches. On this hike, glimpse 50-foot-tall caves near miles 3.4 and 11.2, and 51-foot-long Irish Run Natural Bridge near mile 0.7.

Fall-perfect hardwoods

55: SIGHTS OF SOLITUDE
CHICKENBONE LAKE, ISLE ROYALE NATIONAL PARK, MICHIGAN

Sunsets or sunrises? The answer is yes. Either way you look, a long draw of lake water awaits to reflect the light at site 6 at Chickenbone Lake. This lowland highlight arrives just a third of the way into the Greenstone Ridge Trail, a 42-mile route that takes you from the heights of the island's rocky spine down to the intimacy of its swimming holes and marshes. Follow the sun west to find your private paradise, filling up on summer-perfect thimbleberries, big views—and alone time.

TRIP PLANNER

SEASON Mid-April to October

PERMIT Required for overnight stay ($7 per person per day); pay ahead of time online at pay.gov or obtain from Rock Harbor

COMMERCIAL FERRY *Voyageur II*; book ferry rides from Grand Portage to Rock Harbor and Windigo to Grand Portage at grand-isle-royale.com. For the water taxi, use Rock Harbor Lodge at rockharborlodge.com.

CONTACT Isle Royale National Park, www.nps.gov/isro

Adapted from text by Graham Averill.

Photo: Aaron Peterson

DISTANCE: 42 miles (point to point)

TIME: 4 days

DIFFICULTY: ★★★★

THE PAYOFF: The Lower 48's least visited national park showcases ridges, lowlands, lake views, and deep, *deep* solitude.

TRAILHEAD: Hidden Lake (48.1589, -88.4719); a water taxi will drop you off at the pier.

SHUTTLE FERRY: Windigo (47.9120, -89.1582); a ferry will pick you up at the pier.

MILES AND DIRECTIONS

FROM THE HIDDEN LAKE TRAILHEAD:

1. Pick up the **Greenstone Ridge Trail** from the dock and take it around Hidden Lake and up to Isle Royale's spine near mile 0.7.

2. Follow the main path on a southwest trajectory, wavering between 280 and 800 feet above Lake Superior's deep-blue waters, some 41.3 miles to Windigo, dropping off the catwalk at your leisure to explore lakes, forests, and side trails.

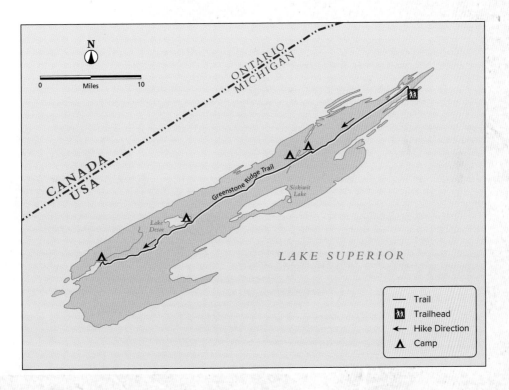

ALL THE EXTRAS

DON'T MISS THIS CAMPSITE: WEST CHICKENBONE LAKE SITE 6 (MILE 15)

Split north off the main drag on the Indian Portage Trail near mile 15 to find your idyllic backcountry digs. Follow the path clockwise around Chickenbone Lake and its north arm to set up on lakeside site 6, where you'll want to wake early to watch the first rays of sunshine raise a curtain of mist from the water.

KEEP YOUR EYES PEELED: WILDLIFE

Moose and elusive gray wolves headline the all-star cast of island inhabitants here. Neither is native and both likely crossed an ice bridge from Ontario years ago, marooning their populations—for all intents and purposes—on the archipelago. Both species are most active at dusk.

GEAR TIP: BRING CASH

The *Voyageur II* makes regular drop-offs at Rock Harbor, across the bay from Hidden Lake. Folks lazy about logistics will start their island traverses here by linking the Rock Harbor and Mount Franklin Trails to meet the Greenstone Ridge Trail near mile 5.5. Don't follow suit. The first 5 miles of the Greenstone Ridge Trail from Lookout Louise are draped in views. Arrange for a water taxi (starting at $58) to cart you across the bay from Rock Harbor to the true starting point at Hidden Lake to savor the 50-mile views over Lake Superior.

Lake Superior licks Isle Royale

56: WATERFRONT PROPERTY
LAKE MONROE PENINSULA
CHARLES C. DEAM WILDERNESS, INDIANA

By Stuart Peck

I understand the attraction of loops—new scenery every step, no retracing your route, a sense of continuity. But out-and-backs are better. Pick the right end point, and an out-and-back is more than a linear hike. It's a mission. Every step brings you closer to the prize, and in the Deam, just an hour and a half outside Indy, the quarry is best-in-class camping: a private peninsula, where I plan to kick my feet up (or maybe dangle them in the water), catch the best star show in Indiana, and cook over an open fire. Then I'll linger lakeside in the morning; no rush, I know exactly how long it will take to retrace my steps.

TRIP PLANNER

SEASON April to November

PERMIT None

CONTACT Hoosier National Forest, www.fs.usda.gov/hoosier

DO IT

DISTANCE: 17.4 miles (out and back)

TIME: 2 days

DIFFICULTY: ★★

THE PAYOFF: Land a private backcountry campsite on the tip of a peninsula on Lake Monroe.

TRAILHEAD: Grubb Ridge (39.0179, -86.3885); 16 miles south of Bloomington on Tower Ridge Road

MILES AND DIRECTIONS

FROM THE GRUBB RIDGE TRAILHEAD:

1. Follow the **Grubb Ridge Loop Trail** 5.9 miles to an intersection.

2. Hang north and pick up the **Peninsula Trail;** take it 2.5 miles to its terminus at a beach on one of the fingers of Lake Monroe.

3. Head 0.3 mile north along the shore to a campsite at the tip of the peninsula.

4. Retrace your steps to the trailhead.

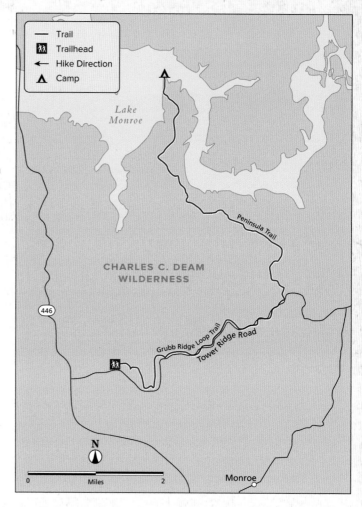

ALL THE EXTRAS

DON'T MISS THIS CAMPSITE: HOOSIER NATIONAL FOREST CAMPSITE #1 (MILE 8.7)

This may be the best campsite in all of Indiana. It might even top the list in the Midwest. Surrounded by water on all but one side, you're almost guaranteed primo sunrise and sunset views across North Fork Salt Creek, the top portion of 10,000-acre Lake Monroe, the state's largest. Seventy-foot hardwoods shelter your camp from lake winds and invite a chorus of birdsong (warblers and wood thrush). There's space for six tents; first-come, first-served.

KEEP YOUR EYES PEELED: WILDLIFE

From your campsite, scan for bald eagles floating on thermals and geese and grebes in the shallows. Look for white-tailed deer and foxes in the nearby trees.

Grebes

57: IDEAL ISOLATION
FRENCH CREEK,
CUSTER STATE PARK, SOUTH DAKOTA

The green water glides through the tight slot like a flume beneath copper-tinted limestone walls that kiss the sky 75 feet above. It's the reckoning, this hike's crux: Will you look for an out and climb above the liquid labyrinth, or will you hoist your pack overhead and venture through? Some of the baddest American desperados—General Custer, Crazy Horse, and others—won battles and fortunes in these untamed Black Hills. We bet we know which they'd choose.

TRIP PLANNER

SEASON August to November and March to June

PERMIT Required for overnight stay ($7 per person per night); self-issue at trailhead kiosk

CONTACT Custer State Park, bit.do/custer-state-park

DISTANCE: 11.6 miles (point to point)

TIME: 2 days

DIFFICULTY: ★★

THE PAYOFF: Spy A-list wildlife as you rock-hop through the Black Hills' seldom-visited narrows.

TRAILHEAD: Horse Camp (43.7161, -103.4513); 13 miles southeast of Custer on Lame Johnny Road

SHUTTLE CAR French Creek East (43.7123, -103.3505); 10 miles west of Fairburn on Wildlife Loop

MILES AND DIRECTIONS

FROM THE FRENCH CREEK TRAILHEAD:

1. From Horse Camp, take the **Centennial Trail** north along French Creek and beneath a canopy of vanilla-scented, 200-year-old ponderosa pines to a junction near mile 1.1.

2. Split east onto the **French Creek Trail** and parallel the path's namesake 10.5 miles—alternating between trailless, tight, watery canyons and aspen-shaded singletrack—to the eastern terminus and your shuttle car.

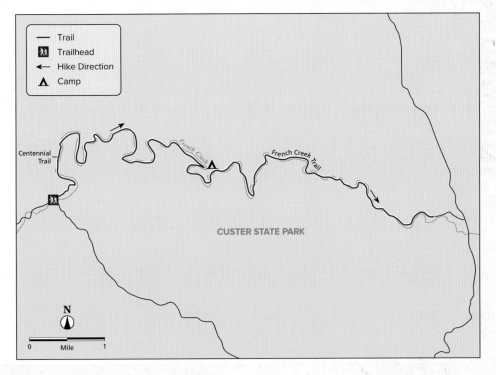

ALL THE EXTRAS

DON'T MISS THIS CAMPSITE: BIRCH GROVE (MILE 5.3)

A particularly idyllic birch grove nestles beneath the cliffs near mile 5.3. Claim the quiet spot and secure both easy water access and a front row to the wildlife show that kicks off every day around dusk. The area typically sees fewer than half a dozen overnight visitors each week in shoulder seasons, so you won't have to share. *Echo-o-o-o-o!*

KEEP YOUR EYES PEELED: WILDLIFE

It's a zoo out there: Look for members of the area's protected, 1,500-strong bison herd roaming through the flats and bighorn sheep balancing on the canyon walls. White-tailed deer and pronghorn graze in the trailside grasses, while orange-colored painted turtles often crawl along the creek. Golden eagles pass through often (scan for them floating on thermals overhead), and, at night, coyotes break the silence with piercing yips.

GEAR TIP: WEAR WATER SHOES

Plan on crossing French Creek at least thirty times and spending a fair amount of time simply wading through it. Amphibious shoes will not only offer supreme grip on slippery stones, but they also allow for more ground feel (for better footing when the water is more opaque) and dry faster than typical midweight hiking boots. Speaking of water: Pack your rod and enjoy French Creek's brown trout bounty.

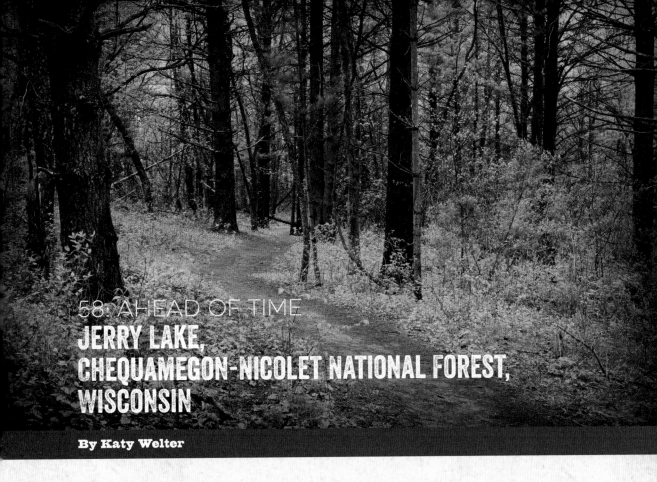

58: AHEAD OF TIME
JERRY LAKE, CHEQUAMEGON-NICOLET NATIONAL FOREST, WISCONSIN

By Katy Welter

It's hard to believe from this cozy perch, but before the dazzling cobalt pool and the brilliant yellow aspens and sugar maples 30 feet below me, there was only a massive glacier here. But the Ice Age left its mark, and I've experienced it on its namesake trail. Earlier in the day, I catwalked across an ancient, bridge-like glacial esker and skirted a swampy ravine of primordial ferns. Now I'm camped above a kettle lake that formed when the glaciers receded. Surrounding it, the trees spring from between milk crate-size erratics, oddball rocks dropped here by moving ice. Time—10,000 years, actually—has added the enchanting forest. Some things are better with age.

TRIP PLANNER

SEASON May to October

PERMIT None

CONTACT Chequamegon-Nicolet National Forest, www.fs.usda.gov/cnnf

Photo: iStockphoto

DISTANCE: 18.7 miles (point to point)

TIME: 2 days

DIFFICULTY: ★★✦

THE PAYOFF: Solitude prevails on this rare, nonmotorized section of the Ice Age Trail, which skirts past erratics, eskers, kettles, and drumlins left by receding glaciers.

TRAILHEAD: Jerry Lake (45.2162, -90.5887); 2 miles northeast of Perkinstown on Sailor Creek Road

SHUTTLE CAR: Mondeaux Dam (45.3334, -90.4519); 20 miles north of Medford off Park Road

MILES AND DIRECTIONS

FROM THE JERRY LAKE TRAILHEAD:

1. Parallel the road north less than 0.2 mile to find the start of the singletrack.

2. Turn west on the **Ice Age Trail,** tracing Jerry Lake, a 26-acre kettle lake, and proceeding through white birch and hemlock forest to a viewpoint overlooking the national forest near mile 2.9.

3. Continue 6.6 miles to a glacial esker; walk along the natural bridge and trek 4.3 more miles north and east to the campsite spur.

4. Back on the main trail, proceed 8 miles to the parking lot at Mondeaux Dam.

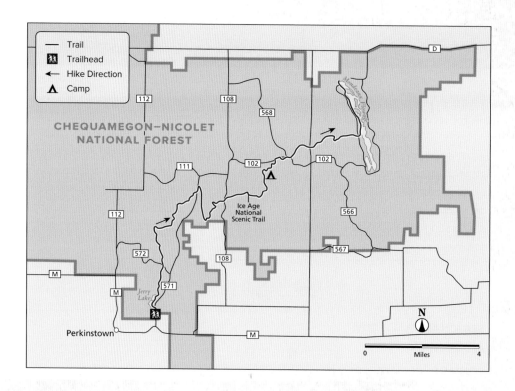

ALL THE EXTRAS

DON'T MISS THIS CAMPSITE: UNNAMED KETTLE (MILE 11.7)

Cap a long day in this glacial playground at a quiet tent site overlooking a little sapphire kettle. The trail curls around the pool near mile 11.7; scan for a faint user trail that climbs uphill to the easy-to-miss perch on the right-hand side. Sixty-foot-tall white birches and pines provide wind protection and privacy from the main trail, while clear water is just a short walk away—and you can't beat the view.

KEEP YOUR EYES PEELED: GLACIAL REMNANTS

On this route, you'll trace three giant eskers (50- to 100-foot-tall embankments of sand and gravel deposited by rivers that flowed beneath glaciers). The first, Hemlock Esker, runs nearly 1.3 miles north to south (around miles 6.3 to 7.6), in the direction of the glacial movement—so you're hiking with the glacial flow from between 10,000 and 60,000 years ago. The kettle lakes on this route, including the campsite above, are like giant potholes formed by the retreating glaciers.

EXTRA CREDIT: TAKE A BREAK

Midway along Hemlock Esker, grab a seat on a bench emblazoned with a quote from the grandfather of the Wilderness Act, Aldo Leopold (who lived in central Wisconsin when he wrote his famous *A Sand County Almanac*): "To those devoid of imagination, a blank place on the map is a useless waste; to others, the most valuable part."

Kettle lake

59: A RIVER RUNS THROUGH IT
HUZZAH VALLEY,
MARK TWAIN NATIONAL FOREST, MISSOURI

Missouri's Ozarks famously feature cave-pocketed limestone bluffs, dense hard-wood forests, and knobby topography riddled with hollows and rivers. And the Ozark Trail—a 350-mile work in progress—hits all the highlights as it careens from near St. Louis to the Arkansas border. But here's a secret: You need not take a month off to experience it. You can sample all the goods on the criminally underrated northernmost stretch of the trail. Better yet? You won't have to share.

TRIP PLANNER

SEASON Year-round

PERMIT None

CONTACTS Mark Twain National Forest, www.fs.usda.gov/mtnf & Ozark Trail Association, www.ozarktrail.com

Adapted from text by Elisabeth Kwak-Hefferan.

Photo: G Michael Lewis

DO IT

DISTANCE: 16 miles (out and back)

TIME: 2 days

DIFFICULTY: ★↗

THE PAYOFF: Climb from ravine to ridge on the Ozark Trail for views of a trio of river valleys.

TRAILHEAD: Onondaga (38.0570, -91.2221); 10 miles south of Bourbon on Highway H/Cave Road

MILES AND DIRECTIONS

FROM THE ONONDAGA TRAILHEAD:

1. Follow the **Ozark Trail** south into an open canopy of white oak, shagbark, hickory, and wild roses (blooming in May and June). The path meanders over ridges and hollows, ultimately paralleling Huzzah Creek to mile 8.

2. Retrace your steps to the trailhead.

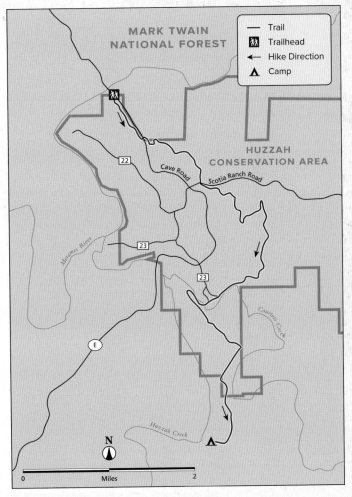

ALL THE EXTRAS

DON'T MISS THIS CAMPSITE: HUZZAH VALLEY PERCH (MILE 8)

Near mile 7.8, keep an eye out for an unnamed social path on the right-hand side of the trail; take it about 0.2 mile toward Huzzah Creek through a dense forest of oak, maple, and pine. It opens like a gateway to reveal a hilltop perch with room for two tents and front-porch views over the valley below. ***Note:*** This spot is dry, so be sure to top off water at the Courtois Creek crossing near mile 5. (Say it like a local: "Code-uh-way" Creek.)

KEEP YOUR EYES PEELED: RUINS

Look for the ruins of the 1870s Scotia Furnace and Iron Works at mile 2.6, just 500 feet south of the trail. The forest around the area was clear-cut for the smelter 150 years ago and is still recovering.

EXTRA CREDIT: MULTISPORT OPTION

If you're an adept paddler—or just a fan of loops—turn this trip into a hike-and-float instead of retracing your steps. From camp, continue 4.1 miles on foot on the Ozark Trail, which deposits you at Bass River Resort. Rent a boat (prices vary; www.bassresort.com) and paddle north along Huzzah Creek and the Meramec River to the original starting point at Onondaga Cave. The paddling is easy, except the waterways can get weedy (read: slow) in late summer.

60 ISLAND TIME
NORTH MANITOU ISLAND, SLEEPING BEAR DUNES NATIONAL LAKESHORE, MICHIGAN

By Stuart Peck

Lounging against my pack while turquoise waves lick my bare feet, I feel like I've been transported somewhere far away—not 12 miles into Lake Michigan. Here, wild Upper Peninsula backcountry meets tropical getaway on North Manitou Island, which features 22 square miles of mostly trailless white-pine woods and white-sand beaches. I've sampled its best on a three-day adventure, camping atop a wooded sand dune and beside a hidden lake. The mandatory ferry ride keeps North Manitou as empty as it is exotic, but when I look up to glimpse a deer loping into pine woods, I'm reminded that it isn't the tropics after all.

TRIP PLANNER

SEASON May to October

PERMIT Required for overnight stay ($10 per party per night); obtain from the ferry ticket office in Leland

COMMERCIAL FERRY Manitou Island Transit; book a round-trip ferry ride from Leland at manitoutransit.com

CONTACT Sleeping Bear Dunes National Lakeshore, www.nps.gov/slbe

DISTANCE: 21.2 miles (loop)

TIME: 3 days

DIFFICULTY: ★★

THE PAYOFF: Start with 20 miles of Lake Michigan's wide, sandy beaches, add towering dunes and pine forests, then subtract the crowds, and you get North Manitou Island, a perfect weekend getaway.

TRAILHEAD: Manitou Village (45.1214, -85.9754); a ferry will drop you off at the pier.

MILES AND DIRECTIONS

FROM MANITOU VILLAGE:

1. Hike 3.6 miles south on the **Manitou Trail** to a clearing just past a small cemetery.

2. You could loop around the island without leaving the singletrack on the Manitou Trail, but then you'd miss the premier campsite on Old Baldy, so veer southwest off-trail at this point. Set your compass bearing toward Old Baldy, near the island's southern tip and walk about 3 miles cross-country to the dune (near 45.0645, -85.9958).

3. From Old Baldy, trek about 0.7 mile southwest to reach the shoreline.

4. Follow the beach 6.2 miles north (merging back with the Manitou Trail near mile 7.6) to an old dock at mile 13.8.

5. Begin wrapping clockwise into the mixed pine and cedar woods on the **Old Grade** path of the Manitou Trail to a T-junction at mile 17.8.

6. Veer south and head 0.8 mile to another intersection.

7. Take the short, 0.3-mile spur to Lake Manitou.

8. Back on the main trail, continue 2 miles east, returning to Manitou Village near mile 21.2.

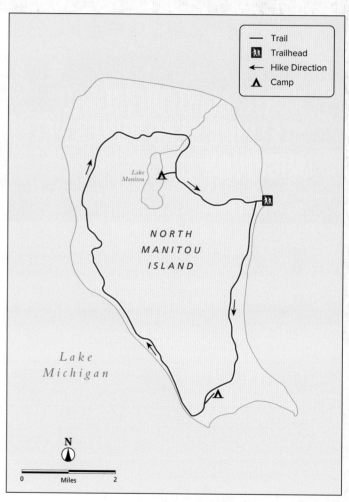

Trail
Trailhead
Hike Direction
Camp

Lake Manitou

NORTH MANITOU ISLAND

Lake Michigan

N

0   Miles   2

ALL THE EXTRAS

DON'T MISS THIS CAMPSITE: OLD BALDY (MILE 6.6)

Bed down on an 850-foot-tall sand dune for 180-degree views that stretch from South Manitou Island (southwest) to the Michigan mainland (east). Cedars protect from prevailing winds, and soft sand means you can skip the pad on warm nights. For the easiest ascent, pass the dune on your left and circle back up its southwestern slope. Don't forget to top off drinking water from Lake Michigan before climbing Old Baldy; it's dry up there.

DON'T MISS THIS CAMPSITE: LAKE MANITOU (MILE 19.6)

Ferry schedules mean you have no choice but to turn this trip into a two-nighter—view that as a blessing because now you need not choose between dune camping and lake camping. Spend your second evening overlooking this lake-within-a-lake from a grove off the eastern shore. Listen for screeching native bald eagles, which nest in the oaks on the western banks between late April and early October.

KEEP YOUR EYES PEELED: RUINS

At mile 17.4, poke around Stormer Logging Camp, a mid-1900s mill that produced timber to power Great Lakes steamers. The relics include 1940s cars that are quickly being reclaimed by the woods.

EXTRA CREDIT: TAKE A BREAK

Walk through Frank Farm and an abandoned mid-1900s orchard near mile 21. The trees still bear juicy apples for visitors to enjoy. (Prime picking season is in August.)

61: CALL YOUR BLUFF
BROWN'S HOLLOW,
YELLOW RIVER STATE FOREST, IOWA

By Korey Peterson

You might not think of Iowa as rugged, but this trail, cut across bluffs and through rutted bedrock, climbs and drops relentlessly. You might not think of Iowa as pretty, but when Paint Creek glides beneath a gilded canopy of oak and hickory, it feels as if even speaking would mar the beauty. You might not think of Iowa as a place to go backpacking—and that's why I won't have to share my easy-access waterfront camp with another soul, save a few songbirds. You might not think of Iowa as wild. That's your loss.

TRIP PLANNER

SEASON Year-round

PERMIT Required for overnight stay (free); self-issue at trailhead kiosk

CONTACT Yellow River State Forest, bit.do/yellow-river-state-forest

DISTANCE: 9 miles (out and back)

TIME: 2 days

DIFFICULTY: ★

THE PAYOFF: Explore the criminally underrated Yellow River State Forest on an easy walk to a riverine camp.

TRAILHEAD: Backpacking (43.1705, -91.2487); 12 miles north of Marquette on State Forest Road

MILES AND DIRECTIONS

FROM THE BACKPACKING TRAILHEAD:

1. Link the **White Pine** and **Forester Trails** 1.6 miles to a junction.

2. Turn east onto **Brown's Hollow Trail** and take it 1.3 miles to where it merges with **Fire Tower Road.**

3. Continue 0.7 mile on the unpaved road.

4. Proceed onto **Brown's Hollow Trail** as it splits east and walk 0.9 mile to the grassy clearing of Brown's Hollow.

5. Retrace your steps to the trailhead.

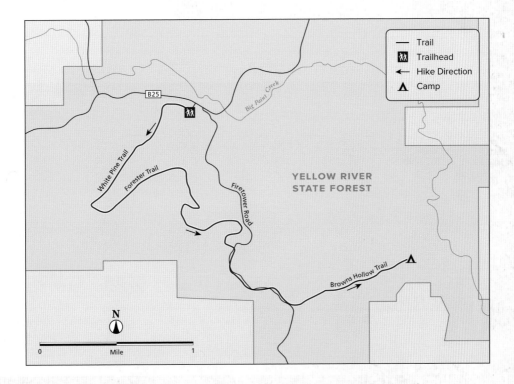

ALL THE EXTRAS

DON'T MISS THIS CAMPSITE: BROWN'S HOLLOW (MILE 4.5)

Pitch a tent (or hammock) in this grove of hickories, oaks, and walnuts north of Paint Creek. Wood benches and a fire ring set this site apart, and you can't beat the easy water access. If you can, time it for mid-October when the trees light up in a fireworks display of fall color.

KEEP YOUR EYES PEELED: WILDLIFE

At night, this area transforms into something from a spooky campfire story, with the coyotes yipping and owls hooting year-round. Come daytime, listen for chattering wild turkeys and keep an eye out for white-tailed deer and nonmigratory birds, such as quail, ring-necked pheasant, and chukar partridge.

FUN FACT: GEOLOGY

Unlike much of the Midwest, the Yellow River area didn't experience glacial activity half a million years ago. Called a "driftless area," it was primarily shaped by wind and precipitation, which is why it has steep bluffs and ravines pockmarked with sinkholes, caves, and springs.

Ring-necked pheasant

62: PIONEER DAYS
MIRROR POOL,
SHEYENNE NATIONAL GRASSLAND, NORTH DAKOTA

By Korey Peterson

I sit against a gnarled oak, resting my eyes on the prairie I waded through to get here. A gentle wind passes through the tan and green grasses, and suddenly it looks less North Dakota than a vast ocean, the prairie swelling and glimmering in the breeze. I walked just 5.3 miles to reach this spot, but out here, remoteness isn't measured in miles. The terrain here is untamed, unmanicured, and wild.

TRIP PLANNER

SEASON April to November

PERMIT None

CONTACT Dakota Prairie Grasslands, www.fs.usda.gov/dpg

DISTANCE: 10.6 miles (out and back)

TIME: 2 days

DIFFICULTY: ★ↄ

THE PAYOFF: Visit one of the country's few remaining tracts of oak savannah—a mixture of grass prairie and small stands of oak—where several threatened and endangered species, such as the Dakota skipper and regal fritillary butterfly, roam.

TRAILHEAD: North Country (46.5236, -97.2033); 46 miles southwest of Fargo on 153rd Avenue SE

MILES AND DIRECTIONS

FROM THE NORTH COUNTRY TRAILHEAD:

1. Pick up the **North Country Trail** and follow it 2.7 miles west to a junction.

2. Veer north (hiker's right) onto an unnamed trail (it appears on topos) and follow it through hilly, short-grass prairie to another intersection at mile 4.5.

3. Split west onto another unnamed trail (also on maps) and take it 0.8 mile to its end at Mirror Pool.

4. Retrace your steps to the trailhead.

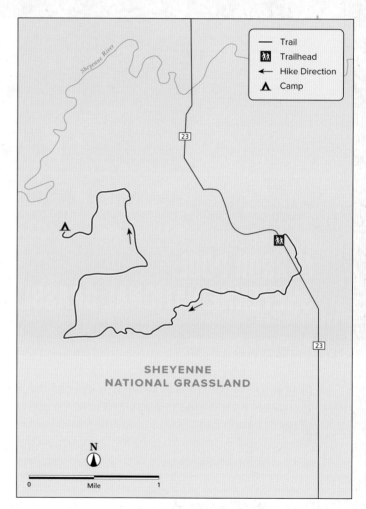

SHEYENNE
NATIONAL GRASSLAND

ALL THE EXTRAS

DON'T MISS THIS CAMPSITE: MIRROR POOL (MILE 5.3)

In a state that's often overlooked for its backcountry virtues, within a land designation that's often cast aside for more banner parks, you'd be hard-pressed to find *any* fellow hikers on the trails. That means the pick of the litter when it comes to dispersed campsites in Sheyenne National Grassland (there are no designated spots). Aim for the flat site amid a grove of gnarled oaks that overlooks the prairie for its obvious views, but the easy walk to water is hard to beat in these parts: It's less than 300 yards to aptly named Mirror Pool.

KEEP YOUR EYES PEELED: WILDLIFE

White-tailed deer, wild turkeys, prairie chickens, and pheasants live here year-round. Scan for eagles and red-tailed hawks floating—and hunting—on thermals overhead, and listen for coyote yips at night.

Prairie chickens

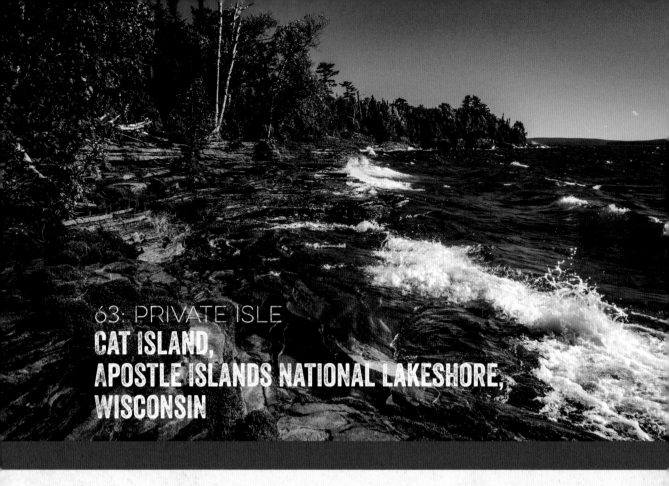

63: PRIVATE ISLE
CAT ISLAND, APOSTLE ISLANDS NATIONAL LAKESHORE, WISCONSIN

One surefire strategy for solitude: Book the place for yourself. Nowhere does this trick work better than in the Apostle Islands, where almost half of the chain's sculpted-rock islands have a single campsite. That means strong paddlers with the skills to navigate Lake Superior's challenging waters can access their own island, complete with sandy beaches, guaranteed tent-door water views, and shady hemlock and pine forests where black bears and red foxes roam.

TRIP PLANNER

SEASON June to October

PERMIT Required for overnight stay ($10 per party plus $15 per night); reserve online at recreation.gov

CONTACT Apostle Islands National Lakeshore, www.nps.gov/apis

Adapted from text by Elisabeth Kwak-Hefferan.

DO IT

DISTANCE: 36 miles (out and back)

TIME: 2 to 4 days

DIFFICULTY: ★★★

THE PAYOFF: Reserve the only campsite on this wooded island and you reserve solitude.

TRAILHEAD: Bayfield Boat Launch (46.8080, -90.8192); 20 miles north of Ashland on South 3rd Street

MILES AND DIRECTIONS

FROM THE BAYFIELD BOAT LAUNCH:

1. Paddle north along the shore through the **West Channel** of the Apostle Islands to Red Cliff Point near mile 7.

2. Bearing northeast, make a straight shot to the sandy southwest shore of Cat Island, weaving between Oak, Hermit, Manitou, Stockton, and Ironwood Islands.

3. Retrace your strokes to the put-in.

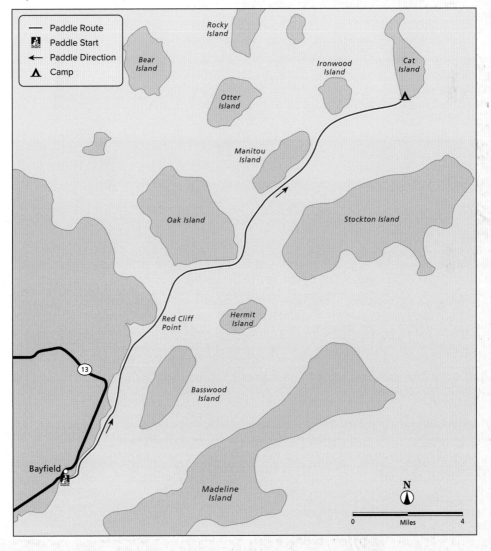

ALL THE EXTRAS

DON'T MISS THIS CAMPSITE: CAT ISLAND (MILE 18)

This outlier near the archipelago's northeastern tip lacks a dock, so you won't even have to share with the occasional boater. Set up your tent in a grove of hemlocks set back off the sandy spit and explore the small island on social trails (tread lightly on sensitive vegetation). Be sure to plan a festive dinner: Cooler-chilled meat, fresh vegetables, and, yes, libations are all on the menu when you have a boat.

EXTRA CREDIT: ADD A HIKE

If the 18-mile paddle out has your arms and abs seizing just reading this, stop en route. (The Apostle Islands' sea caves and arches, remote beaches, and rusty sandstone cliffs deserve more of your time, anyway.) Manitou is an option near the tail-end of the paddle, but Oak (mile 10) is better: From the island's overlook (a 3.5-mile hike from the dock), you can see as many as ten islands in the viewshed, as well as the Hole-in-the-Wall arch. Oak has eight campsites, including three right near the dock (can't beat the convenience) and others as far as 3.7 miles away (if you want solitude).

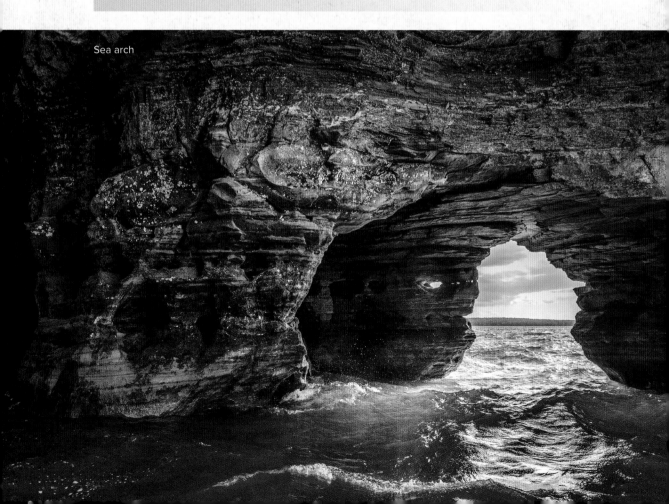

Sea arch

64: SPOILED FOR CHOICE
HOIST LAKES,
HURON NATIONAL FOREST, MICHIGAN

By Stuart Peck

When your hiking route winds past half a dozen jade pools, you need to be a little more selective in picking where to camp for the night. For starters, you want a view of the water so you can see both colorful foliage and the moon reflected on the surface (neither of which gets old, ever). Second, you want seclusion—a sense of privacy, like you have the lake entirely to yourself. So when I land at Byron Lake midway through this loop, I know I've hit the jackpot. I even add a new criterion to the list: You want a sandy beach campsite so you can walk around without shoes and lounge comfortably when contemplating what makes a great campsite.

— DO IT —

DISTANCE: 16.6 miles (lollipop-loop)

TIME: 2 days

DIFFICULTY: ★★

THE PAYOFF: Most backpackers to central Michigan will land at the Manistee River area—overlooking these hardwood forests that thread together more pools than you can count on two hands.

TRAILHEAD: Hoist Lake East (44.6484, -83.7486); 35 miles north of Whittemore on MI 65

MILES AND DIRECTIONS

FROM THE HOIST LAKE EAST TRAILHEAD:

1. Head east on **Trail #1,** following blue blazes to a fork at mile 0.7.
2. Continue 1.8 miles clockwise on **Trail #14** through a hardwood forest to South Hoist Lake.
3. Merge onto a logging road and walk 0.2 mile south.
4. Continue wrapping clockwise on **Trails #12** and **#13** to reach the original junction at mile 15.9 (merge with a logging road at mile 12.6 for 0.3 mile).
5. Retrace your steps 0.7 mile to the trailhead.

ALL THE EXTRAS

DON'T MISS THIS CAMPSITE: BYRON LAKE (MILE 6.9)

Peel off Trail #13 to snag the trophy campsite on Byron's broad, sandy northeastern shore. You might awake to a maze of various animal tracks in the sand: This lake attracts white-tailed deer, beavers, red foxes, otters, and mink.

GEAR TIP: PACK A ROD

This route passes seven named lakes (and a handful of unnamed ones), so opportunities abound for swimming and fishing. For the latter, cast for sunfish in North Hoist and brown trout in South Hoist.

EXTRA CREDIT: ADD A HIKE

If you milk this loop out over three days instead of two (say, with a Friday afternoon start), spend the first night at Hoist Lakes: From the main path (near mile 2.5), follow wooden signposts to the twin lakes. The best campsite overlooks South Hoist from a rock shelf, like box seats at a baseball stadium.

Beavers

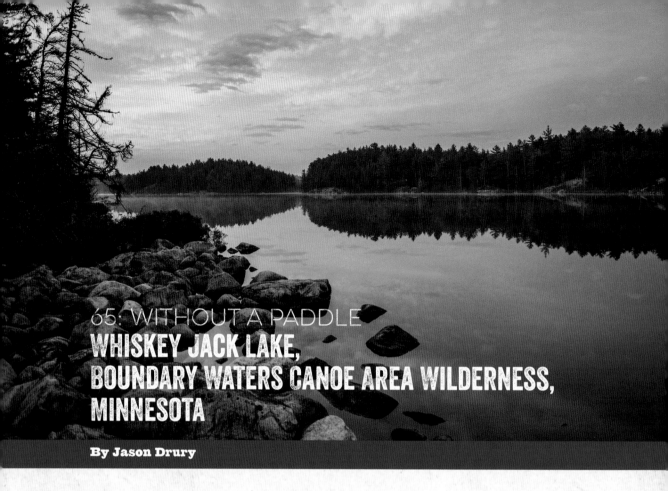

65: WITHOUT A PADDLE
WHISKEY JACK LAKE, BOUNDARY WATERS CANOE AREA WILDERNESS, MINNESOTA

By Jason Drury

The black water is so calm that I skip a stone across its surface to remind myself it's not a sheet of obsidian. I watch the ripples propagate out toward the opposite shore, where the aspens and tamaracks are just starting to turn. It'd be a nice place to camp, but I know there's a better spot just a few miles farther: at a tiny tarn shrouded in maples and pines that's only accessible by foot. Without paddlers and, this time of year, mosquitoes, I'm happy to share with just loons and beavers.

TRIP PLANNER

SEASON June to October

PERMIT Required for overnight stay ($16 per party plus $6 reservation fee); obtain from the Kawishiwi Ranger Station in Ely

CONTACT Superior National Forest, www.fs.usda.gov/superior

DISTANCE: 13.2 miles (lollipop-loop)

TIME: 2 days

DIFFICULTY: ★✈

THE PAYOFF: Skip the crowds—and the hassle of portaging a boat—on this hiking-only loop past three named lakes and half a dozen unnamed.

TRAILHEAD: Angleworm (48.0632, -91.9292); 17 miles north of Ely off Echo Trail (CR 116)

MILES AND DIRECTIONS

FROM THE ANGLEWORM TRAILHEAD:

1. Take the **Angleworm Trail** 1.9 miles northeast to a fork near the southernmost point of the finger lake.

2. Do the loop portion of the lollipop clockwise: Split around the western shore of Angleworm Lake and continue through boreal forest around Home Lake to a faint trail junction near mile 6.3.

3. Keep hiking clockwise on the Angleworm Trail to the eastern shore of tiny Whiskey Jack Lake at mile 7.9.

4. Continue 3.4 miles south on the main trail to the junction of the lollipop-loop. (Since this portion of the Angleworm Trail doesn't appear on many topo maps, expect solitude.)

5. Retrace your steps 1.9 miles to the trailhead.

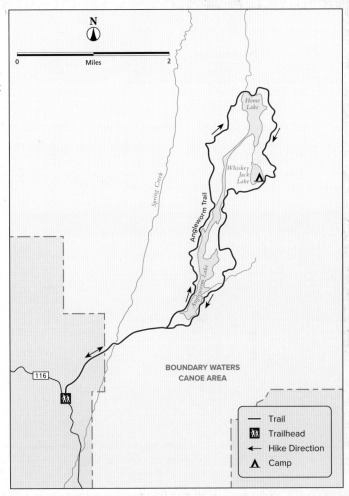

ALL THE EXTRAS

DON'T MISS THIS CAMPSITE: WHISKEY JACK LAKE (MILE 7.9)

With no portage connections to surrounding lakes, Whiskey Jack Lake remains a relative ghost town in Boundary Waters. In fact, only two permits are issued for this area each day, so it's guaranteed to be quiet. Find the one campsite nestled amid the pines on the eastern shore (marked with a fire ring). On the unlikely chance it's taken, keep going about a mile to select any of the sites along Angleworm Lake (the best ones are near the middle).

KEEP YOUR EYES PEELED: WILDLIFE

Massive glaciers carved the rugged scene here, and beavers are continuing their work. Many of the beaver projects—like the one on Angleworm Lake's eastern bank—are staggering in scope, stretching hundreds of feet across. Loons begin to migrate south in September, but you're likely to hear them laughing through summer evenings and into fall. Also listen for moose bellowing: They begin mating in early fall.

Loon

66: ANIMAL CROSSING
DEER HAVEN,
BADLANDS NATIONAL PARK, SOUTH DAKOTA

Home to the largest mixed-grass prairie in the United States, Badlands masquerades as an open-air zoo for classic North American game like bighorn sheep and bison. The trailless Sage Creek Loop leads from one rangeland vista to the next, but wait until Deer Haven to set up your tent. Hemmed in by striated bluffs, it sits high above the plains on a 2,950-foot-high uplift that's dominated by a juniper forest. The animals come for the grass, the trees, and the water, allowing for opportunities to observe interactions between bison herds, coyotes, bighorn and pronghorn sheep, and foxes.

TRIP PLANNER

SEASON September to November and April to May

PERMIT None

CONTACT Badlands National Park, www.nps.gov/badl

DISTANCE: 23-plus miles (lollipop-loop)

TIME: 3 days

DIFFICULTY: ★★★★

THE PAYOFF: Stage dayhikes to explore the badlands from a basecamp in a lush oasis where wild animals flock.

TRAILHEAD: Conata Picnic Area (43.8348, -102.2015); 5 miles south of the Pinnacles Entrance on Conata Basin Road

MILES AND DIRECTIONS

FROM THE CONATA PICNIC AREA:

1. No trails here: Circle clockwise around an obvious badlands formation to a wash that leads north near mile 2.7 (roughly 43.8398, -102.2358).

2. Pick a path of least resistance up the bluffs to **Deer Haven** at mile 3.2.

3. Make a 16.7-or-so-mile loop from camp: Thread together the arid **Sage Creek** and **Tyree Basins** back to the park's southern boundary, which you'll parallel to the wash that leads back to Deer Haven.

4. Retrace your steps to the picnic area.

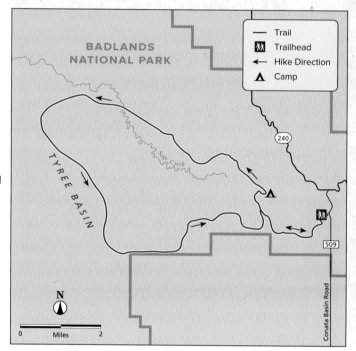

Trail
Trailhead
← Hike Direction
▲ Camp

BADLANDS NATIONAL PARK

TYREE BASIN

Sage Creek

240

509

Conata Basin Road

N

0   Miles   2

Adapted from text by Graham Averill.

ALL THE EXTRAS

DON'T MISS THIS CAMPSITE: DEER HAVEN (MILE 3.2)

Spend the night on this forested perch that looks south over the badlands to Buffalo Gap National Grassland. The short mileage into this spot should make for more time spent watching the big boys (most likely to mosey through at dawn and dusk) and ogling the heavens (the remote park means darker skies). **Note:** Though it's a veritable oasis, pools and streams are unreliable. Plan on packing in all water.

GEAR TIP: BRING A MAP AND COMPASS

Consider this route more a general framework: The serpentine washes that splinter across the badlands will determine your path. Only occasionally will you be able to cross them perpendicularly; more often than not, you'll have to trace their courses until you reach an easy exit. Brush up on your map-and-compass skills and make sure you have a detailed topo (and preferably a GPS unit). It's easy to get turned around in the monochromatic badlands.

Deer Haven

67: WATER'S EDGE
PICTURED ROCKS NATIONAL LAKESHORE, MICHIGAN

On Lake Superior's southern shore, mineral-laden sandstone meets the unrelenting waves and weather of the world's largest freshwater lake. The result: a delicate sculpture of sea caves, stone arches, and polychrome cliffs stretching along the shoreline of the mightiest of the Great Lakes. Find solitude among it all with tips and tricks from local expert **Michael Neiger**. By Elisabeth Kwak-Hefferan

THE INSIDER

Few can claim to know the nooks and crannies of Michigan's wild Lake Superior shoreline better than Michael Neiger. After decades spent exploring the region as a volunteer canoeing and backpacking guide, an investigator for Michigan Backcountry Search and Rescue, and the author of *Exploring Pictured Rocks: West Half,* the almost-lifelong local has logged nearly as many hours in "the bush" as he has in civilization.

1. TOP DAYHIKE

The loop circling Chapel and Mosquito Beaches is "the best cliffside hiking in the Midwest," Neiger says—and that's not even the half of it. The 10.4-miler also encompasses a pair of waterfalls, wavy sandstone formations, and pristine, singing-sand beaches. From the Chapel Road trailhead, hike counterclockwise through orange-yellow jewelweed (blooming late summer into fall) to 60-foot Chapel Falls. Continue on to see Chapel Rock, a sandstone pillar marking the start of Chapel Beach, at mile 2.1. Swing west along the sandy stretch (when it's dry, the sand will squeak or "sing" underfoot), then stroll 200 feet above the shoreline to "the most spectacular part of the park," where views stretch to the cliffs' coves and sea caves in both directions. Descend to Mosquito Beach, then loop back past Mosquito Falls—a wide shelf where you might spy river otters.

Photo: John McCormick

2. BEST MULTIDAY TRIP

Pictured Rocks is a long, skinny park, and the North Country National Scenic Trail spans the whole thing—making it the best bet for extended backpacking. Neiger's favorite segment links Sand Point to Little Beaver Lake for a leisurely 22-mile, four-day shuttle route. From Sand Point (beachy and sheltered, it's a top spot for a dip in the lake), follow the NCT northeast along the bluff to Miners Castle. Take the short spur to a series of overlooks to check out the solitary sandstone pillar, then continue down to Miners Beach. Camp at the clifftop Potato Patch site at mile 7 (there's no water up there, so top off at Miners Beach 0.4 mile back). Day two, hike the shoreline section of the Chapel-Mosquito Beach Loop (see "Top dayhike," previous) and snag a coveted site in the pines near Chapel Beach for a grade-A Lake Superior sunset (reservation required). Follow the bluff 4.3 miles to the sandy Coves site for night three, nabbing views of 70-foot Spray Falls along the way. Finish by connecting with the spur to Little Beaver Lake in the Beaver Basin Wilderness and hiking out to your shuttle car.

3. SECRET BEACH RAMBLE

The 5-square-mile expanse of Grand Sable Dunes, a rare "perched dune" system of sand deposited on top of a bluff, "will blow your mind," Neiger says. "You'll think you're in the desert." For the best access, start at the Sable Falls lot and head 1 mile north to wander through the fragile dune ecosystem, a rolling landscape dotted with stands of jack pine. (Tread lightly.)

4. BEST CAR CAMPGROUND

Tent-door lake views, epic sunsets, a sugary beach: Midwestern camping doesn't get much better than Twelvemile Beach. The first-come, first-served sites sit on an elevated plateau shaded by white birch and fill up fast, so show up early and beeline it for sites 12, 15, 16, 24, 25, or 26 for the best water views.

5. POST-TRIP REFUELING

At Falling Rock Café & Bookstore in Munising, locals hang their own coffee mugs on the walls, smoked whitefish headlines the menu, and a "super selection" of ice cream replenishes lost calories, Neiger says.

TRIP PLANNER

SEASON May to October

PERMIT Required for backpacking ($5 per person per night plus $15 reservation fee); obtain at recreation.gov. Car campgrounds are $16 per night.

COMMERCIAL SHUTTLES ALTRAN (altranbus.com/backpack.html) and Trailspotters (trailspotters.com) both run hiker drop-offs and pickups. Prices vary.

CONTACT Pictured Rocks National Lakeshore, www.nps.gov/piro

Swaths of rhododendron, far-reaching panoramas over seas of gentle green peaks, and wild ponies make this region a sensory delight. Photo: Adam Mowery

MID-ATLANTIC

68: DEEPEST 'DAKS
WEST CANADA LAKE WILDERNESS, ADIRONDACK PARK, NEW YORK

By Casey Lyons

The other side of the stream looks too far to me, but Adam thinks he can jump it.

"Don't worry," he says, sizing up the 5-foot-wide torrent of muddy water and muscling his 40-pound pack back into the reeds to give himself a proper two-step launch pad. "I used to run track in high school."

I want to point out that high school was a long time ago, but I think what he needs right now is my support. I know the precise reason I'll give it to him.

Here on the Sucker Brook Trail, not 3.5 miles from our trailhead at Lewey Lake, we're about to enter some of the deepest forests the Adirondaks have. This lake-filled corner of the 6.1-million-acre park isn't the place to rub elbows with dayhikers looking to bag a pretty peak. It's the least visited corner of the East's largest natural area. Even the name sounds out there: West Canada Lake.

We'd planned to stay on trails for the first four days, skimming Cedar Lake en route to the Adirondacks' highest lake basin, then circle back to Lost Pond over hardwood-forested ridges popping with Candy Land fall colors. On day four—if we were up to it—we'd turn abruptly east, hike to where the dotted line ends, and bushwhack a backside ascent of 3,899-foot Snowy Mountain, the tallest peak in the southern 'Daks.

It's the kind of wilderness that requires more commitment than a casual weekend on the trails. And it's the kind of trip I need during the conflicted time I've recently entered. Having just turned 30, I'm nagged by all sorts of questions about life: I want to know if I've lived up to the promise and potential I had when I was younger.

Mostly, I want to find out if my 18-year-old self would punch the man I've become in the face. The optimal way I've found to measure myself against the past is to try something harder than what I've done before.

Here, without even knowing it, Adam, a 31-year-old who's been between internships lately, has neatly encapsulated this messy mix of potential and current reality into the space between this bank and the far one. His jump is my experiment. "All right," I say, "let's see what you got."

Like a guy about to shoulder through a door, Adam shifts his momentum back and forth. Then, without another word, he takes two giant steps and commits his mass to gravity.

It's the kind of jump that takes place in slow motion, viewed from underneath and lit from above, even if it isn't. Flecks of dirt fall off his Asolos and into Colvin Brook. He reaches the zenith of his arc and sails toward the far bank. His body blots out the sun.

But then he lays up short. His left foot goes forward, but the other slips back, shears the grass off the bank, and dunks in the stream. He comes to rest briefly in a near-textbook hurdlers' split—though flat on the ground.

I think what Adam probably needs right now is my indifference (he'd probably lobby aggressively for a mulligan), and I'd give it to him—if I could control the spasms of laughter. I drop to a knee. I'm wiping tears from my eyes. It's like I've been tear-gassed.

I'm guessing the 18-year-old version of Adam would join me and my teenaged self laughing—though perhaps he might be a little shocked that twelve years could translate to such a loss of linear leap. Then he snaps me out of it.

"OK," he says, scraping the mud off his shin. "Your turn."

FOR ONE IN SIX PEOPLE IN AMERICA, "Adirondacks" defines wilderness. These woods, with their rugged but reachable mountains, forests, and fish-packed lakes, provide the counterpoint to all the parts of the Northeast beset with signs, cities, and interstates.

Leaf-peeping trips (starting in early September in the northernmost parts of the park, then expanding south) anchor the seasonal must-do list. But daytrippers stick mostly to the fringes. Even in the hot months, the interior hangs with a silent immensity that's hard to grasp and hard to resist, but sometimes hard to find.

As an efficiency-minded Northeasterner myself—I grew up in Connecticut—I planned this route to carry us to the deepest interior in the most direct way. It already feels far away, partly because the trail keeps disappearing, partly because of the rain.

Almost immediately after Adam's failed jump (hubris be damned, I scouted a dry crossing), the cold October rain begins. It dumps on us as we pick our way across slick, moss-covered rocks over serial crossings of Colvin Brook. It taps our hoods as we reach the Northville-Placid Trail, heading south toward Cedar Lakes. We stop for a dry break in its lean-to at mile 9.5.

The water, scenic against a backdrop of conifer green and spent-autumn yellow, is blurry with tiny explosions. The lean-to sags in the rain like an old mule. Adam's got the wild-eyed look of mutiny rising. We need fire.

A few minutes later, he returns with a sodden armful of branches and a bundle of stuff he'd protected in his jacket. I lurch into a thicket tinseled with ribbons from the paper birch above. With a few dry twigs scavenged from under the shelter and with our bodies as a rain break, we'll have our fire.

As Adam sets his stream-soaked boot to braise, I think about what this 5-miles-too-early camp really means: The weather is drowning the grand, 68-mile loop I'd come to do. Compromise comes early.

As I fall asleep under the leaky roof that night, I can picture teenaged me reaching back for the haymaker. It was always all or nothing back then. No one ever taught that kid to jab.

WE OPEN OUR EYES TO MORE RAIN THE NEXT MORNING. Across Cedar Lake, fog clings to Good Luck Mountain and Noisey Ridge like smoke rising from one hundred campfires. Last night's thoughts seem silly, and the idea of an either/or world childish. It's not either it rains, or you hike. Sometimes it's both. I feel invigorated and ready to push deeper.

We suit up and head south on the Perkins Clearing Trail into a forest of young birch. Their skinny boughs hang like low-slung arches over a yellow-brown mosaic. The trail slowly disappears under half a foot of water that widens into a lagoon.

My heels slurp inside my boots with each step as I swashbuckle through. The bridge at mile 12.4 is washed out, and the grass on the lower side looks like slicked-back hair. We enter stands of older hemlocks and maples after we turn west on the Pillsbury Lake Trail. Adam spots a fire-colored red eft newt in the leaf litter. They only come out when it's wet.

By my fourth step into Mud Creek on the third morning, the water reaches my thigh. By the fifth, I'm yelping as the cold envelopes my waist.

Adam's around the corner putting his clothes back on. The clouds are fragmenting now, but after two days of rain we've decided a few things: We're not going to let our skivvies get wet, and we're not going to let deep, slow-moving water lock us out.

I can't say that was always the case. Teenaged me would have strode up to that bank and plunged in—fully clothed and come-what-may. Now I just chuck a rock into the current and know it's a go. At moments like this, it's striking to realize how time converts what's merely possible into wisdom and skill.

Dressed again, we start to crank, like our skin is converting the rays that penetrate the canopy into energy. As we gain a little elevation, the trail emerges from ankle-deep puddles and looks paved in gold for all the fallen leaves. To our right, we get occasional glimpses of mirror-shine lakes where few people go.

Then we arrive at a stream, 5 feet across with milky swirls covering the rocks we're supposed to step on. "Looks like we have two options," I tell Adam. "We can take the easy route and cross up there." We both look upstream to a fallen tree encased in a brushy tangle. "Or, we can take the sporting approach and jump it."

"Me first," I add.

I count three steps back, as deliberately as a placekicker, dig the toe of my back boot into the dirt and push off hard. Call it a calculated incaution. Call it whatever you want, because the next thing you know, you're airborne. Committed.

I extend my right foot mid-leap and find the far shore. I run out the momentum for the rest of the day to Beaver Brook Lean-to, which sits 20 feet above the water and has an impossibly red sugar maple framing our cross-lake vista of Blue Ridge, a sloping nub in a rolling forest.

I'll need that momentum for the rest of the trip. The next two days will take us off the well-known Northville-Placid Trail, into second-growth forests pooled with beaver ponds, and finally across a river to where the trail fades, a few miles southwest of Snowy Mountain.

ON OUR FINAL MORNING, we're standing at the edge of Little Squaw Brook. The map shows the trail continuing, but neck-high grass disagrees.

"Good a place as any," I say to Adam. We start off-trail, uphill and east, toward Snowy's long southern ridge, which we'll follow to the summit. The leaves crunch under our feet in the wide-open forest dotted with suitcase-size boulders and crossed by thin drainage brooks still gurgling with fresh rainfall.

White pines thread in with the hardwoods the higher we climb, closing off the cross-valley view to Buck Mountain until we reach a 30-foot-tall cliff band near the top. Just short enough to hide between topo lines.

It'd be easy for Adam and me to turn back here, give in to doubt, re-ford the chest-deep Cedar River like we did yesterday afternoon, take the NPT back to the Colvin Brook Trail, and blame it on something besides ourselves.

But that's not what we're going to do.

After a few minutes of grunting and scraping fingernails, Adam joins me on a ridge so crowded by white pines that light barely penetrates. In their race for open air, these 40-foot-tall, Nalgene-skinny trees let the bottom branches die to feed the crown. The tight, 2-foot space between trunks is now barbed with hundreds of skewers. They poke our arms and legs and whip our faces.

Mossy logs flatten to mush when we step on them. Cliff bands on both sides keep us on the ridge. We take turns breaking branches. We don't talk much. Hours pass. Frustration gives in to doubt. Doubt collapses into exhaustion.

The sun is on its way down by the time we stand below the last 200-foot broken rock face on the backside of Snowy. I take inventory: both water bottles missing, right leg of shorts ripped off, bleeding from both forearms, scratched and swollen left eye. I look like

Fall in the West Canada Lake Wilderness

a kid fresh from a hiding spot in the prickers, or a man returned from clearing them away. Then I realize: I am both. I can hold fast to my teenaged taste for risk, but inform it with the things I've learned; I can convert my ideas into adventures better than ever before. Growing up doesn't mean getting soft. There's nowhere to go from here but forward.

Testing each step, Adam leads up the steep, tree-filled seam between sheer rocks. We shift boulders and uproot tiny saplings. We never look back or down. Adam smells something familiar. "Campfire," he says. "We're close."

And then, leading to the cliff we've just scaled, we see a faint trail that delivers us to the base of an 80-foot fire tower. We scale it in seconds; it's like being borne into the sky. The southern 'Daks stretch out before us. To the east, Indian Lake shines like a sword below rolling hills splotched with yellows, oranges, and forest-greens. To the north, the High Peaks chip the horizon.

Far away on those slopes, the ant paths deliver dayhikers—teenagers and seniors alike—to popular summits with finer views than the one here. But we're the ones who gained perspective.

TRIP PLANNER

SEASON May to November

PERMIT None

CONTACT West Canada Lake Wilderness, bit.do/west-canada-lake-wilderness

DISTANCE: 52.1 miles (loop)*

TIME: 5 days

DIFFICULTY: ★★★★★

THE PAYOFF: Find rare solitude in America's most accessible wilderness on this challenging loop in the southern Adirondack Mountains.

TRAILHEAD: Sucker Brook (43.6518, -74.3975); 12 miles north of Speculator off NY 30

*This trip info follows the loop that the author and his partner ended up actually doing, not the one they originally planned.

MILES AND DIRECTIONS

FROM THE SUCKER BROOK TRAILHEAD:

1. From Lewey Lake, hike 5.6 miles west on the **Sucker Brook Trail** to the Colvin Brook Lean-to.

2. Pick up the **Northville-Placid Trail** and head 3.9 miles south to the Cedar Lake Lean-to.

3. At the Cedar Lakes, veer south on the **Perkins Clearing Trail** for 2.8 miles.

4. Turn west onto the **Pillsbury Lake Trail** and continue 7.4 miles until you rejoin the Northville-Placid Trail.

5. Circle back north on the **Northville-Placid Trail** back around Cedar Lakes to an inconspicuous junction near mile 25.9.

6. Peel off to the north and keep hiking on the **Cedar Lakes Trail** around Lost Pond and Little Moose Lake to reconnect with the **Northville-Placid Trail** near mile 35.5.

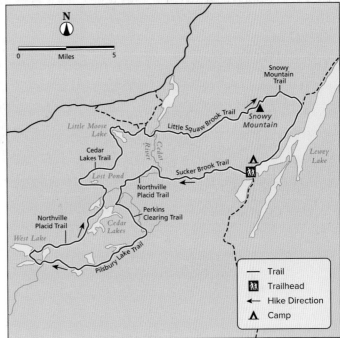

7. Ford the Cedar River and trek east on the **Little Squaw Brook Trail** to its terminus near mile 41.1.

8. Begin ascending southeast up Snowy Mountain's tail-like southern ridge; at the top, continue bushwhacking northeast to the fire tower at the true summit near mile 43.3.

9. Follow the **Snowy Mountain Trail** 3.9 miles off the ridge to NY 30.

10. Walk the final 5.2 miles south along the road to close the loop at the original trailhead (or hitch a ride or leave a second car at the Snowy Mountain trailhead for a 46.9-mile shuttle hike).

69: HIDE-'N'-SEEK
GAP RUN,
SHENANDOAH NATIONAL PARK, VIRGINIA

Crystalline swimming holes, secluded hollows, monster trout, see-forever ridgelines, showy fall color—every trademark of the Shennies is up for the taking on the Rocky Mount Loop in the park's southern corner. Even better? This insulated piece of paradise is an hour's drive from the metro mobs at the northern end of Shenandoah, making it quiet, even by South District standards. Classic Appalachian wonders, no Appalachian crowds.

TRIP PLANNER

SEASON April to November

PERMIT Required for overnight stay (free); obtain from any park visitor center

CONTACT Shenandoah National Park, www.nps.gov/shen

Photo: iStockphoto

DISTANCE: 9.8 miles (lollipop-loop)

TIME: 2 days

DIFFICULTY: ★★

THE PAYOFF: Dodge the crowds on this loop in the underrated South District, where you'll sample both high ridges and low valleys.

TRAILHEAD: Rocky Mount (38.2990, -78.6468); 10 miles southwest of the Swift Run Gap Entrance on Skyline Drive

MILES AND DIRECTIONS

FROM THE ROCKY MOUNT TRAILHEAD:

1. Ramble 5.3 miles north along the **Rocky Mount Trail,** savoring views across Gap Run Valley, Shenandoah Valley, and the main crest of Shenandoah's Blue Ridge, to Gap Run.

2. Turn south, following the water on the **Gap Run Trail** to rejoin the Rocky Mount Trail near mile 7.6.

3. Retrace your steps 2.2 miles to the trailhead.

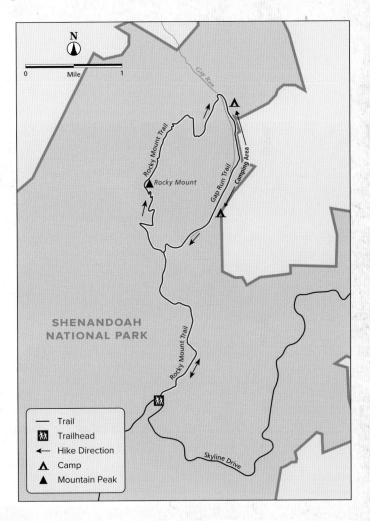

ALL THE EXTRAS

DON'T MISS THIS CAMPSITE: GAP RUN (MILES 5.4 TO 6.4)

Pinpoint a secluded piece of waterside real estate anywhere along Gap Run. Scout for an impacted spot among the hardwoods, or, better yet, sling a hammock: It can be hard to find a flat, rock-free spot, but there's no shortage of ideally positioned trees. You'll have prime access to clear swimming holes and excellent fishing for native brook trout.

KEEP YOUR EYES PEELED: FOLIAGE

Blue Ridge Mountains? Not in fall. Instead, think scarlet (maple), gold (sassafras), amber (hickory), and vast swaths of ruby (oaks) when Shenandoah's hardwood forests show off their changing leaves in mid-October.

Fall in the hollows

70: WALK IN THE WOODS
PINE BARRENS,
PINELANDS NATIONAL RESERVE, NEW JERSEY

The water is the color of tea. That's the observation everyone makes when they first see the springs and creeks along the Batona Trail, 50 miles of almost preternaturally peaceful hiking through the Pine Barrens. But there's something almost enchanting about the deep-brown color, the gentle current, and the cedar smell that hangs in the pinelands. It's intimate, the way hiking should be. The world around the Batona opens up as the trail journeys alongside the country's largest cranberry bogs and climbs the region's highest fire tower, but it's the secret, soothing pinelands that infiltrate your psyche.

TRIP PLANNER

SEASON April to November

PERMIT Required for overnight stay ($5 per person per night); reserve ahead of time and pick up at the state forest offices

CONTACTS Bass River State Forest, Wharton State Forest, and Brendan T. Byrne State Forest, bit.do/nj-parks-and-forests & New York-New Jersey Trail Conference, www.nynjtc.org

DISTANCE: 50 -plus miles (point to point)

TIME: 3 to 5 days

DIFFICULTY: ★★

THE PAYOFF: Explore a mosaic of dark, secret forests and swamps on a long, but beginner-friendly, trail across the coastal plain.

TRAILHEAD: Dans Bridge (39.6280, -74.4361); 2 miles north of Bass River on Dans Bridge Road

SHUTTLE CAR Ong's Hat (39.9113, -74.6206); 4 miles southeast of Pemberton on Turkey Buzzard Bridge Road

MILES AND DIRECTIONS

FROM THE DANS BRIDGE TRAILHEAD:

1. The Batona Trail is unfinished, a patch-work of preexisting and new trails and, yes, some roads (make sure you have the latest beta before you head out). Depending on campsite spurs, expect it to be between 50 and 60 miles end to end. Do it south to north by starting in Bass River State Forest: Pick up the new **Batona Trail** from Dan Bridge Road and follow it north and west past swamps and through—you guessed it—pine woods into Wharton State Forest to overnight at Buttonwood Hill Camp, near mile 16.

2. Next day, continue generally north through Wharton, paralleling the lazy, tea-colored Batsto River along sugar-sand paths to the best campsite on the route: Lower Forge (mile 25 or so; see right for more info).

3. From Lower Forge, hike northeast through cedar swamps and pine forests into Brendan T. Byrne State Forest, over-nighting at the frontcountry campground at mile 45.

4. Tick off the final section by proceeding 9 or so miles northwest on the Batona to Ong's Hat.

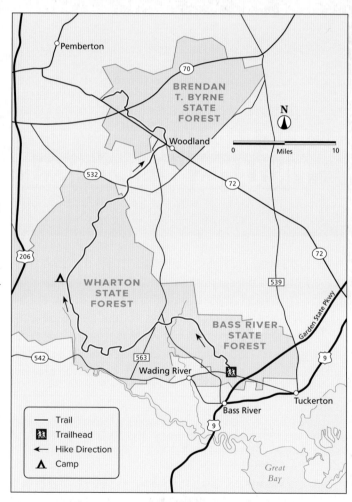

ALL THE EXTRAS

DON'T MISS THIS CAMPSITE: LOWER FORGE CAMP (MILE 25)

The long trail's best backcountry digs is at the exact midpoint: Pitch your tent in the spacious, pine-ringed clearing near a narrow, shallow section of the Batsto River, which burbles from beyond a wall of shrubs and low trees. One of the remotest campsites on the route, Lower Forge is at the end of a 0.4-mile spur in Wharton State Forest.

KEEP YOUR EYES PEELED: WILDLIFE

Scan for wading birds like great blue herons along the various riverbanks, as well as the endangered purple-and-green Pine Barrens tree frog—which you can identify by its distinctive "quonk-quonk-quonk" call and the flash of bright orange on its hind legs when it jumps.

FUN FACT: GEOLOGY

The Pine Barrens, a 1.1-million-acre tract of pine woods and swamps, used to be the floor of a massive sea. When the water retreated, it left behind various layers of sand and gravel that still exist today. While the soil is too dusty and acidic—called "sugar sand"—to support crops (hence the name), many plants thrive in the Pine Barrens. In addition to stunted conifers, look for sassafras, sweetgum, and oak trees, as well as carnivorous plants like pitcher plants, sundews, and bladderworts. In midsummer, snack on trailside blueberries and huckleberries.

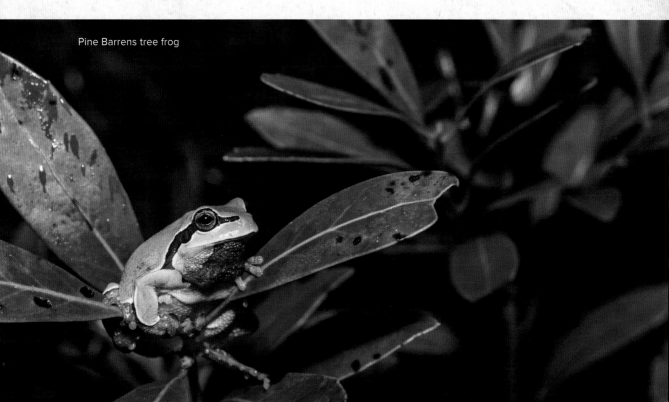

Pine Barrens tree frog

71: EASY SUMMITS
TERRACE MOUNTAIN, SLIDE MOUNTAIN WILDERNESS, NEW YORK

By Ryan Wichelns

I spy a cairn through a small opening in the stand of yellow birches ahead. I take my cue and walk through the leafy tunnel, pausing a minute to enjoy the view of the 11-mile-long blue expanse of the Ashokan Reservoir and the pastel tones of the farmlands that surround it. The hardwoods flutter near me as I try to count the steeples in the sleepy country towns below. Views in the Catskills, like this one along serpentine Cross Mountain, aren't as extreme as those from the Adirondacks to the north, but they may be better. Between the mellow, shaded ridges and open forests, the beauty is close at hand on summits like these, which is why I'm stringing together six of them on this overnight. It's a peakbagging mission, but it feels oddly relaxing.

TRIP PLANNER

SEASON April to November

PERMIT None

CONTACT Slide Mountain Wilderness, bit.do/slide-mountain-wilderness

Photo: Greg Miller

DISTANCE: 19.2 miles (point to point)

TIME: 2 days

DIFFICULTY: ★★

THE PAYOFF: Enjoy an easy peakbagging mission—complete with a deserted campsite—in the under-rated Catskills.

TRAILHEAD: Phoenicia East Branch (42.0801, -74.3207); 25 miles west of Kingston on Lane Street

SHUTTLE CAR Denning (41.9658, -74.4525; 13 miles northeast of Grahamsville at the end of Denning Road

MILES AND DIRECTIONS

FROM THE PHOENICIA EAST BRANCH TRAILHEAD:

1. Take the **Phoenicia East Branch Trail** 8.3 miles, undulating across the gentle spines of Romer Mountain, Mount Pleasant, and Cross Mountain, to a small junction.

2. Turn north onto the **Terrace Mountain Trail** and take it 1 mile to the Terrace Mountain Lean-to.

3. Retrace your steps to the junction.

4. Continue southwest on the **Burroughs Range Trail** across Wittenberg, Cornell, and the Catskill's tallest, 4,180-foot Slide Mountain, to an intersection at mile 14.6.

5. Descend 4.6 miles on the **Phoenicia East Branch Trail** to your shuttle car.

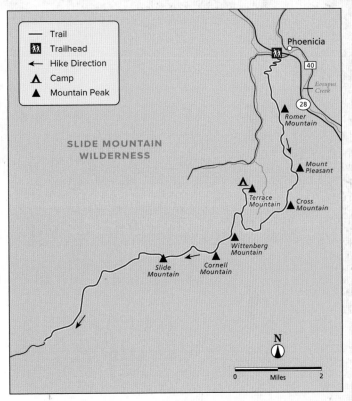

Neversink River

ALL THE EXTRAS

DON'T MISS THIS CAMPSITE: TERRACE MOUNTAIN LEAN-TO (MILE 9.3)

Hiking an extra mile to a shelter might seem like a lot. Luckily, in this case, it's more about the journey than the destination. Meadows, blueberry bushes (ripe in July), and views back to the day's earlier summits are worth the trip. But the lean-to (free; first-come, first-served) isn't bad, either: It sleeps eight, and the roundabout spur to get there means it's generally vacant. Top off water at one of the creeks on Cross Mountain beforehand; it's dry.

GEAR TIP: PACK A ROD

After descending to the crystal-clear East Branch of the Neversink River on day two, take a break beneath the hemlocks to cast for brown, brook, and rainbow trout.

EXTRA CREDIT: MAKE IT LONGER

In the 1930s, when the Long Path was created, you wouldn't have seen any blazes or signposts. Instead, it was a succession of points of interest that intrepid hikers could link however they chose: trails, roads, or bushwhacks. Today the 357-mile route from Fort Lee, New Jersey, to Altamont, New York, mostly threads together preexisting trails, including the first half of this route from Phoenicia to Wittenberg Mountain, which was added to the Long Path in 2014.

72. LESS IS MORE
ENDLESS MOUNTAINS, PENNSYLVANIA

By Jim Gorman

Unexpectedly and abruptly, at around mile 30, we run into a group of backpackers in their mid-20s. They are from West Chester, Pennsylvania, and they're the first people my buddy Alan and I have seen in days. They smell like shampoo. They seem to be in a hurry.

"How far ya' going?" one says.

"How many miles to Angel Falls?" asks another.

The trail chatter snaps me out of a thru-hiker's hypnosis—I'm not sure what time it is or exactly where we are on the map. My mind has been floating and drifting, pleasantly void of stress or boundaries as my feet pad methodically through mile after mile of hemlock and hickory laced with rushing creeks. This is long-trail bliss.

The crazy thing? This "long trail" is only 59 miles end to end, and we're already about halfway through. Our trip isn't a traditional multi-month, foot-long-beard-growing, trail name-acquiring, complicated-mail-dropping, job-quitting thru-hike. My friend Alan and I have families, careers, and mortgage payments that can't be put on hold for six months. But we also have aspirations for long-trail satisfaction—accomplishment, adventure, scenic variety, disconnection, and the bone-weary exhaustion that rewards a hard effort. The solution: a point-to-point hike of about a week. By passing the aches-and-pain break-in period of the weekend, getting to know one trail intimately, and hiking into new territory, we hope to arrive at a place where contemplating the fuzzy caterpillar crossing the trail is infinitely more important than deciding whether granite or engineered stone countertops will better enhance resale.

Judging by the looks on the twentysomethings' faces, our lofty plan appears to be working. They move on while I'm still trying to pinpoint our precise location.

Alan and I are on the Loyalsock Trail, a little-known route through the Nowheresville of north-central Pennsylvania. The path rolls and dips along the Allegheny Plateau in the heart of one of the biggest green blobs Google Earth shows south of Maine. The scene past the trailhead, near Hilsgrove Township, is straight out of the Carboniferous Period. A colony of fledgling ground pines—Joshua tree-like evergreens—projects weird lime-green antennae skyward. Stands of spruce, their arching branches studded with needles, cast shadows on an understory of spongy, star-shaped mosses. It's a fascinating prologue, but we didn't linger.

"We better get moving if we're going to finish this thing," Alan had said.

The Loyalsock is diverse. It visits 31 waterfalls, countless drips and runnels, and one impressive set of class IV rapids. It pings to this beaver pond, pongs to that clearing, then shoots into an open forest of tall maple and black cherry underplanted in ferns nipped with autumn gold. The variety creates the illusion of covering more ground than we'd thought possible, a point driven home as Alan and I take out the maps while relaxing beside a small fire at a campsite in Dutters Run. We listen to a 5-foot waterfall and play rewind on our adventure.

"Wow, still 32 miles to go?" I point out while tracing my finger back along the squiggling red line.

"Perfect."

"That climb right there was a killer," adds Alan, jabbing a finger at the map. "And there's where we got the apples off that old tree."

But the best is yet to come. Going west to east, the Loyalsock's highlights go from high to higher. The valleys are deeper, the streams more acrobatic, and the views more extensive. Fans of the trail are divided in pinpointing its apex. For some, it's the collision of seven mountain spines at Canyon Vista, at mile 43 in Worlds End State Park. For others, it's the Haystacks at mile 57, a sandstone outcrop in Loyalsock Creek that forms a snowmelt-charged, class IV+ rapid that kayakers paddle in spring.

I say it comes at mile 34 at the head of Ketchum Run, where the trail teeters between darkness and light. Cupped in a west-facing bowl carved into steep hillsides, the east and

TRIP PLANNER

SEASON Year-round

PERMIT None

COMMERCIAL SHUTTLE Locals and volunteers for the Alpine Club of Williamsport (alpineclubofwilliamsport.com) run hiker drop-offs and pickups. Prices vary.

CONTACTS The Alpine Club of Williamsport, alpineclubofwilliamsport.com & Loyalsock State Forest, bit.do/loyalsock-state-forest

west branches of translucent Ketchum Run converge in an intimate glen. It's made dusky even at midday by steep walls of schist and a dense canopy of hemlock. Licks of cool air and the muffled roar of Lee Falls below drift up on a breeze. And there's a campsite, too.

Debating a trail's best spot can start a campfire brawl. But as we descend the final 2 miles, alongside Loyalsock Creek, I recall that sweet spot by Ketchum Run and realize that only one truth matters: You can never be sure until you've hiked the whole thing."

DO IT

DISTANCE: 59.2 miles (point to point)

TIME: 4 to 6 days

DIFFICULTY: ★★★★

THE PAYOFF: Undulate through an immense deciduous woodland replete with mountain streams, tiered waterfalls, gardens of maidenhair and Christmas ferns, and deep ravines.

TRAILHEAD: Loyalsock West (41.3619, -76.8759); 14 miles northeast of Williamsport on PA 87

SHUTTLE CAR Loyalsock East (41.4489, -76.4498); 3 miles northeast of Laporte off US 220

MILES AND DIRECTIONS

FROM THE LOYALSOCK WEST TRAILHEAD:

1. The beauty of a thru-hike: Pick up the **Loyalsock Trail** and follow its yellow-and-red blazes 59.2 miles to the eastern terminus. (Reality check: The path is at times a patchwork of other trails and does involve junctions and road-walking, so don't shirk proper map-and-compass navigation.)

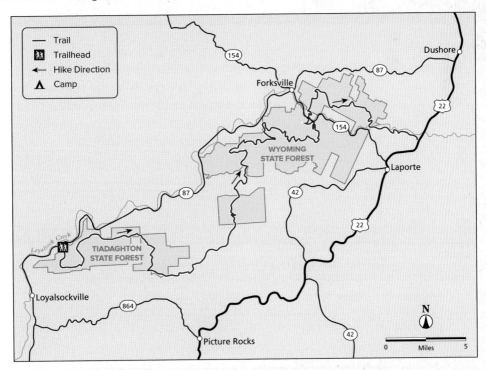

73: ABOVE GROUND
SAL HOLLOW,
MAMMOTH CAVE NATIONAL PARK, KENTUCKY

Put "cave" in your name, and most visitors head straight underground—leaving the trails lacing the bumpy karst landscape above blissfully quiet. Embrace this truth on a two-day loop that explores Mammoth Cave National Park's Sal Hollow, where the sun *does* shine. The above-ground tour takes you across riverside bluffs and through stands of beech, maple, and hickory, proving once and for all that Mammoth Cave's topside features are just as attractive as its subterranean labyrinth.

TRIP PLANNER

SEASON Year-round

PERMIT Required for overnight stay (free); obtain from the visitor center

CONTACT Mammoth Cave National Park, www.nps.gov/maca

DISTANCE: 11.7 miles (loop)

TIME: 2 days

DIFFICULTY: ★↙

THE PAYOFF: Dodge the cave crowds on this easy loop that tours the above-ground landscape of this national park.

TRAILHEAD: Maple Springs (37.2057, -86.1391); 15 miles east of Sweeden on Maple Springs Loop

MILES AND DIRECTIONS

FROM THE MAPLE SPRINGS TRAILHEAD:

1. Hike south toward the Green River on the **Sal Hollow Trail,** passing small streams, dark hollows, and limestone formations, to a junction near mile 8.6.

2. Return to the trailhead via the **Buffalo Creek Trail.**

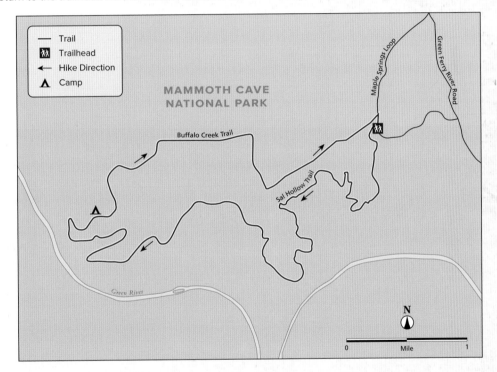

ALL THE EXTRAS

DON'T MISS THIS CAMPSITE: SAL HOLLOW (MILE 7.4)

Snag this spot on the rim for a quiet night, just a short walk from an airy perch over Sal Hollow. It's set back from the trail for solitude and tucked in a stand of hard-woods that are either piercingly green in summertime or bright orange in fall. (Come late fall, the fallen leaves make for a pretty cushy mattress, though.) Be sure to top off water before starting the climb up the rim.

EXTRA CREDIT: ADD A HIKE

Near mile 3.6, veer south on the 2-mile Turnhole Bend Trail to gain a view over an oxbow bend in the Green River. (**Tip:** Go after the leaves fall in mid-September, when you can see the Green on both sides of the ridge for the last 1.5 miles of the detour.) At trail's end, cross a 200-foot-wide choke point flanked by cliffs on both sides before picking a path down to the water to picnic or cast a line. On day two, venture off the main drag near mile 8 to take a short spur to Miles-Davis Cemetery, a settler's graveyard dating back to the mid-1800s. Poke around the old tombstones and restock your campfire story archives before returning the way you came.

Wild turkey

74: MOUNTAIN MAGIC
BREATHED MOUNTAIN, DOLLY SODS WILDERNESS, WEST VIRGINIA

By Nathan Pipenberg

I puff my way up a short, steep climb through hardwood forest and pick a route through a rock garden, hiking poles clacking against stone. When I look up from the slopes of 3,848-foot Breathed Mountain across the Monongahela, it feels as though I've been transported to the far reaches of the Northeast: The wide view is replete with upland bogs and red spruce. One place it doesn't bring to mind is West Virginia. But locals know the best of our state looks a world away. I'm midway through a 16-mile loop across the high plateau of the Alleghenies, and it's something I need to keep reminding myself when I wend through blueberry thickets and rock outcroppings that put other states to shame. I don't want to be anywhere else.

TRIP PLANNER

SEASON April to November

PERMIT None

CONTACT Monongahela National Forest, www.fs.usda.gov/mnf

DISTANCE: 16 miles (lollipop-loop)

TIME: 2 days

DIFFICULTY: ★★

THE PAYOFF: Enjoy the Northeast-like Dolly Sods— with its stunted forests and scalped rocks—without Northeast-like crowds.

TRAILHEAD: Blackbird Knob (39.0335, -79.3144); 15 miles southwest of Maysville on FR 75

MILES AND DIRECTIONS

FROM THE BLACKBIRD KNOB TRAILHEAD:

1. Follow the **Blackbird Knob Trail** 2.3 miles west through rhododendron tunnels to a Y-junction.

2. Peel off to the south (hiker's left) on the **Red Creek Trail** and take it 1.1 miles south to another intersection.

3. To do the loop around Breathed Mountain counterclockwise (saving the best scenery for day two), head 2.7 miles west on the **Breathed Mountain Trail.**

4. Veer south onto the **Big Stonecoal Trail** and take it 3.2 miles to a junction.

5. Turn onto the **Rocky Point Trail** and follow it around Breathed Mountain and past views of the Sods to its end at the Red Creek Trail near mile 11.3.

6. Follow the **Red Creek Trail** 1.3 miles north back to complete the loop portion of the lollipop.

7. Retrace your steps 3.4 miles to the trailhead.

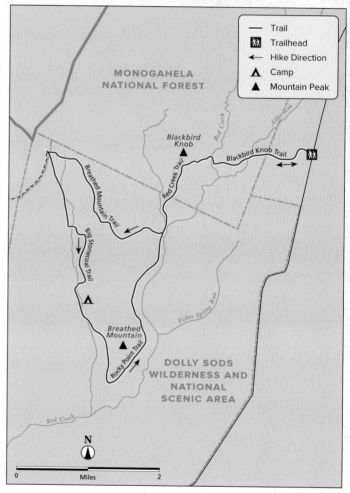

MONOGAHELA NATIONAL FOREST

Blackbird Knob

Blackbird Knob Trail

Red Creek Trail

Red Creek

Alder Run

Breathed Mountain Trail

Big Stonecoal Trail

Fisher Spring Run

Breathed Mountain

Rocky Point Trail

DOLLY SODS WILDERNESS AND NATIONAL SCENIC AREA

Red Creek

| Trail |
| Trailhead |
| Hike Direction |
| Camp |
| Mountain Peak |

N

0 — Miles — 2

ALL THE EXTRAS

DON'T MISS THIS CAMPSITE: BIG STONECOAL (MILE 8.6)

Find a quiet site east of the Big Stonecoal Trail near a thick stand of red spruce, along a sandy bank of the river. This flat expanse was a lumber camp at the turn of the twentieth century, and it's just a short spur away from an 18-foot waterfall south of camp.

KEEP YOUR EYES PEELED: WILDLIFE

You're not the only one who prizes the vast stretches of blueberries (fruiting July and August) in this neck of the woods. Four-legged foragers like black bears harvest their fill, too. (Forest rangers in the Monongahela say they hear reports of more bear encounters in the Dolly Sods than anywhere else in the state.) Also, due to the relatively high elevation, the Sods are home to species like snowshoe hares and saw-whet owls, which are more commonly found several degrees of latitude to the north.

Red creek

75· NEW OUTLOOK
THATCHER'S PINNACLES, DANBY STATE FOREST, NEW YORK

Name be damned—you won't see any lakes on this section of the Finger Lakes Trail, but you'll get open ridgeline views, wilderness solitude, and chances to spot black bears. The area is great year-round, but you'll be rewarded for adventuring there in spring, when water is reliable and woodland wildflowers like sarsaparilla and red trillium burst with color. Of course, no one would fault you for waiting until fall, when the ridges and hollows light up in a living tapestry of color. After, stick around town to sample the region's legendary selection of cider—just be sure to save the hard stuff for *after* your hike. The deceptively strenuous trail sports more than 3,000 feet of elevation gain.

TRIP PLANNER

SEASON May to November

PERMIT None

CONTACT Danby State Forest, bit.do/danby-state-forest

Adapted from text by Paul Chisholm.

DO IT

DISTANCE: 12.4 miles (lollipop-loop)

TIME: 2 days

DIFFICULTY: ★★⟋

THE PAYOFF: Skip the state's better-known range for backyard virtues in underrated Danby State Forest, where seldom-visited bluff-top campsites await.

TRAILHEAD: Finger Lakes (42.3081, -76.4433); 10 miles south of Ithaca on South Danby Road

MILES AND DIRECTIONS

FROM THE FINGER LAKES TRAILHEAD:

1. Head west on the **Finger Lakes Trail,** gaining an easy 500 feet en route to the lollipop-loop's apex at mile 2.2.

2. Tackle the 8-mile **Abbott Loop,** which circles around Michigan Creek through bluffy hardwoods before reconnecting with the **Finger Lakes Trail** at mile 10.2. (Do it counterclockwise to savor the hike's best views in peak daylight on day two.)

3. Retrace your steps 2.2 miles to the trailhead.

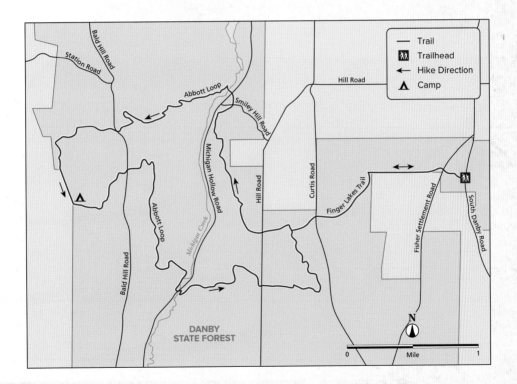

ALL THE EXTRAS

DON'T MISS THIS CAMPSITE: THATCHER'S PINNACLES (MILE 5.7)

Perched 800 feet above the Inlet Valley, the Thatcher's Pinnacles overlook offers throne-like camping above the rolling hills and hardwood forests of upstate New York. The best site opens like a theater stage toward the valley view, so you don't even need to leave your tent to cash in. Spin around to watch for woodland birds like scarlet tanagers and blue-gray gnatcatchers flitting through the sugar maples and red pines behind your shelter. ***Note:*** Top off water at the Michigan Creek crossing beforehand; this site is dry.

KEEP YOUR EYES PEELED: RUINS

European settlers and Revolutionary War veterans cleared this area—originally a super-dense, treed corridor—almost entirely to use as farmland, though the upland soils and steep slopes never supported fruitful agriculture. Eventually the farmers abandoned the area, though you can still spy evidence of the region's farming history if you look closely. Scan for family cemeteries and old fence lines.

Blue-gray gnatcatcher

76: LONG SHOT
TROUT RUN VALLEY, GEORGE WASHINGTON NATIONAL FOREST, WEST VIRGINIA/VIRGINIA

In late March and April, when the Appalachians' highest peaks remain under snow, this lower-elevation circuit delivers a supremely satisfying consolation prize with its catwalk above wanderlust-stirring vistas and glades festooned in trillium. But even if you hold out for summer when the numerous runs and brooks make for a clutch wet-'n'-wild adventure—or fall when reds and oranges paint the mountainsides—chances are good you won't have to share. There's always consolation in that.

TRIP PLANNER

SEASON March to November

PERMIT None

CONTACT George Washington National Forest, www.fs.usda.gov/gwj

DISTANCE: 24.5 miles (loop)

TIME: 2 or 3 days

DIFFICULTY: ★★✯

THE PAYOFF: Bask in big views as you undulate through remote hollows in this Shenandoah look-alike.

TRAILHEAD: Wolf Gap (38.9244, -78.6890); 13 miles west of Woodstock, Virginia, off VA 675

MILES AND DIRECTIONS

FROM THE WOLF GAP TRAILHEAD:

1. Pick up the **Mill Mountain Trail** (called "Wolf Gap Trail" on older topos) and take it 6.4 miles north to an intersection.

2. Continue straight on the **Tuscarora Trail** to link up with the **Halfmoon Trail.**

3. Loop 0.6 mile around Halfmoon Run to the **Bucktail Connector** near mile 9.1.

4. Take it 2.6 miles to the **Buckhorn Trail,** which downclimbs briefly to the road.

5. Cross Trout Run Road and follow the **Long Mountain Trail** (called "Crack Whip Furnace Trail" on older topos) up Cherry Ridge to parallel the path's eponymous mountain to FR 691 near mile 20.

6. Trek 2.5 miles south on the rough, one-lane road to a trailhead.

7. Trace the ridge north some 2 miles on the **Tibbet Knob Trail** to close the loop at Wolf Gap.

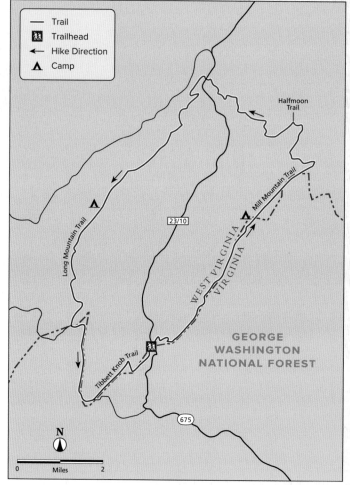

ALL THE EXTRAS

DON'T MISS THIS CAMPSITE: SANDSTONE SPRING (MILE 4.6)

The only thing that could possibly put a damper on this ridge walk is water weight, so plan a night at this spot near a reliable spring and keep your pack light. Set up your tent on a flat spot in a grove of hardwoods amid dense ferns—if you didn't already, now you'll know why thru-hikers call this area the Green Tunnel. (If you're going on a late-fall or winter trip, you'll still want to haul in water.)

DON'T MISS THIS CAMPSITE: BENS RIDGE (MILE 16.6)

Cap off a long day in a grassy area near an unnamed stream in the shadow of 2,200-foot Bens Ridge. There are no designated campsites and, for all intents and purposes, no people. Throw down wherever suits and sit back to watch the setting sun dip behind Bens Ridge.

EXTRA CREDIT: ADD A HIKE

Tack on as many as six short spurs to overlooks on this route. The string of soul-stirring vistas begins early on the Mill Mountain Trail (don't miss the Big Schloss detour near mile 1.9) and continues through day two. The eagle-eye views over a web of forested ridges and pristine Trout Run Valley—a dead ringer for Shenandoah—add overall mileage, but since you don't have to throw elbows to secure them, they're all the sweeter.

By Stephen Edwards

77: FALL FANTASY
PHARAOH LAKE, ADIRONDACK PARK, NEW YORK

This can't be right. From my peak-top vantage in the eastern Adirondacks, there's enough crimson and gold wrapped around a half-dozen cloistered lakes to stress my DSLR's color settings. Yet I have this sun-drenched Saturday scene entirely to myself. A few quacks from migrating geese break the silence, then it's still again. This is the way leaf-peeping should be done: solitude on a crisp Saturday morning, relishing a cool breeze that carries the scent of damp pine so distinct I know I'm not dreaming.

← DO IT →

DISTANCE: 11.7 miles (lollipop-loop)

TIME: 2 days

DIFFICULTY: ★★

THE PAYOFF: Savor solitude when you skip the High Peaks in favor of this lower-relief corner of the Adirondacks where hardwoods and ponds rule.

TRAILHEAD: Crane Pond (43.8513, -73.6624); 5 miles east of Schroon Lake at the end of Crane Pond Road

MILES AND DIRECTIONS

FROM THE CRANE POND TRAILHEAD:

1. Proceed 0.7 mile south on the **Crane Pond Trail** to a junction and the apex of the loop.
2. To hit the Pharaoh Mountain summit on the morning of day two, do the loop clockwise: Turn east onto the **Long Swing Trail,** which meanders south to 440-acre Pharaoh Lake and an intersection near mile 4.3.
3. Circle around Pharaoh Lake on an obvious user trail, passing lean-tos, to its southern tip at mile 6.4.
4. Veer onto the **West Shore Trail** to keep circumnavigating the lake before reaching the summit turnoff.
5. Take the **Pharaoh Mountain Trail,** which ascends 1,400 switchback-less feet in 1.2 miles to the 2,556-foot summit.
6. Downclimb the north face on the same trail, closing the loop near mile 11.
7. Retrace your steps to the trailhead.

Photo: Jessica Tabora

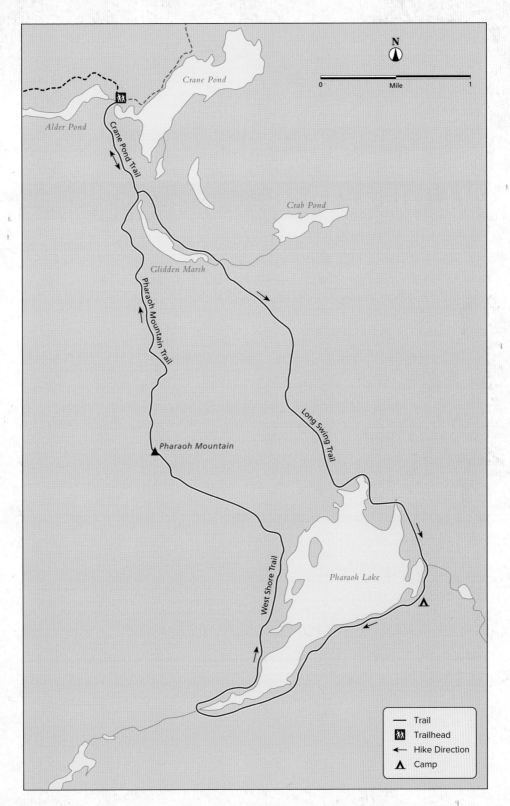

ALL THE EXTRAS

DON'T MISS THIS CAMPSITE: PHARAOH LAKE LEAN-TO #3 (MILE 4.7)

This three-sided shelter opens to Pharaoh Mountain's buffalo-back profile, which looms above one of the eastern Adirondacks' biggest undeveloped lakes. Cook dinner around a fire pit as the sun's last rays disappear behind the peak and stars begin to pop like kernels in the dark sky.

KEEP YOUR EYES PEELED: FOLIAGE

This broccoli-patch canopy of maples and birches typically erupts into a fiery palette of yellows, oranges, and reds the fourth week of September through the second week of October. Savor the half-mile-long corridor of golden, three-story-tall maples at mile 1.5 on this itinerary. And next morning, don't snooze the alarm: You won't want to miss the sun's first rays on Pharaoh Mountain's forested east face, which often set low-lying fog below bright orange.

FUN FACT: EVOLUTION

Coyotes around here don't howl—they bark. Some scientists think these canines, also 10 pounds heavier than average, could be hybrids blending western coyotes and eastern wolves. Listen for them after dusk.

HIKE SMARTER
4 WAYS TO CAMP IN COMFORT

1. Pitch the perfect camp. Choose a site 200 feet from lakes and streams. Camp at established sites and on durable surfaces whenever possible. Hang your bear bag or stash your canister at least 200 feet downwind from camp. (See number 3 for bear bag tips.) In grizzly country, cook 200 feet or more downwind from your tent. In calm conditions, orient your tent door to the east for early sun. Look up to make sure no dead trees or branches threaten to fall on your site (especially in beetle-damaged forests in the West). Find a flat rock, preferably with a windbreak, for your kitchen.

2. Beat the wind. Spend extra time searching out a sheltered site, like in a low-lying forest. Above treeline, seek protection on the lee side of a rock outcropping or ridgeline. Orient your tent so the smallest side is facing the wind. If it's not raining, wait until the winds die down (often at sunset) to pitch your tent. You'll reduce the risk of damage from a big gust. Guy out your tent securely. Here's how: Tie small overhand loops at each end of a nylon cord (4 to 8 feet). Pull one end through a guy loop, then pass the other end through the loop in the cord to fasten it. Anchor the other end tautly to a stake.

3. Hang a bear bag. Select a pair of branches 20 feet apart and at least 15 feet off the ground. Attach one end of a 100-foot utility cord (3 millimeter) to a fist-size rock that's heavy enough to drag the line through dense boughs. Tie the other end to a tree trunk or any nearby sturdy anchor. Throw the rock over both branches in succession. Tie a knotted loop (bight) in the cord midway between the branches. Attach the food bag (the stuff sack for a tent works fine) to the loop using a simple overhand or slip knot, or a carabiner. Pull on the unsecured end of the cord to lift the bag high enough up to be out of a bear's reach from the ground (at least 10 feet) or in either tree (4 feet). Tie off.

4. Easy ways to improve the menu: Pack a few fresh, lightweight add-ins to boost the taste of any dehydrated meal. Ideas: cilantro, jalapeno, parsley, basil. Serve an appetizer. Soup is a no-brainer in cool weather. Upgrade any lunch wrap with an avocado; pack it in your pot to prevent squishing. Add butter. Use extra water in dehydrated meals (there's nothing worse than not-quite-rehydrated stroganoff). Flame control: If you must cook in your vestibule during a storm, prime a liquid-fuel stove outside and then pull it under cover.

INSIDER'S GUIDE

78: BLUEGRASS ESCAPE
DANIEL BOONE NATIONAL FOREST, KENTUCKY

The wilderness draped across eastern Kentucky's Cumberland Plateau is a hiker's playground of sandstone cliffs, tiered waterfalls, swimming holes, and rock arches. Get it to yourself with these recommendations from local expert **Matt Able.**
By Elisabeth Kwak-Hefferan

THE INSIDER

Matt Able fell in love with this area as a college kid who spent his spare weekends climbing in the Red River Gorge. These days, he's the Trails Program Manager for the Daniel Boone—in other words, he now explores the forest's quietest corners for work.

1. BEST WATERFALL

Lacy waterfalls riddle the Daniel Boone, but 40-foot Van Hook Falls is Able's favorite because you can walk right behind it. To feel the spray, start the 6-mile Rockcastle Narrows East Loop clockwise. At the junction near mile 1.5, cross the bridge over Van Hook Branch to reach the grotto cradling the falls. Grab a perch on one of the boulders lining the stream to dip your toes in the water, or poke around the cool cavern behind the cascade. Close the loop on Rockcastle Narrows.

2. TOP OVERNIGHT

A pair of natural sandstone arches, a bluff-lined river, and the state's tallest waterfall—the only way to make this 13-mile loop more *Kentucky* is to add a flask of bourbon. Hike west on Lick Creek Trail (#631) in the forest's southern corner, dropping under rocky over-hangs to a junction. Take the 0.5-mile spur to see an 80-foot cascade plunge over an amphitheater, then continue on to wide Princess Falls at mile 3.4. Swing north along the banks of the Big South Fork of the Cumberland River, crossing into the Big South Fork National Recreation Area. Pick up the Yahoo Falls Loop to see the state's tallest waterfall, a 113-footer, then turn east on Yahoo Arch Trail (#602). The ridgeline between miles 7 and 8 offers good dispersed camping in the pine-oak woods. Next day, hike past 70-foot-long Yahoo Arch before hooking up with the southbound trail #612. Follow it back to the Shel-towee Trace Trail before reconnecting with the Lick Creek Trail.

3. BEST VIEW

Savor 360-degree vistas atop Auxier Ridge, a sandstone spine in the northern Daniel Boone's cliffy Red River Gorge. A 6-mile loop via the Auxier Ridge and Double Arch Trails will land you atop a stone fin with views that stretch to Courthouse Rock and Raven Rock (two islands in a sea of foliage), Haystack Rock (which resembles a giant beehive), and Double Arch. Nab up-close views of the arch-within-an-arch later in the loop.

4. BEST SOLITUDE

Alone time in the northern stretches of the forest can be hard to come by, but not in the Beaver Creek Wilderness, a hardwood forest circled by sandstone cliffs and streaked with creeks. Able's favorite path in is the 6.5-mile (one-way) Middle Ridge Trail (#518). "I'm a glutton for rough trails—the rockier and tougher it is, the more I enjoy it," he says. Take it along Beaver Creek, keeping an eye out for foxes and black bears. Scout a site after mile 4.5, or link up with Trail #512 at mile 6.5 and continue deeper into the wilderness.

5. MULTIDAY TREK

For the full Daniel Boone experience, you can't beat the 290-mile Sheltowee Trace Trail, which bisects the national forest from north to south like the guyline on a pup tent. The long path links clifftop overlooks, wild creeks, waterfalls, and habitats for deer, bald eagles, and river otters. Able's pick for the most primo miles with the fewest road cross-ings: the 70-mile stretch from Holly Bay Marina to the Great Meadows Campground on the Tennessee border. "In late May and June, you're sure to see blooming rhododendrons and trillium," Able says.

TRIP PLANNER

SEASON Year-round

PERMIT None

CONTACT Daniel Boone National Forest, www.fs.usda.gov/dbnf

The Smokies' glut of airy balds (page 259) each offer long-range views. Photo: iStockphoto

SOUTHEAST

79: IN TOO DEEP
CONGAREE NATIONAL PARK, SOUTH CAROLINA

By Eddie Nickens

I'm paddling lazily and daydreaming, idly gazing through the hardwoods, when Lee starts shrieking. "Whoa!" he hollers from up in the canoe's bow. "Backpaddle! Fast!" I dig in deep, bringing the boat to a skidding stop, and follow the trajectory of Lee's index finger to a thick, forked sapling. The cottonmouth is dangling about eye-high.

"Man, you gotta stay on your toes in here," Lee hisses as we detour safely around the snake. This was the latest of a number of close encounters with Congaree National Park's many crawling and slithering denizens.

In theory, Lee is right—it's wise to be alert in here. But in practice, Congaree Swamp is a fascinating fusion of eye-popping flora and fauna and serene, even hypnotic landscapes. It's a place where eerie, afternoon-long silences amid trees as imposing as the Parthenon's columns are followed by nights filled with the shrieking cacophony of the park's winged and many-legged occupants.

I quickly came to embrace all of this on a two-night float-and-hike in Congaree with three buddies. I'd always wanted to go to the park, but when the time came, I'd started off somewhat warily. In 2003, the floodplain forest was upgraded from national monument to national park, a significant bit of recognition that can nonetheless be a mixed blessing. With the higher profile of national park status often comes increased concessions and more campgrounds, which in turn bring more tourists. I didn't know whether the RV-outfitted throngs had already descended on these untamed, unruly 27,000 acres of swamp woods I'd heard so much about, but fortunately, these being the days of ever-shrinking park budgets, I'd arrived to find that not much new had happened in terms of frontcountry infrastructure.

WE LAUNCH A PAIR OF CANOES INTO A SIDE CHANNEL of Cedar Creek at Bannister's Bridge, far up in the park's northwest corner, just as late morning sunlight filters through the ironwood trees. Up ahead, a sunbeam has worked its way through the tangle of branches and mossy tree trunks and glints on the creek's main stem. The passage is as kinked up as a rattler with rickets. "Looks like some tricky stickwork," I mutter to Lee, up in the bow, as we adjust dry bags for trim.

South Carolina's only national park forms an oblong chunk of terra not-so-firma snugged up against the north shore of the Congaree River, just downstream of Columbia, in the bull's-eye center of the state. There, 160 river miles from the sea, the broad, mud-brown Congaree spills from the rolling hills of the Piedmont region into the flat terraces of the upper coastal plain. As the river slows, it broadens, loops, and meanders through the East's finest expanse of old-growth floodplain forest. For 13.2 miles, a single, occasion-ally marked canoe trail traverses the primeval forest via the wandering channel of Cedar Creek. Canoeists navigate banks studded with cypress knees, the sky smothered by tow-ering hardwoods and loblolly pines. At mile 13, the route takes a hard turn south through a feeder slough, and for 13 more miles, paddlers float the wide Congaree, the south bank soaring up to 300-foot bluffs.

Over the centuries, both river and creek have migrated across the lush flood-plain, carving isolated oxbow sloughs and seasonally wet "guts" into rich alluvial soils. Negotiating that labyrinth with several days' worth of gear and water requires equal parts finesse and brute strength. One moment we're threading tight spaces, Lee lean-ing far over the starboard gunwale to drawstroke the bow around tall cypress knees and through hairpin twists. The next, Bill and John are vanishing behind walls of lichen-flecked tree trunks and muscadine vine. Then both boats are breaking out into broad dead-river lakes pinched into canyons of gray tree trunks draped with Spanish moss and resurrection fern.

The forest overhead tends to overhaul your idea of what a tree can and should be. There are 11,000 contiguous acres of old-growth here, and the virgin woods boast a canopy that reaches as high as 160 feet—comparable to the Amazon's. There are more than twenty trees in here large enough to set records; five of them are national cham-pions for their species. They shade a dense understory of river cane, dwarf palmetto, and more vines than have appeared in all the *Tarzan* movies combined. Drifting under gnarly, centuries-old cypress trees, their crowns shattered by lightning, Lee cranes his head back. "Indians with longbows and dugout canoes probably paddled under here," he muses. Extinct passenger pigeons and Carolina parakeets probably perched in their boughs, as well.

The current occupants are equally compelling, but in a much more visceral way—like the spider we spot that looks like an eight-legged mouse, it's so big. I try to scoop it up with a paddle to photograph it with the creek and the Spanish moss as a backdrop, but it slips off and tumbles onto my toes, prompting me to yelp and hop onto the canoe seat.

Eventually, the late-day sun starts coming through on a slant, signaling that it's time to look for higher ground. We take a rough stab at our position on a topo map, but the featureless terrain yields few clues.

"You could put a dollar bill down on that map, and it wouldn't touch a contour line," I tell Lee.

We make camp under a twisted old beech tree on a low ridge heavy with the musk of stinkhorn fungus. As a stove hisses to life, a barred owl cranks up its unmistakable call, "Who-cooks-for-you? Who-cooks-for-you-all?" Soon another owl answers, and then another, their throaty pleas giving way to a raucous mélange of monkey-like cries and howls. They're still at it hours later as I make my way to the tent, headlamp beam blazing green in spiders' eyes.

TO MANY, A FLOODPLAIN FOREST MIGHT LOOK LIKE a monochromatic landscape, a featureless diorama of brown water, gray trees, and mud a shade of muted red. But our second morning spent drifting through Congaree's hoary woods offers a series of landscapes worthy of Renoir. Firebursts of wine-colored catkins hang heavy in maples. Painted turtles bask in the sun, their shells embroidered with crimson hieroglyphics. Prothonotary warblers flit through trees like gold doubloons tossed from the sky. We paddle slowly, savoring scene after kaleidoscopic scene.

Then Lee breaks the reverie. "Hey, y'all, anybody know where the creek went?"

We lay our paddles across the gunwales, baffled. For hours we'd cruised Cedar Creek's well-defined banks. But gradually the creek had risen, spilling over its sides, until we were paddling through an ocean of trees. At some point we must have crossed over the levee and continued through open woods, until a curtain of cypress knees and briers descended.

Now, water covers the forest floor as far as we can see. I shove a paddle into the murky soup, and can't find bottom. We are afloat in a surging Congaree flood.

Congaree is actually a wetland that's typically covered with water, not a true swamp like Georgia's Okefenokee or Louisiana's Atchafalaya Basin. Its forest floor is dry enough during lean rainfall seasons for backpackers to piece together loops on 25 trail miles. If there are storms in the uplands, though, the Congaree goes swimming. The floodplain drains more than 8,000 square miles of the western Carolinas, which means massive, days-long floods some ten times per year. Water spreads like a brown sheet, swallowing all but the highest bluffs. Deer, bobcats, and canoe campers vie for high ground. A ranger once watched three wild pigs ride out the floodwaters on a log. As we sit there puzzling over what to do next, it hits me: This park, purely because of its inherent challenges, is practically immune to crowds. My fears about this place were blissfully unfounded.

Right now, though, we wouldn't mind seeing someone with a GPS, or maybe even a crew of porcine trailblazers to guide us out of this morass. We turn to map and compass, but they're nearly useless given that we don't know which side of the stream we're on. Next we study the flow of water, trailing pale-pink maple seeds as they drift downstream. But with the flood, however, we aren't sure whether to paddle upcurrent or down. Finally we decide to bend the rules, sending one boat north and the other south. Lee and I push through tangles of vine, briers, and blown-down tree trunks. Just before heading into a gloomy tunnel of brambles, we hear Bill's distant call: "Hey, over here! We found it!" We backtrack through the maze.

That night, after we set up camp, we try to piece together where we'd gone wrong. Somewhere along the way, it appeared, we'd turned the boats away from the creek channel as the flood reversed its current.

Indeed, it's easy to be seduced by the seemingly gentle creek wending through the trees, but this dynamic system is demanding of visitors. It requires routefinding and strong paddling skills, and a tolerance for mud, murky water, fang-baring opossums, featureless bogs, creeks that run backward, and two dozen species of arachnids. A decade ago, a travel-and-lifestyle magazine published a feature on the place, prompting a rush of visitors who were shocked to discover snakes in the swamp.

I welcome every such sighting, down to the last day, when we suddenly burst onto the Congaree's broad back and roll seaward. We squint in the sunlight, watching vultures trace black spirals in the sky. Along the riverbank, wild pigs snort as we pass.

Our final push is one for the books. The rising flood has the Congaree roiling. Fortunately, there's a stiff breeze at our backs, so we lash the boats together, jam a paddle in between to serve as a makeshift rudder, and raise a space-blanket sail.

Our little armada covers 13 miles in three hours, riding a red mud river home fast enough to throw out a wake. On the prettiest Sunday of the young spring, we pass only a pair of johnboats and a single family camping on the riverbank. In a landscape that changes by the hour, the remoteness of this wild, wet place is, happily, the only constant.

TRIP PLANNER

SEASON Year-round

PERMIT Required for overnight stay (free); obtain at the Harry Hampton Visitor Center

CONTACT Congaree National Park, www.nps.gov/cong

DISTANCE: 26.2 miles (point to point)

TIME: 3 days

DIFFICULTY: ★★★↙

THE PAYOFF: Wet-and-wild Congaree is never the same park twice—if you venture into the water.

TRAILHEAD: Bannister's Bridge Landing (33.8399, -80.8613); 16 miles southeast of Columbia on Roger Myers Road

SHUTTLE CAR Route 601 Landing (33.7536, -80.6446); 3 miles south of Wateree off US 601.

MILES AND DIRECTIONS

FROM BANNISTER'S BRIDGE LANDING:

1. Launch your canoe into **Cedar Creek** and follow the channel downstream roughly 13.2 miles to the **Congaree River.**

2. Float 13 miles downstream to the takeout at the Route 601 Landing.

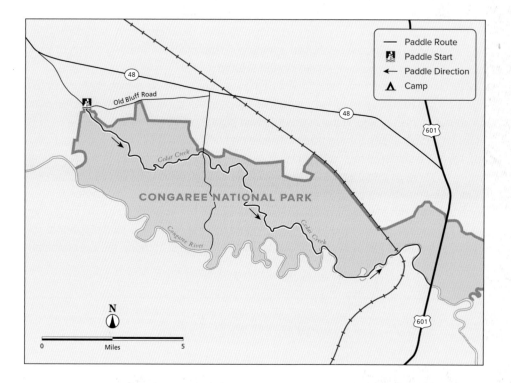

80 FLOWER POWER
SHEEP PEN GAP,
GREAT SMOKY MOUNTAINS NATIONAL PARK,
TENNESSEE/NORTH CAROLINA

While the origin of the southern Appalachians' high-elevation balds remains a mystery, one thing's for sure: Divine intervention could scarcely have made better picnic spots. And Gregory Bald, which sits above the Smokies' repeating ridges like a throne wreathed in pink and orange flame azaleas, is best among them.

TRIP PLANNER

SEASON April to October

PERMIT Required for overnight stay ($4 per person per night); reserve online

CONTACT Great Smoky Mountains National Park, www.nps.gov/grsm

DISTANCE: 12 miles (out and back)

TIME: 2 days

DIFFICULTY: ★★✔

THE PAYOFF: Steer clear of the Appalachian Trail corridor and stage an out-and-back to a flora hot spot from an underrated trailhead.

TRAILHEAD: Gregory Ridge (35.5625, -83.8458); 18 miles southwest of the Townsend Entrance, Tennessee, on Forge Creek Road

MILES AND DIRECTIONS

FROM THE GREGORY RIDGE TRAILHEAD:

1. Duck beneath leaf canopies on the **Gregory Ridge Trail** to a junction near mile 4.8 at Rich Gap.

2. Catwalk west along the state line on the **Gregory Bald Trail,** coming up on Sheep Pen Gap near mile 6.

3. Retrace your steps to the trailhead.

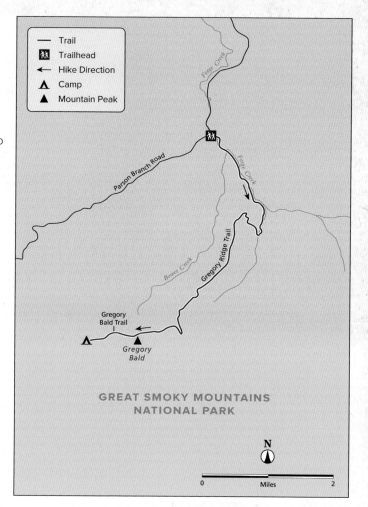

Trail
Trailhead
Hike Direction
Camp
Mountain Peak

Forge Creek

Parson Branch Road

Forge Creek

Gregory Ridge Trail

Bower Creek

Gregory Bald Trail

Gregory Bald

GREAT SMOKY MOUNTAINS NATIONAL PARK

N

0   Miles   2

Adapted from text by Graham Averill.

ALL THE EXTRAS

DON'T MISS THIS CAMPSITE: SHEEP PEN GAP (MILE 6)

The Smokies are busy, plain and simple, but this itinerary keeps you 3 miles away from the Appalachian Trail corridor and has you at a trailhead that services only one footpath. That doesn't spell out complete solitude, necessarily, but it means Sheep Pen Gap #13, the closest campsite to Gregory Bald, remains relatively quiet. From Gregory Bald, continue some 10 minutes west to the campsite, which has room for fifteen partitioned among the yellow birches.

KEEP YOUR EYES PEELED: FLORA

This trip is OK year-round, but it's a showstopper in mid- to late June, when the rare flame azaleas on Gregory Bald burst into an inferno of blooms. The rhododendron shrubs are on the tall side, with some creeping up to shoulder height, and packed with the showy, funnel-shaped flowers. Fair warning: This yearly show is becoming a hit on Pinterest and Instagram, so time your visit for midweek and head out early (from Sheep Pen Gap, *shhhh*) to secure solitude.

FUN FACT: MAINTENANCE

Gregory Bald is one of only two balds in the Smokies that the park service keeps cleared of woodlands, since reforestation would threaten its crown of rare azaleas. The 10-acre meadow makes for clear views over the psychedelic-colored flowers into the endless ridges and blossomy reaches of the Smokies.

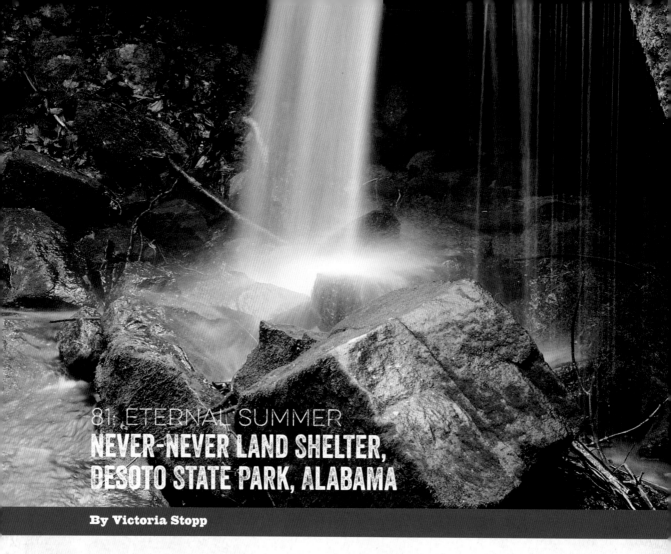

81: ETERNAL SUMMER
NEVER-NEVER LAND SHELTER, DESOTO STATE PARK, ALABAMA

By Victoria Stopp

Stretching out across a sun-soaked boulder, I consider going for another dip in Laurel Creek. A 6-foot waterfall spills over a limestone ledge into the pool, tempting me. I'm midway through a short overnight, and though the summery scene is perfect, the deep-gold hickories and reddish maples give away my secret: It's late October. Idyllic air temps in the 70s, year-round falls, empty trails and shelters, and this scene have me convinced that fall is prime time in the South. That settles it: One more soak.

TRIP PLANNER

SEASON Year-round

PERMIT None

CONTACT DeSoto State Park, bit.do/desoto-sp

══ DO IT ══

DISTANCE: 7.2 miles (dumbbell loop)

TIME: 2 days

DIFFICULTY: ★

THE PAYOFF: Finally, a backcountry shelter where you don't need to fight for sleeping-pad space: Only one party at a time can book this three-sided hut tucked into northeastern Alabama's rolling hardwood forest.

TRAILHEAD: DeSoto Picnic Area (34.5010, -85.6185); 13 miles west of Cloudland, Georgia, on DeSoto Parkway

MILES AND DIRECTIONS

FROM THE DESOTO PICNIC AREA:

1. Like many backpacking trips in the Deep South, this one requires creativity: Begin at the easternmost end of the dumbbell and follow the **Laurel Falls Trail** south as it wraps clockwise to the park road at mile 2.

2. Join the **Family Bike Loop Trail** and continue 0.4 mile north to a junction.

3. Head west on the **Never-Never Land Trail,** which bends counterclockwise to a fork at mile 3.9.

4. Turn south onto the unnamed path and walk 0.6 mile to the Never-Never Land Shelter.

5. Retrace your steps to the junction.

6. Walk less than 0.1 mile east to another T-intersection, closing the western loop of the dumbbell.

7. Rejoin the **Laurel Falls Trail** and take it 0.4 mile south.

8. Instead of continuing 1.6 miles to the trailhead (creating a 7.2-mile lollipop-loop), savor new scenery and close the east loop of the dumbbell: Take the **Lost Falls Trail,** which wends 1.2 miles south of Laurel Creek before merging with the Laurel Falls Trail again for the final 0.4 mile to the trailhead.

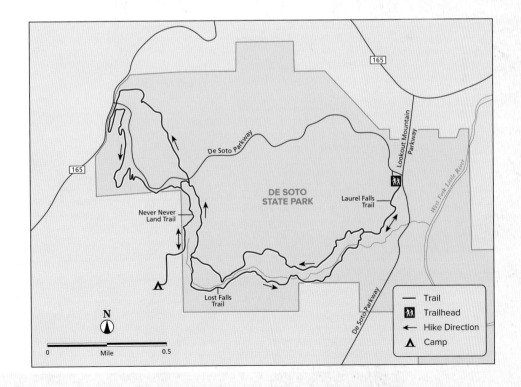

ALL THE EXTRAS

DON'T MISS THIS CAMPSITE: NEVER-NEVER LAND SHELTER (MILE 4.5)

Sharing is for kindergarten: Park rules state that only one party may book this hut at a time (and camping is only allowed in the park's two shelters), which means solitude is guaranteed. That's good news for you because Never-Never Land is the swankiest shelter in the area: three walls, wood floor, and metal roof. Top off water at a seasonal stream 0.2 mile south (usually flowing through winter, but call ahead to check). Reserve online ($17).

KEEP YOUR EYES PEELED: FOLIAGE

Hickories and red and silver maples hit peak fall color by mid-October, but foliage lingers into mid-November.

EXTRA CREDIT: ADD A HIKE

Check out a 1930s Civilian Conservation Corps quarry midway through this route on a 2-mile, round-trip detour. From the fork at mile 2.4 (step 2 on the itinerary on previous page), head a mile east to the stadium seating-like ledges that surround the football field-size quarry. Pick a lunch spot and peer across the basin for a primo foliage view. ***Note:*** The park's other shelter is here, too, but it doesn't have walls, so bring a tent if you plan on camping here in iffy weather.

Rhododendron

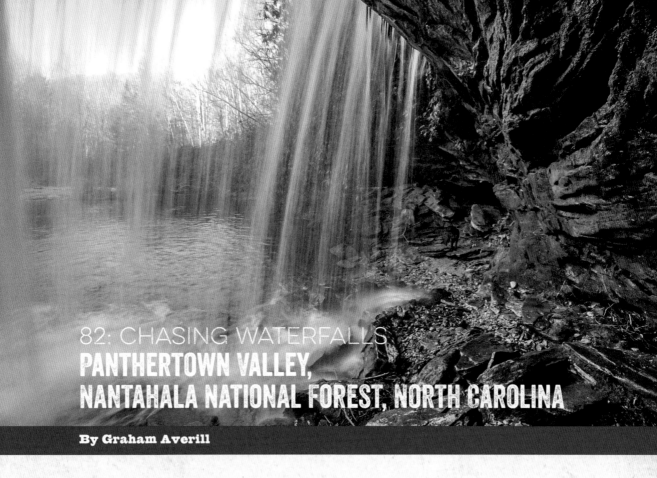

PANTHERTOWN VALLEY, NANTAHALA NATIONAL FOREST, NORTH CAROLINA

By Graham Averill

Granite domes surround a tannin-colored pool, which gleams like gold. I ditch my boots and ease into the cool, spring-fed water for the second time today. Earlier, I backstroked beneath a remote, 30-foot-tall cascade. Later this afternoon, I plan to relive my childhood with laps on a waterslide—only now, I'm not in a crowded water park, and I'll have this rhododendron-lined granite flume to myself. So what if I'm not making miles on this short, weekend-size loop? I'd rather spend more time barefoot than booted, swimming than slogging. There's more than one way to escape, and on a Carolina summer day, I'll choose this one every time.

TRIP PLANNER

SEASON April to October

PERMIT None

CONTACT Nantahala National Forest, www.fs.usda.gov/nfsnc

Photo: Brad Kuntz

DISTANCE: 10.8 miles (dumbbell loop)

TIME: 2-3 days

DIFFICULTY: ★↗

THE PAYOFF: Splash through the Blue Ridge Mountains on a wet-and-wild tour that evades the national park hordes.

TRAILHEAD: Cold Mountain Gap (35.1579, -82.9992); 6 miles northwest of Lake Toxaway off Cold Mountain Road

MILES AND DIRECTIONS

FROM COLD MOUNTAIN GAP:

1. Follow the **Panthertown Valley Trail** 1.4 miles northwest to a T-junction.

2. Turn north onto the **Power Line Road Trail** and follow it 0.4 mile to another intersection.

3. Tackle loop one: Thread together the **Power Line Road Trail, Carlton's Way,** and the **North Road Trail** on a 3-mile counterclockwise circuit through the hardwoods beneath Blackrock Mountain.

4. Retrace your steps 0.4 mile southwest on the **Power Line Road Trail** to the start of the second leg.

5. Loop two: Link the **Panthertown Valley, Big Green, Mac's Gap,** and **Little Green Trails** into a 4.6-miler that rejoins the **Panthertown Valley Trail** from step 1.

6. Retrace your steps 1 mile back to the trailhead.

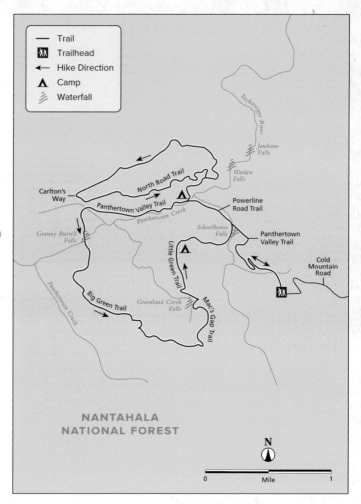

ALL THE EXTRAS

DON'T MISS THIS CAMPSITE: PANTHERTOWN CREEK (MILE 5.2)

Bed down at one of six waterside sites in the soft sand north of Panthertown Creek at the front end of the second loop. Just steps off the trail, these tree-protected, established spots (complete with fire rings and blowdown benches) are easy to locate.

DON'T MISS THIS CAMPSITE: LITTLE GREEN MOUNTAIN (MILE 8.9)

If time suits, stretch this trip over three days, spending the second evening near a pine-shrouded cliff edge on 4,040-foot Little Green Mountain. Find Tranquility Point, a west-facing granite ledge overlooking the valley, 20 yards away. The overhang offers the best sunset view in these woods. **Note:** Carry in water from Greenland Creek before ascending the mountain.

EXTRA CREDIT: ADD A HIKE

In this case, consider the "extra credit" mandatory: At least a dozen waterfalls, named and unnamed, litter this route, transforming it from a workaday piece of Blue Ridge scenery into one of the South's best. Near the apex of loop one, head east down an unnamed-but-marked footpath to see 30-foot Warden and 50-foot Jawbone Falls. Warden sports a near-vertical slide and wading pool, while Jawbone has a low-angle flume and a deep basin—making the 0.8-mile detour entirely worth it. On loop two, budget time to see 10-foot Granny Burrell Falls (and its 100-foot-long slide) on a 0.6-mile detour; two-tiered, 60-foot Greenland Creek Falls (and its cave) on a 1.2-mile detour; and trailside, 20-foot Schoolhouse Falls, which has a lap pool-like basin.

83: UNDER COVER
RED HILLS,
BLACK CREEK WILDERNESS, MISSISSIPPI

The deepest part of the Deep South comes alive in the wilds of Black Creek, a tea-colored river that seems to force its way through emerald-green forests so dense, they seem impenetrable. Squeezing through the low-hanging cypresses on its banks and twisting around the sweetgums and into the piney uplands is the 40-mile Black Creek Trail, a designated National Recreation path and tour de force that at times feels like it belongs more in New Zealand than the Magnolia State. Spend a week knocking out the whole thing or savor a weekend-size bit when you sluice across the trail's best section in the 5,000-acre Black Creek Wilderness, where your biggest concern will be whether to throw down on a sandbar island or among the loblolly pines that seem to sentinel over the floodplain. Truth be told, this trip is wilder than a feral hog.

TRIP PLANNER

SEASON Year-round

PERMIT None

CONTACT De Soto National Forest, www.fs.usda.gov/mississippi

DISTANCE: 16 miles (point to point)

TIME: 2 days

DIFFICULTY: ★★✦

THE PAYOFF: Explore the Gulf Coast's jungle-like low-lands before camping in West-like pine woods on this underrated National Recreation Trail.

TRAILHEAD: Black Creek (30.9883, -89.0515); 11 miles northeast of Wiggins on MS 29

SHUTTLE CAR through the Red Hills

MILES AND DIRECTIONS

FROM THE BLACK CREEK TRAILHEAD:

1. Pick up the **Black Creek Trail** heading south to loop around Beaverdam Creek before following the path's namesake downstream through the Red Hills to the parking lot at Fairley Bridge, 16 miles away.

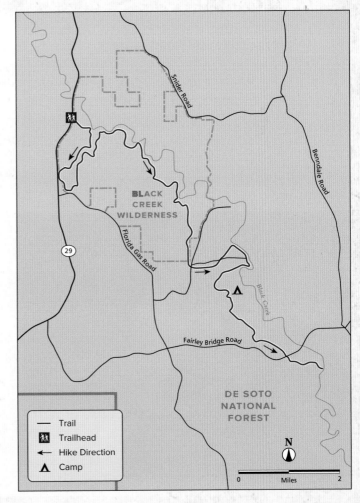

ALL THE EXTRAS

DON'T MISS THIS CAMPSITE: RED HILLS (MILES 11.3 TO 12.6)

If you spy other recreationists on this trip, chances are high they're canoeists floating the Black, a designated Wild and Scenic River. If they're overnighters, the boaters will gun for campsites on the bleached-white sandbars that poke out of the water—leaving the trail's most rugged terrain up for the taking for those traveling on foot. The ups and downs through the ravines of the Red Hills make for the hike's most challenging hiking, but pick a flat spot snugged against the pines and the total solitude will feel totally worth it.

KEEP YOUR EYES PEELED: FOLIAGE

While the understory of yaupon holly shines brilliant green year-round, not much else does. The bottomland hardwood forests are composed of gums, oaks, hickories, dogwoods, tulips, cypresses—the list goes on. See the river valley erupt into a chorus of reds, oranges, yellows, and even purples in October—or wait until winter, when the bare trunks mean long-range water views through windows among the evergreen magnolia, bay, and pine trees.

Flowering dogwood

84: SWAMP SEASON
FLOYDS ISLAND, OKEFENOKEE NATIONAL WILDLIFE REFUGE, GEORGIA

By Kathy Kyle

Cypress trees shawled in gray moss shield my crew of eight from the sunshine. We float through a cluster of lily pads as our aluminum canoes clunk off roots in the narrow canal of coffee-colored water. A doe looks up at us while nibbling on some moss, unconcerned with our intrusion. Here, in the Lower 48's largest blackwater swamp, she must not get many visitors. We're less than an hour into an 18-mile paddle and we've already seen a group of tumbling otters, a hawk, and a gator—each one more disinterested in us than the last. Given that our only intention was to flee the cold for T-shirt weather, I'll consider this a landslide win.

TRIP PLANNER

SEASON October to May

PERMIT Required for overnight stay ($15 per person per night); reserve at recreation.gov

CONTACT Okefenokee National Wildlife Refuge, www.fws.gov /okefenokee

DISTANCE: 18 miles (out and back)

TIME: 2 days

DIFFICULTY: ★★⌇

THE PAYOFF: This refuge's 120 miles of water trails remain virtually untouched by recreationists, which bodes well not only for solitude, but wildlife sightings too.

TRAILHEAD: Kingfisher Landing (30.8278, -82.3611); 18 miles northeast of Fargo off GA 177

MILES AND DIRECTIONS

FROM KINGFISHER LANDING:

1. Paddle 0.3 mile north to the dark-water **Suwannee River.**

2. Turn east into the flatwater and go 1.1 miles to another confluence.

3. Split north into the **Middle Fork Suwannee River** and follow it 4.3 miles.

4. Veer east into a signed, 4-foot-wide channel and paddle 3.3 miles to Floyds Island.

5. Retrace your strokes 9 miles to the put-in.

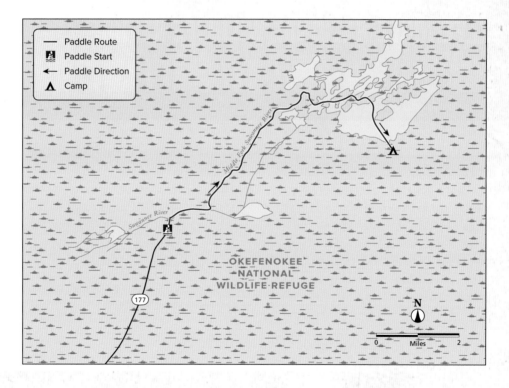

ALL THE EXTRAS

DON'T MISS THIS CAMPSITE: FLOYDS ISLAND (MILE 9)

Leave the tent at home and spend the night in this simple, metal-roofed hunting cabin built in the 1920s. There are four rooms (no furnishings; bring a pad) that surround a living room with a wood-burning stove. Pack something for happy hour on one of the covered porches and your boots so you can explore the island's 5-mile-long trail on foot. (Be prepared for ankle-deep mud.)

KEEP YOUR EYES PEELED: WILDLIFE

November to March is best for viewing because the birds are more active and the alligators are dormant (making their prey, such as otters, more active). Keep an ear out for the trilling of sandhill cranes, and scan for red-shouldered hawks surveying the swamp from tree branches. Yellow-bellied sliders and snapping turtles lounge on waterside logs.

EXTRA CREDIT: MAKE IT LONGER

The best spot for tent camping in the area is near Kingfisher Landing, but west. When you return to the original junction from step 1 of this route on day two (near mile 17.7), instead of turning south to the put-in, keep going: Paddle another 1.5 miles west through the flatwater to Mixons Hammock, a tiny island ideal for throwing down. Pull your boat ashore and follow the footpath less than 0.5 mile to a clearing amid the saw palmettos to set up your tent. At night, listen for barred owls—or any of the other 234 birds that call the refuge home.

85: SOLITUDE SUPREME
CATALOOCHEE DIVIDE,
GREAT SMOKY MOUNTAINS NATIONAL PARK,
NORTH CAROLINA

By Graham Averill

The trout in the stream next to my campsite were elusive, but not the elk. Six of the ungulates strolled past me at the trailhead as I geared up for an overnight on the Cataloochee Divide in the eastern corner of Great Smoky Mountains National Park. I took it as a good omen and began the ridge walk, which undulates across grassy balds and passes some of the biggest, oldest poplars in the park. While Great Smoky Mountains might be the most visited park in the system, Cataloochee is far from the crowds that flock to the Appalachian Trail and gateway towns at the western entrance. With a bit of luck, you can see as many elk as people. It's enough to make me forget those wily trout.

TRIP PLANNER

SEASON April to November

PERMIT Required for overnight stay ($4 per person); obtain from smokiespermits. nps.gov.

CONTACT Great Smoky Mountains National Park, www.nps.gov/grsm

DO IT

DISTANCE: 14.2 miles (loop)

TIME: 2 days

DIFFICULTY: ★★

THE PAYOFF: One of the least visited backcountry camping destinations in the most visited park, this ridge walk offers rare quietude—without shirking Smoky Mountain hallmarks like views and wildlife.

TRAILHEAD: Polls Gap (35.5632, -83.1616); 18 miles northwest of Dellwood on Heintooga Ridge Road

MILES AND DIRECTIONS

FROM THE POLLS GAP TRAILHEAD:

1. Head south on the **Hemphill Bald Trail** to a junction at mile 5.7.
2. Take a sharp turn and head west, staying on the **Hemphill Bald Trail** 3.1 miles to a fork.
3. Continue 1.8 miles on the **Caldwell Fork Trail** to another junction.
4. Veer south onto the **Rough Fork Trail** and take it 3.6 miles back to the trailhead.

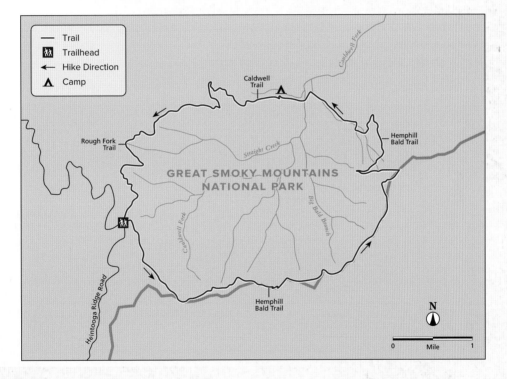

ALL THE EXTRAS

DON'T MISS THIS CAMPSITE: BACKCOUNTRY CAMPSITE 41 (MILE 9)

Bring your fly rod (and patience); this site is steps from Caldwell Fork, a stream with knee-deep pools full of brook trout. It's one of a few sites by the creek, and you'll be just 0.3 mile east of some of the biggest poplars in the park (some have trunks 10 feet in diameter).

KEEP YOUR EYES PEELED: WILDLIFE

Reintroduced to the park in 2001, Manitoban elk are thriving: The population stands at an estimated 200 animals. Scan for the 700-pound ungulates in pastures and clearings near forested areas and streams at dawn and dusk.

EXTRA CREDIT: ADD A HIKE

From Gooseberry Knob, a grassy bald equipped with Adirondack chairs, you can see 50 miles into the Black Mountain Range. It's worth the 0.7-mile spur from the Hemphill Bald junction at mile 5.7 on this route. In summer the hardwood canopy is at its most lush (and the high elevation means you'll escape the Smokies' notorious heat), but fall brings a kaleidoscopic color show.

Gooseberry Knob

YANKEE PARADISE, CUMBERLAND ISLAND NATIONAL SEASHORE, GEORGIA

Moss-draped oak forests, soothing saltwater marshes, trickling tidal creeks, and broad white-sand beaches, all on a 37,000-acre barrier island—sounds like the perfect place for a resort with hotels and golf courses. But Cumberland Island on the south Georgia coast remains steadfastly wild and pristine. Only 300 campers are permitted each day, and the 45-minute ferry ride across Fancy Bluff Creek keeps even those few away: Cumberland sees only 60,000 or so visitors every year. That leaves its 50 square miles of oak canopies, palmetto groves, and sand dunes virtually untouched—and a haven for hikers.

TRIP PLANNER

SEASON Year-round

PERMIT Required for overnight stay ($2 per person per night); obtain from the Sea Camp Visitor Center

COMMERCIAL FERRY Cumberland Island Ferry; book a round-trip ferry ride from St. Marys at cumberlandislandferry.com

CONTACT Cumberland Island National Seashore, www.nps.gov/cuis

Photo: iStockphoto

DISTANCE: 15 miles (out and back)

TIME: 2 days

DIFFICULTY: ★↗

THE PAYOFF: Discover one of the country's least visited public lands before this white-sand beach paradise becomes a classic.

TRAILHEAD: Dungeness Wharf (30.7543, -81.4740); a ferry will drop you off at the pier.

◄═══►

MILES AND DIRECTIONS

FROM DUNGENESS WHARF:

1. Pick up the **River Trail,** heading north along the Cumberland Sound, to an intersection at mile 0.8.

2. Veer onto the **Parallel Trail,** a main vein that bisects the island north-south, and take it beneath live oak branches hung with Spanish moss and over sandy ridges to Yankee Paradise at mile 7.5.

3. Retrace your steps to the trailhead.

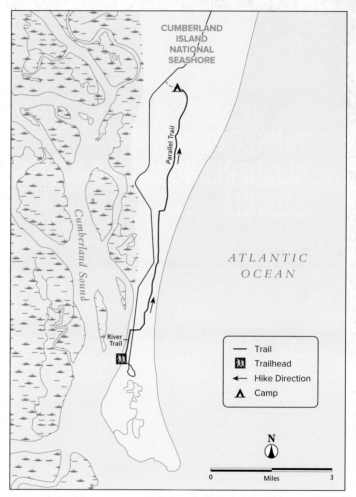

ALL THE EXTRAS

DON'T MISS THIS CAMPSITE: YANKEE PARADISE (MILE 7.5)

Tent at a shaded campground close to a beach where sea turtles nest April to August. From here, not only are you well past where most overnighters pit stop, but you're also in prime position for the dayhikes described below. **Note:** Top off water at the well roughly 1.3 miles before Yankee Paradise.

KEEP YOUR EYES PEELED: FAUNA

Hit the beach to see the island's resident seabirds like oystercatchers and plovers and—from April to August—nesting loggerhead sea turtles. You may spot dolphins or manatees in the water if you're lucky. Throughout this journey, scan for Cumberland's primary crowd-pleasers: a 150-strong herd of feral ponies.

EXTRA CREDIT: ADD A HIKE

During the early twentieth century, Cumberland Island was a tale of contrast: Huge, sprawling estates owned by the Carnegie family dominated the southern end, while a segregation-era society of poor African American laborers known as The Settlement lay in the north. Today, ruined remnants of both communities remain along the island's 50-plus miles of trail. From camp, venture down the Roller Coaster Trail to explore the historic First African Baptist Church, a restored one-room chapel, and the ruins of the old Cumberland Wharf for a taste. Birders may want to budget a day for the 9-mile out-and-back from camp to Table Point, a promontory where you can spyglass species like the wood stork, American oystercatcher, and saltmarsh sparrow.

87: HEAD FOR THE HILLS
LITTLE GRAND CANYON,
KISATCHIE NATIONAL FOREST, LOUISIANA

By Jonathan Olivier

Cresting yet another sandstone bluff, I witness the day's first light peek over the outcroppings to the east, setting the emerald hills alight. It seems like something I'd find just north in the Ozarks until suddenly, as if on command, the fog lifts from the valley, allowing the amber sunshine to jet through the cypress trees where it glints off the swamp below. Many Bayou State hikers head to Arkansas for outdoor escapes, but our backyard is just as wild, if not more. On this shuttle hike alone, I've toured lush mesas, pine savannahs, and bottomland forests. The best part? I only have to share it with black bears, foxes, and otters. There's more to Louisiana than Mardi Gras.

TRIP PLANNER

SEASON Year-round

PERMIT Required for overnight stay (free); self-issue at trailhead kiosk

CONTACT Kisatchie National Forest, www.fs.usda.gov/kisatchie

Photo: Aubrey Bolen

DISTANCE: 17.8 miles (point to point)

TIME: 2 days

DIFFICULTY: ★★

THE PAYOFF: Explore bayous and sandstone outcroppings in this wild neck of the woods where bears still roam.

TRAILHEAD: Kisatchie Bayou (31.4445, -93.0902); 18 miles west of Derry on Bayou Camp Road

SHUTTLE CAR Backbone (31.5090, -93.0332); 5 miles south of Montrose on Montrose Road

MILES AND DIRECTIONS

FROM THE KISATCHIE BAYOU TRAILHEAD:

1. Take the **Caroline Dormon Trail** 10.2 miles past overlooks and through various bayous to its terminus at Longleaf Trail Scenic Byway.

2. Cross into the Kisatchie Hills Wilderness and link up with the **Backbone Trail** on the other side of the road, continuing 7.6 miles on a counterclockwise circuit through the Little Grand Canyon to the trailhead and your shuttle car on Montrose Road.

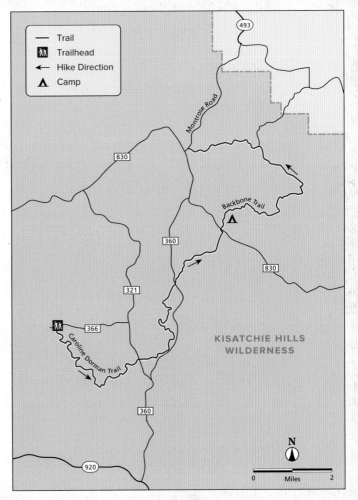

- — Trail
- 🚶 Trailhead
- ← Hike Direction
- ▲ Camp

ALL THE EXTRAS

DON'T MISS THIS CAMPSITE: SANDSTONE OUTCROP (MILE 10.9)

Make like an outlaw during Louisiana's territorial days and camp out on a hidden mesa complete with a fire ring and view of the sandstone hills known to locals as the "Little Grand Canyon." Since the hilltop is only sparsely vegetated, the evening's agenda calls for killer stargazing. Find the faint user trail to the site shortly after crossing Longleaf Vista Road and switching onto the Backbone Trail. *Tip:* Since this site is dry, leave yourself a water cache (named and dated) in the parking lot off Longleaf Trail Scenic Byway (Par Road 830), at the start of the Backbone Trail.

KEEP YOUR EYES PEELED: WILDLIFE

If you're lucky, you'll spot a Louisiana black bear in the foothills. Fewer than 500 of the threatened bruins roam the state, but a handful call the Kisatchie Hills home. Catch them feeding on berries in summertime and acorns in fall. (They're most active at twilight.)

Yellow lady's slipper

88: SURF AND TURF
BOSTON MOUNTAINS, HURRICANE CREEK WILDERNESS, ARKANSAS

Brimming with clear, boulder-studded streams and turquoise pools that would entice any hiker to take a dip, northern Arkansas's little-known Boston Mountains set the scene for an ideal warm-weather escape. Trace the range's spine on this weekend-long section of the 230-mile-long Ozark Highlands Trail, where deep hollows and sky-kissing outcroppings hide wonder of their own.

TRIP PLANNER

SEASON March to November

PERMIT None

COMMERCIAL SHUTTLE Hagarville Grocery and Station (hagarvillegrocery.com) runs hiker drop-offs and pickups for around $50.

CONTACT Ozark National Forest, www.fs.usda.gov/osfnf

Adapted from text by Paul Chisholm.

DISTANCE: 19 miles (point to point)

TIME: 2 days

DIFFICULTY: ★★⁀

THE PAYOFF: Catwalk a ridgeline past ribbon-like waterfalls and limestone bluffs in the underrated Boston Mountains.

TRAILHEAD: Haw Creek Falls (35.6793, -93.2594); 23 miles north of Lamar off AR 123.

SHUTTLE CAR Fairview Recreation Area (35.7373, -93.0940); 1 mile north of Sand Gap off AR 123/AR 16/AR 7

MILES AND DIRECTIONS

FROM THE HAW CREEK FALLS TRAILHEAD:

1. Walk east on the **Ozark Highlands Trail** as it contours along a rocky hillside before crossing wide, lazy Big Piney Creek via AR 123 at mile 1.7.

2. Turn north onto a gravel road for 0.2 mile.

3. Link back up with the **Ozark Highlands Trail** as it crosses into the Hurricane Creek Wilderness, wending through an oak-hickory forest punctuated by stands of pungent shortleaf pine and dropping down to 50-foot-wide Hurricane Creek near mile 7.

4. Scout a crossing downstream where it's gentler and go another 3.1 miles east to another crossing.

5. Back on the east side of Hurricane Creek, continue 8.9 miles through bottomland forest and around bluffs and house-size limestone boulders to Fairview Recreation Area and your shuttle car.

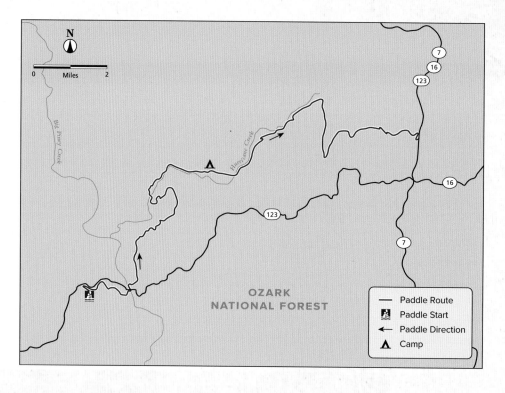

ALL THE EXTRAS

DON'T MISS THIS CAMPSITE: CONFLUENCE OF HURRICANE AND GREASY CREEKS (MILE 9)

Set up your backcountry digs in a hickory grove at the rocky ruins of a late-1800s homestead beside both Hurricane and Greasy Creeks. Just downstream, cool off in an 8-foot-deep swimming hole (natural diving boards abound).

KEEP YOUR EYES PEELED: WILDLIFE

Scan for brightly colored greenside darters and Ozark minnows flashing through calmer pools and eddies along Hurricane Creek. Pileated woodpeckers provide the soundtrack in the bottomland forest, while bobcats, white-tailed deer, foxes, and black bears lurk in this wilderness's quietest recesses.

EXTRA CREDIT: TAKE A BREAK

Shortly after the Hurricane Creek crossing, find a natural, 60-foot-long sandstone arch that juts out from the moss-covered cliffs. When you find it, scan the ground for chunks of chert—arrowhead remnants from 1600s Osage residents.

Pileated woodpecker

89: WILD COAST
CAPERS AND BULL ISLANDS, CAPE ROMAIN NATIONAL WILDLIFE REFUGE, SOUTH CAROLINA

By David Kuczkir

I dip my paddle into the brackish water and cut through the surf, trying to keep pace with my companions—a pod of bottlenose dolphins. The outgoing tide propels my kayak through an estuary in the Lowcountry, a low-lying coastal area outside of Charleston where land, sea, and river converge. I'll float 10.5 easy miles through the Intracoastal Waterway and a slew of tidal creeks to the sandy north end of Capers Island today before tenting on the beach. Tomorrow, I'll explore the next island by foot, where I hope to see loggerhead turtles and alligators. Then I'll retrace my strokes—maybe I can keep up with the dolphins on the way out.

TRIP PLANNER

SEASON Year-round

PERMIT Required for overnight stay (free); obtain from the South Carolina Department of Natural Resources Charleston office.

CONTACT Cape Romain National Wildlife Refuge, bit.do/cape-romain

DO IT

DISTANCE: 35.8 miles (lollipop-loop; 21 miles paddling, 14.8 miles hiking)

TIME: 2 to 3 days

DIFFICULTY: ★★✎

THE PAYOFF: Camp on an undeveloped barrier island not accessible to ferries before exploring a wildlife mecca on foot.

TRAILHEAD: Isle of Palms Landing (32.8051, -79.7592); 16 miles east of Charleston off 41st Avenue

MILES AND DIRECTIONS

FROM THE ISLE OF PALMS LANDING:

1. Wait for an outgoing tide and paddle 4 miles northeast through the **Atlantic Intracoastal Waterway** to marker #103. *Tip:* Hug the bank for an easier time avoiding other boats and their wakes.

2. Veer east into deep-water **Watermelon Creek** and continue 0.9 mile toward Capers Island.

3. Head 1.4 miles into **Capers Creek.**

4. Turn east into **Santee Pass,** a deep-water, narrow tributary, and float 3.1 miles past the mudflats of Mark Bay to an intersection with **Price Creek.**

5. Head 0.7 mile south into Price and paddle ashore at **Capers Island.**

6. Navigate across 0.2-mile-wide Price Creek to the southern shore of **Bull Island** at mile 10.5. *Tip:* Paddle diagonally into the tide if flow is swift.

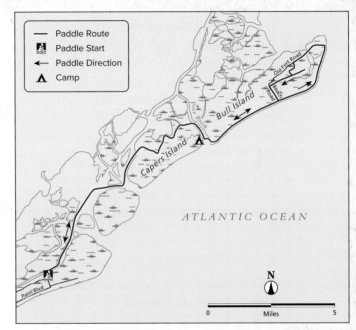

7. Leave your boat above the high-tide line and hike 3.3 miles northeast on **Front Beach.**

8. Turn northwest on sandy **Beach Road** and follow it 0.7 mile. (Only federal service vehicles are allowed on Bull Island, so don't expect car traffic on these "roads.")

9. Veer northeast on grassy **Sheepshead Ridge Road** and take it 1.6 miles to its terminus for a view from the 16-foot-tall observation tower.

10. Retrace your steps 0.5 mile to **Alligator Alley** and follow the sandy trail 0.7 mile as it zigzags north to an intersection.

11. Turn northeast onto grassy **Old Fort Road** and take it 1.5 miles to the tip of the island at Northeast Point.

12. Follow the shore 6.5 miles south and west to the south beach of Bull Island and your boat.

13. Retrace your strokes across Price Creek to camp and, next day, to the put-in.

ALL THE EXTRAS

DON'T MISS THIS CAMPSITE: NORTH BEACH ON CAPERS ISLAND (MILE 10.3)

You won't have to throw elbows to get the best spot on this island. Capers is only accessible by watercraft, so nab a space above the high-tide line on the north beach. Gators don't live on Capers, but don't push your luck: Follow Leave No Trace guidelines and don't wash your dishes in any body of water.

KEEP YOUR EYES PEELED: WILDLIFE

Bull Island is replete with exotic animals. For birds—there are more than 290 species here—stay awhile at Jacks Creek (near mile 18). Highlights include ring-necked teals, canvasback ducks, plovers, American oystercatchers, and black skimmers. Also at Jacks Creek: alligators. The big lizards, which don't hunt on land, often sun themselves on the banks here. Then there are the loggerheads: Bull is one of the most active nesting sites for these reddish-brown turtles. Back on Capers, bobcats lurk in the maritime woods and deer browse in the forest fringes.

GEAR TIP: PACK IN WATER

Hey, at least it's not all on your back. Bring at least one gallon per person per day (in mild conditions) in your boat because the creeks on Capers and Bull Islands are brackish. In a bind? There's a picnic area with running water on Bull Island just north of the intersection of Beach and Sheepshead Ridge Roads (mile 14.5). Need to rent a boat? Coastal Expeditions (coastalexpeditions.com) in Isle of Palms rents kayaks for about $55 per day. The shop is less than a football field from the put-in.

EXTRA CREDIT: TAKE A BREAK

Both islands have a "boneyard beach," or expanse of coastline that has eroded to the point where the skeletal remains of the maritime forest are now in the surf. On this itinerary, you'll hike through Bull's boneyard beach on day two (miles 20 to 21); time it for low tide so you can wander among the fossilized trees. Capers' boneyard makes for a great time-killer if you miss the incoming tide to paddle back to the put-in: From camp, follow the coastline 0.8 mile southwest on foot to reach the haunting thickets of sun-bleached oaks, cedars, and pines.

90: SECRET GARDEN
OAK HILL CAMP,
BIG CYPRESS NATIONAL PRESERVE, FLORIDA

By Melanie Radzicki McManus

The water is cool against my calves and shockingly clear, reflecting the tangle of cypress roots, pond apples, and Jamaican dogwoods above. But I don't have time to stop and stare—I need to make miles. I average roughly a mile per hour in the wet segments of this section of the Florida National Scenic Trail, and today the path has been mostly underwater. I wade through Big Cypress Swamp until dusk before looking for a dry patch. When I finally spot a mound of soil that peeks just above the coffee-colored, tannic drink, I sling my hammock. It's unusual to camp so close to the water's surface, a feeling that catches an edge as the night sucks the colors out of the day. Sure, it'd be easier to do the Florida Trail in spring, when the water has nearly dried up, but what's the fun of hiking through a dry swamp?

Photo: Paul Marcellini

DISTANCE: 31.4 miles (point to point)

TIME: 3 days

DIFFICULTY: ★★★★

THE PAYOFF: Leave the paddle at home: Nowhere else can you explore the Lower 48's only subtropical rainforest on foot.

TRAILHEAD: Oasis Visitor Center (25.8573, -81.0338); 55 miles west of Miami on US 41

SHUTTLE CAR Florida Trail on I-75 (26.1679, -81.0723); 43 miles west of Andytown on I-75

MILES AND DIRECTIONS

FROM THE OASIS VISITOR CENTER:

1. Pick up the **Florida National Scenic Trail** and follow it 9.7 miles north through sawgrass prairies and pine flats to 10 Mile Camp.

2. Continue 13.3 miles north beneath stands of cypress and through calf-deep water to Oak Hill Camp.

3. Alternate hiking on dry land and wading through water to mile 30.2, where an unnamed, gravel doubletrack crosses the trail (near 26.1538, -81.0685).

4. Turn north on the doubletrack and follow it 1.2 miles to the trailhead on I-75.

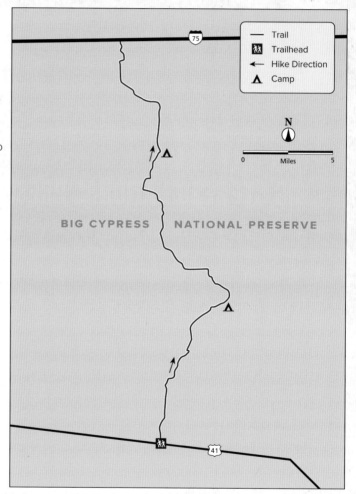

Legend:
— Trail
🚶 Trailhead
← Hike Direction
⛰ Camp

N

0 — Miles — 5

BIG CYPRESS NATIONAL PRESERVE

ALL THE EXTRAS

DON'T MISS THIS CAMPSITE: 10 MILE CAMP (MILE 9.7)

Find this spacious, trailside spot tucked in a pine grove. The easy (dry) miles leading to it are a perfect warmup for the swamp. Top off water in the nearby cypress dome (a watery, cypress-filled bog)—you may want to pre-filter through a handkerchief if it's muddy.

DON'T MISS THIS CAMPSITE: OAK HILL CAMP (MILE 23)

Set up camp on this blessed bit of dry land: a forested bump that rises just inches above the water. The smallest campsite in Big Cypress, it can fit only a handful of tents, but the feeling of being so closely surrounded by water is life list-worthy for any backpacker. **Warning:** It can be buggy here before the first hard freeze. Mesh netting is recommended.

KEEP YOUR EYES PEELED: WILDLIFE

Look for alligators and water moccasins near the trail (give each a wide berth). Elusive Florida panthers and black bears also call this preserve home. There are cool plants here, too: In the latter half of this route, look for swamp natives like bromeliads, orchids, and airplants, the latter of which grow on the trunks and branches of cypress trees. The cardinal airplant (Big Cypress's largest) provides a pop of red amid the swamp's greenery.

GEAR TIP: PACK PANTS

Florida or not, the first half of this route passes through tall, thick sawgrass, a sedge plant with blades edged with tiny, sharp teeth. You'll want to wear pants and long sleeves when passing through or you might end up looking like an extra in an action flick.

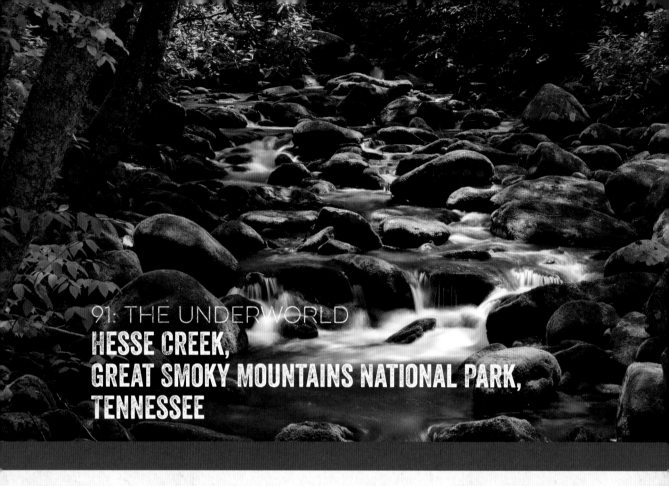

91: THE UNDERWORLD
HESSE CREEK, GREAT SMOKY MOUNTAINS NATIONAL PARK, TENNESSEE

True: Great Smoky Mountains is the most visited national park, year in and year out. Also true: Rangers issue hundreds of permits each month for backcountry campsites in the bustling folds of the park. *Still* true: Only three or so people claim permits monthly for peaceful Hesse Creek, tucked under a hemlock canopy that provides habitat for grouse, black bears, and deer. So follow the numbers. Let everyone else head for the Smokies' mountain meadows and airy perches while you cash in on this solitude-seeking counterprogram. Why? This riverine camp is as private as they come—the numbers don't lie.

TRIP PLANNER

SEASON Year-round

PERMIT Required for overnight stay ($4 per person per night); reserve online

CONTACT Great Smoky Mountains National Park, www.nps.gov/grsm

Photo: iStockphoto

DISTANCE: 11.2 miles (out and back)

TIME: 2 days

DIFFICULTY: ★✈

THE PAYOFF: Hit the Smokies' less-used northwest corner for flowing creeks all to yourself.

TRAILHEAD: Rich Mountain Gap (35.6456, -83.8053); 29 miles south of Knoxville on Old Cades Cove Road, which becomes Rich Mountain Road

MILES AND DIRECTIONS

FROM THE RICH MOUNTAIN GAP TRAILHEAD:

1. Trek 5.6 miles northwest on the **Ace Gap Trail,** which undulates past numerous creeks and through lush gorges, toward the confluence of Cane and Hesse Creeks.

2. Retrace your steps to the trailhead.

DON'T MISS THIS CAMPSITE: HESSE CREEK #003 (MILE 5.6)

You'll be hard-pressed to find another campsite as convenient to the trail and as little-used. Set up your tent in the clearing beyond the fire ring and top off water from the nearby creek. Curious wildlife unaccustomed to humans will likely mosey through around dusk; make use of the bear hang.

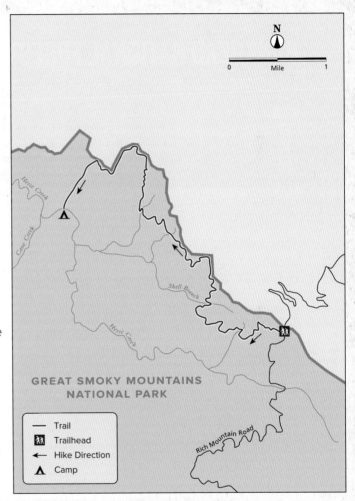

92: SOUTHERN CHARM
BANKHEAD NATIONAL FOREST, ALABAMA

The hardwood forests, scalped cliffs, and sandstone caves of northern Alabama are good any time of year, but they're hard to beat with fall's mild temperatures and electric foliage. Reap the rewards of the South's best season with these tips and trips from local expert **Janice Barrett**. By Elisabeth Kwak-Hefferan

THE INSIDER

The Bankhead—which includes the Sipsey Wilderness—is Janice Barrett's backyard. And as outreach coordinator for the advocacy nonprofit Wild South, she takes full advantage of it. Barrett leads hikes exploring the wilderness's caves and ridges all year long.

1. TOP CANYON HIKE

The swimming hole below 40-foot Caney Creek Falls is no secret. But most hikers stop at the falls 1 mile in—leaving the off-trail extension deeper into the canyon all for you. Continue downstream on the social trail along the South Fork of Caney Creek another 0.8 mile to reach a 20-foot cascade Barrett calls Lower Caney Creek Falls (there's no official name). From here, the trail disappears and the sandstone walls deepen to 50 feet. Hike on and keep your eyes peeled for shallow overhangs; these rock shelters were used by prehistoric inhabitants 10,000 years ago. Turn back at the junction with the North Fork of Caney Creek for a 5.9-mile out-and-back.

2. OFF-TRAIL OVERNIGHT

In the Sipsey Wilderness's little-tracked northern reaches, "you can drop down any canyon, follow a stream, and find beautiful places to camp," Barrett says. Her top pick for those with navigation chops: the roughly 5-mile, partially off-trail loop linking the Lick Branch and Thompson Creek areas. From the Braziel trailhead, immediately head cross-country to the southwest and follow the unnamed creek. Pick your way down into the canyon, where ankle-deep Lick Branch flows between sandstone walls and limestone outcroppings. Scout an established campsite under the trees, then ditch your pack and explore the side canyons riddling the area—you might find unnamed waterfalls and more rock shelters. Next day, head west to Thompson Creek, then climb Warlick Ridge back east to hook up with the Gum Pond Trail back to the road and your car.

3. SECRET FOLIAGE HIKE

Toward the end of October, you'll find a fiery palette of fall colors on any trail in the Bankhead. But for a view that's next-level idyllic, make like a photographer and chase the light: "The Rippey Trail runs north–south, and on a fall afternoon, when the sun is shining from the west, it's a beautiful scene," Barrett says. For a 7.5-mile out-and-back, follow Rippey Trail (#201) along a ridge thick with northern red oak, hickory, sugar maple, and American beech. Then hang a left on Trail #206 to descend into the Sipsey Fork canyon, a short-but-steep drop with expansive views over the forest's mosaic of reds, oranges, and yellows. Trace the river for a half mile, then head back on Trail #206 to link back to #201.

4. BEST MULTIDAY TRIP

Get a grand tour of the Sipsey on Barrett's favorite epic: a four-day, 40-mile loop that meanders through each of the region's ecosystems, from upland forests to sandstone canyons to fern-filled gullies. The logistics are a bit intense, but it's worth it: You also get abundant seasonal waterfalls (November through May) and a firsthand look at the area's human history, from post-Ice Age shelters to nineteenth-century whiskey stills. Follow Trail #203 from the Flannagin trailhead on the wilderness's eastern edge down to Borden Creek, then link Trails #207, #208, and #210 to camp under the forest canopy near mile 9.5. Day two's hike stays high on a ridge for almost 7 miles, connecting Trails #210 and #223. Day three, follow Trails #208 and #206 past Eye of the Needle (a tight boulder squeeze) and Ship Rock (a prominent, prow-shaped bluff) before taking Trail #209 east along the Sipsey Fork. To finish, link Trails #209, #200, and #203.

5. BIRDER'S CAMPGROUND

Avian enthusiasts pitch their tents at the quiet, thirteen-site Brushy Lake Campground for a peek at great blue herons, kingfishers, and, in spring and fall, migratory species such as orchard orioles, yellow-throated vireos, and warblers.

TRIP PLANNER

SEASON Year-round

PERMIT None

CAR CAMPING $5 per night (first-come, first-served)

CONTACT Bankhead National Forest, bit.do/bankhead-nf

If it's fall color you seek, Maine's North Woods (page 320) are your prize.

NORTHEAST

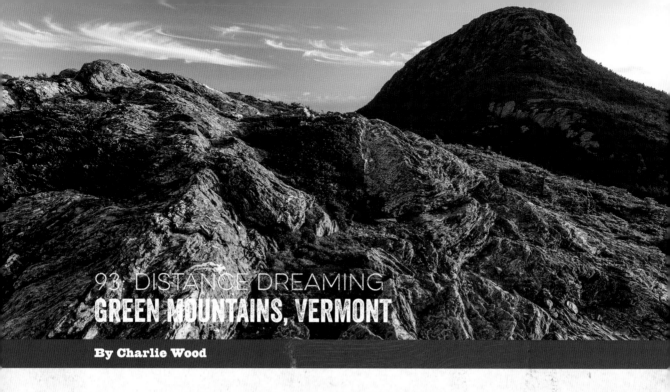

93. DISTANCE DREAMING
GREEN MOUNTAINS, VERMONT

By Charlie Wood

As I gaze into Canada from my vantage point in northernmost Vermont, the Great White North lives up to its name. Fog and clouds blanket the thickly forested valley beneath my feet, and a few treetops barely peek out. I pause to soak up the scene—briefly, since a light rain makes standing still a chilly proposition—then turn and head for Massachusetts with the perfect plan in mind: Beginning on this, the first day of autumn, I'll follow fall through Vermont as it colors the Green Mountains in shades of crimson and gold. And in the process, I'll satisfy my hunger for a long-distance hike as I chase the season along the 272-mile Long Trail.

While most foot travelers assume the Appalachian Trail was the first long-distance footpath, that honor actually belongs to the Long Trail. Years before the AT was even marked, before the Pacific Crest Trail was a germ of an idea, the Green Mountain Club marked, cut, and blazed a route along the length of the Green Mountains. Not only did the Long Trail inspire the creation of the AT, but for 100 miles the two run concurrently.

Between 1910 and 1930, Green Mountain Club (GMC) trailblazers plotted the route to run near existing vacation cabins and three-sided hunting shelters so the new trail would be readily accessible to Vermonters. More small lodges and lean-tos sprang up as the trail's popularity grew, and, after just one day out, I'm glad they did. The four walls and roof of Jay Camp Shelter seem like the Ritz, and I'm thankful to be out of the rain that's pummeling northern Vermont.

Warm sun burns through the fog the next morning, and for two days, I don't see a soul, unless you count the occasional owl, osprey, or salamander. The Long Trail's slogan is, after all, "a footpath in the wilderness," but I knew going into this hike that I would encounter "urban" parts of the trail where I'd cross a few roads. At times, I hear and see signs of civilization in the form of chain saws and distant town lights at night, but those intrusions are minor and don't discount the slogan's truthfulness.

My pace slows considerably as I ascend yet another ladder installed by the GMC to aid a grueling climb over another peak. Halfway up, I wonder if I should have hiked a less punishing trail somewhere else. As it turns out, the trail's jagged design is not an accident. When the path was being plotted, a casual observer had suggested that more switchbacks and a gentler grade might better suit pack animals. "This isn't the West!" was the angry retort from one GMC'er.

A WEEK INTO THE HIKE, I emerge from hemlock forests onto the open tundra of Mount Mansfield, Vermont's highest peak and one of the few spots in the Green Mountain State that's above treeline. Panoramic views in all directions greet me—as do dozens of dayhikers. Folks from all over make the trip to Mansfield, by far the most popular mountain in Vermont, with almost 60,000 visitors annually.

I get it: From this bird's-eye perspective, I can see Canada to the north, New York to the west, and New Hampshire to the east. Crisp air fills my lungs. Geese are heading south. The first third of the rugged Long Trail has humbled me plenty, but I'm making progress and finally hiking with the New England fall as planned.

The bright colors tickle my eyes, and the smell of decomposing leaves is in the air as I crunch through the forest and down Mansfield's flank to the Winooski River. The Mansfield dayhikers are quickly a distant memory. Three days later, my quest to walk with autumn ends abruptly when winter arrives. Snow, sleet, and freezing rain frost the woods, making an arctic ordeal out of a 100-foot trip to the privy outside Skyline Lodge, where I've holed up for the night. The next day, Travis, the GMC caretaker, and I sit and read in silence inside the chilly shelter, occasionally making small talk and listening to the weather report on a battery-powered radio. It's a day not fit for man nor beast, and I wonder whether my end-to-end hike will have to be put on hold until the weather breaks.

"Hey, y'all in there?" comes a voice from out in the cold.

Jennifer and Bret, a couple from Louisville, Kentucky, out for an overnighter, are on the front porch. They're wearing flannel shirts, corduroys, and bandannas, and are just begging for a lecture from a self-righteous outdoorsperson on the evils of cotton. Even so, the supposedly thin-blooded Southerners appear to be enjoying the scenery.

"It's a little cold out here, but it's beautiful!" they rave. "Just look at Skylight Pond in the fog!"

I decide that the cotton-clad interlopers aren't about to out-tough me. Mumbling my mantra ("Today is a good day to hike"), I don my high-tech clothing and follow Bret and Jennifer back to the trail.

As my blood pumps and the altitude drops, warmth returns. Autumn, however, does not. Winter hangs in the air and offers a few more dustings of snow before milder weather ushers in Columbus Day weekend—the unofficial fall-foliage holiday. Only 100 miles and a week on the trail lie ahead of me, but I'm not about to battle the crowds of holiday leaf-peepers. Instead, I give up walking for a few days and hook up with a GMC trail crew to "give something back," as they say.

Five volunteers and I lug rocks of all shapes and sizes to create a trail to crew leader Greg's exacting specifications. "Make it easy to walk, but hard to break down," he says. "It should look as though it belongs here."

By day's end, my body aches and I'm covered with dirt, but the stone staircase and smoother section of trail do me proud. Working like this makes me all the more grateful for the sweat others shed so that I might enjoy a few weeks of backpacking along this route.

The Long Trail was originally conceived by schoolteacher James P. Taylor in 1909 "to make the Vermont mountains play a larger part in the life of the people." Soon after, Taylor and some prominent citizens formed the GMC to establish and manage the trail. By 1930, the trail officially stretched from border to border, and the GMC had published eight editions of the *Long Trail Guide*. Ever since, the club has vigilantly maintained the path, relocating parts from valley bottoms to mountain peaks, building shelters, educating the public, and keeping the myriad side trails in tip-top shape.

I leave the work party just south of Maine Junction, where the Long Trail and the Appalachian Trail merge. Green Mountaineers possess a fierce sense of pride for Vermont's gift to hikers and even refused to rename it to the suggested "Green Mountain Trail" when the longer AT outdid the Long Trail by some 1,800 miles. The Long Trail existed first, GMC'ers retorted, insisting that it was still the longest trail in the state and that the Appalachian Trail was merely a side footpath.

I had hiked the AT/Long Trail overlap portion four years previously, so I decide to finish up this adventure by taking some of the side trails that loop back to the Long Trail. Less traveled but no less beautiful than the Long Trail proper, the Old Job, Branch Pond, and Stratton Pond Trails ease along streams and lakes instead of climbing rugged ridgelines.

AFTER THREE-AND-A-HALF WEEKS OF SOUTHBOUND HIKING, I noticed that the trees in the mountains are nearly bare, but in the valleys, the birches and maples blaze. My hike with autumn is done.

I consider what waits—work, bills, a computer—and my body doesn't want to submit. I've gotten into the rhythm of the trail, and want to keep going for another 1,000 miles. But I don't have time to disappear into the woods again. Fortunately, the Long Trail will be there, its short stretches waiting for those with calendars and commitments, and its longer sections available to those who have the time to return to the simple life.

TRIP PLANNER

SEASON June to October

PERMIT None

CONTACT Green Mountain Club, greenmountainclub.org

DO IT

DISTANCE: 44 miles (point to point)

TIME: 4 to 5 days

DIFFICULTY: ★★★↙

THE PAYOFF: Get a taste of the granddaddy of long paths when you tackle the Long Trail's least-trodden soil. The northernmost section features summit panoramas, a lush gorge, and a wide view down the Champlain Valley.

TRAILHEAD: Journeys End (45.0016, -72.4644); 9 miles north of Troy on Journeys End Road

SHUTTLE CAR VT 15 (44.6418, -72.7215); 9 miles northwest of Morristown on VT 15 at West Settlement Road

MILES AND DIRECTIONS

FROM THE JOURNEYS END TRAILHEAD:

1. Do the hike southbound like the author: Take the **Journeys End Trail** a mile or so west to the Long Trail's northern terminus at the border.

2. Ramble 17 miles south along the spine of the Green Mountains on the **Long Trail,** crossing Jay Peak, Buchanan Mountain, Sugarbush Mountain, Haystack Mountain, and Tillotson Peak, to VT 118.

3. Cross the road and continue southwest through boulder-pinched Devils Gulch, across Laraway Mountain (lookout tower here), and past the open vista from Prospect Rock to the section end and your shuttle car at VT 15.

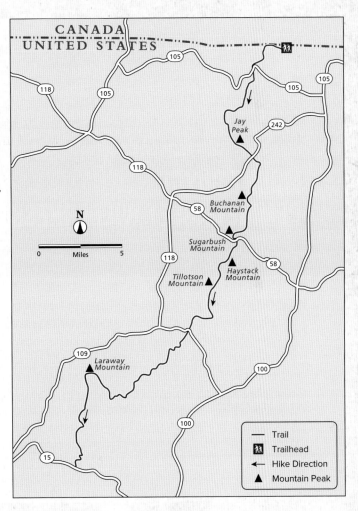

94: KISS THE SKY
MOUNT GUYOT,
PEMIGEWASSET WILDERNESS, NEW HAMPSHIRE

That moment of glory when you emerge out of the forest to wide-open vistas? Multiply that euphoria by 7 miles—the distance you'll spend above treeline on this version of the Semi-Pemi—and you get the East's most viewtastic hiking, across summits clustered close and ripe for the picking. Even the lowlands dazzle, with waterfalls and quiet brooks where moose wade. And in fall, swamp maples and other hardwoods erupt into a sizzling display of fiery reds and yellows. Western mountains never throw confetti like this.

TRIP PLANNER

SEASON June to October

PERMIT None

CONTACT White Mountain National Forest, www.fs.usda.gov/whitemountain

Adapted from text by Kelly Bastone.

DISTANCE: 26.3 miles (lollipop-loop)

TIME: 2 or 3 days

DIFFICULTY: ★★★

THE PAYOFF: The 32-mile Pemigewasset (or "Pemi") Loop is the pride of the Whites, but this slightly shorter version offers a similar alpine tour—with a fraction of the traffic.

TRAILHEAD: Lincoln Woods (44.0640, -71.5878); 5 miles east of Lincoln off NH 112

MILES AND DIRECTIONS

FROM THE LINCOLN WOODS TRAILHEAD:

1. Follow the **Lincoln Woods Trail** 2.9 miles north along the Pemigewasset River to a Y-junction and the apex of the loop.

2. Do it counterclockwise, splitting east onto the **Wilderness Trail** to mile 4.9.

3. Head up the southern flank of 4,698-foot Mount Bond on the **Bondcliff Trail,** summiting Bondcliff near mile 9, Bond near mile 9.8, and 4,508-foot Mount Guyot near mile 11.

4. Descend the northern slope of Guyot on the **Appalachian/Twinway Trail,** cresting 4,902-foot South Twin Mountain near mile 12.8. (It's an optional 2.6-mile out-and-back from here to tag North Twin Mountain.)

5. Take the **Appalachian/Garfield Ridge Trail** west off the peak to a T-junction at mile 15.3.

6. Split onto the **Franconia Brook Trail,** which coasts 8.1 easy miles back to the original junction.

7. Retrace your steps 2.9 miles to the trailhead.

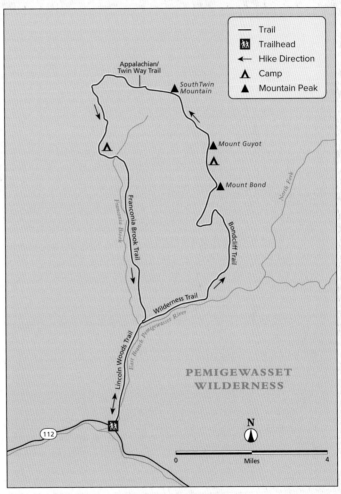

ALL THE EXTRAS

DON'T MISS THIS CAMPSITE: GUYOT CAMPSITE (MILE 10.4)

Camp at 4,360 feet near a reliable spring at one of the Whites' few high-elevation tenting options ($10; first-come, first-served). Guyot (and Bond, for that matter) is one of the remotest peaks you'll find in the Whites, so no roads or buildings propose to mar the view. Best part? The airy, east-facing perch offers one of the best sunrise vistas in the range.

DON'T MISS THIS CAMPSITE: 13 FALLS TENTSITE (MILE 17.3)

Find this hideaway deep in the Franconia Brook valley near several tiered cascades and swimming holes. After claiming a platform ($10; first-come, first-served), find a sunbaked rock ledge near an opening in the canopy to take a break with a view south to aptly named Owls Head.

KEEP YOUR EYES PEELED: FOLIAGE

Expect peak fall color between the fourth week of September and the first week of October. Time it right and the beeches, birches, and sugar maples will provide kaleidoscopic pops of color among the spruces and balsam firs.

EXTRA CREDIT: MAKE IT LONGER

By skipping the west half of the true Pemi, you avoid most of the peakbaggers and Appalachian Trail crowds that flock to Franconia Ridge. But if you wanted to do the full circuit, instead of taking the Franconia Brook Trail off the Garfield Ridge Trail (step 6 on this route), keep going, looping over Mount Garfield, Mount Lafayette, Mount Lincoln, Little Haystack Mountain, Mount Liberty, and Mount Flume en route to the trailhead.

95: SPRING GLORY
ROARING BROOK,
TUNXIS STATE FOREST, CONNECTICUT

One surefire way to solitude? Connecticut. Hikers in the area flock to the New York's mighty summits, leaving the more accessible Tunxis State Forest in Connecticut's northern reaches vacant. There mountain panoramas, flower-filled groves, and piles of giant boulders are up for grabs on the Tunxis Trail, where moose outnumber people. Elevations are high by Constitution State standards (1,400 feet), but low enough to melt out by April—meaning you can cruise down the Tunxis along a plateau that's covered with white blooms of mountain laurel when most of the area's hikers are still hibernating for winter. As though you needed another reason to visit.

TRIP PLANNER

SEASON April to November

PERMIT Required for overnight stay (free); apply online

CONTACT Tunxis State Forest, bit.do/tunxis-sf

─ DO IT ─

DISTANCE: 14 miles (out and back)

TIME: 2 days

DIFFICULTY: ★✦

THE PAYOFF: Plumb Connecticut's wildest woods in solitude on this ridge walk.

TRAILHEAD: Tunxis (42.0156, -72.9166); 9 miles northwest of Granby on CT 20

MILES AND DIRECTIONS

FROM THE TUNXIS TRAILHEAD:

1. Pick up the blue-blazed **Tunxis Trail** and hike 7 miles south through dense hemlocks and past small cascades and a steep gorge to Roaring Brook.

2. Retrace your steps to the trailhead.

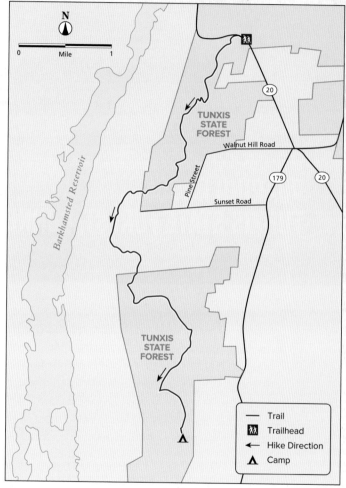

ALL THE EXTRAS

DON'T MISS THIS CAMPSITE: ROARING BROOK (MILE 7)

Tucked beneath hemlocks and white pine boughs, this secluded spot is a rare, true backcountry campsite in Connecticut. You'll be simultaneously alone and in good company: Curious moose, deer, and black bears may wander through this riverine camp.

EXTRA CREDIT: ADD A HIKE

From your camp at Roaring Brook, continue south on the main trail another 0.5 mile to the Indian Council Caves, where a 40-foot-tall rock overhang and heaps of massive boulders offer cave-like exploration opportunities. Whether Native Americans actually used the area as a council site is a matter of conjecture, but artifacts have been found tucked within the recesses.

Witch-hazel in bloom

96: SNEAKY SOLITUDE
STEPSTONE FALLS, ARCADIA MANAGEMENT AREA, RHODE ISLAND

By Ryan Wichelns

A narrow flume of water slides across the trail, echoing off the hills. It's the only noise I hear apart from the shuffling of my boots—and that doesn't happen often in the country's second most densely populated state. Just this afternoon I was stuck in I-95 traffic outside Providence, and now, only a few hours later, I'm hiking through quiet forest and old farmland on the remotest section of Rhode Island's end-to-end North-South Trail. The best part about being a hiker in the smallest state? You're never more than an hour from the trailhead.

TRIP PLANNER

SEASON Year-round

PERMIT Required for overnight stay (free); call ahead to reserve

CONTACT Arcadia Management Area, bit.do/arcadia-management-area

---

DISTANCE: 13.2 miles (point to point)

TIME: 2 days

DIFFICULTY: ★

THE PAYOFF: Escape dayhikers and road walks on arguably the only section of Rhode Island's North-South Trail that caters to backpackers.

TRAILHEAD: Hazard Road (41.6174, -71.7807); 30 miles southwest of Providence on Hazard Road

SHUTTLE CAR Buttonwoods Road (41.5224, -71.6765); 29 miles southwest of Providence on Buttonwoods Road

MILES AND DIRECTIONS

FROM THE HAZARD ROAD TRAILHEAD:

1. Head southeast on the **North-South Trail,** following blue blazes to a fork at mile 1.8.

2. Veer northwest onto the social path and hike 0.2 mile to the log shelter.

3. Return to the main path and continue 11 miles southeast along the Wood River to Buttonwoods Road. (The trail merges with old logging roads periodically.)

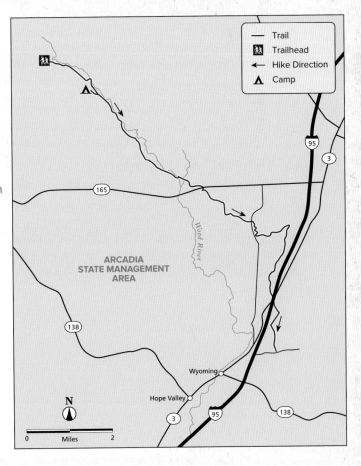

ALL THE EXTRAS

DON'T MISS THIS CAMPSITE: STEPSTONE FALLS (MILE 2.5)

The park's only permitted backcountry campsite is a short walk from the trailhead—which makes it ideal for late-starters and basecampers (you could spend an entire day exploring the web of trails surrounding the Wood River). There's room for a few tents in a handful of wooded sites around an open-sided wooden shelter (communal). Watch for white-tailed deer, foxes, and grouse around the primitive site.

KEEP YOUR EYES PEELED: RUINS

Thousands of miles of stone walls snaked through this region in the mid-1800s—when it was some of the still-tiny country's best farmland, despite its shallow, rocky soil. After the Civil War, agriculture moved west and the woods took control again. See dilapidated stone foundations and remnants of walls and mills near the trail.

EXTRA CREDIT: TAKE A BREAK

Pass three-tiered, 10-foot-tall Stepstone Falls at mile 1.5. Find the best view of the year-round flow on the east side of the Wood River atop a van-size pile of rectangular, quarried stones. Bonus: Brown trout swim in these waters.

EXTRA CREDIT: MAKE IT LONGER

The blue blazes continue from either end of Arcadia to form the 77-mile North-South Trail, linking the Massachusetts state line to the north with the Atlantic Ocean in Charlestown to the south by trails, logging paths, and roads. To the north: dense forests and sleepy towns. To the south: farmland and beaches. This 12.8-mile section is smack in the middle—meaning fewer roads.

97: GREEN LIGHT
GLASTENBURY MOUNTAIN, GLASTENBURY WILDERNESS, VERMONT

Venture off the main drags and find solitude deep in southeastern Vermont's hardwood forests, where showers and fog transform the old-growth into a rainforest with a patina of moss, reminiscent of the Pacific Northwest. Fall, of course, brings different colors—which you won't have to share, thanks to a little creativity.

TRIP PLANNER

SEASON June to November

PERMIT None

CONTACT Green Mountain National Forest, www.fs.usda.gov/gmfl

Photo: Ken Norden

DISTANCE: 21 miles (loop)

TIME: 2 days

DIFFICULTY: ★★★

THE PAYOFF: Experience the hallmarks of the Appalachian and Long Trails before savoring the best of the Greens on a private tour through the hardwoods.

TRAILHEAD: Appalachian/Long (42.8852, -73.1154); 4 miles east of Bennington on VT 9

MILES AND DIRECTIONS

FROM THE APPALACHIAN/LONG TRAILHEAD:

1. Pick up the **Appalachian/Long Trail** and ascend Maple Hill and Little Pond Mountain to the Goddard Shelter at mile 9.3.

2. Track 0.6 mile out and back to the 3,747-foot summit of Glastenbury Mountain.

3. Follow the faint **West Ridge Trail**—you guessed it—west off Glastenbury. Free from the hiker traffic along the Appalachian and Long Trails, the forest and quiet close in around the dirt path, offering an intimate close-up of the beech woods. Summit Bald Mountain near mile 16.8.

4. Head 2.1 miles downhill on the **Bald Mountain Trail** to a trailhead on Harbor Road.

5. Turn south at the water tank and follow the dirt road 0.9 mile to VT 9.

6. Veer east and follow the road 1.2 miles to close the loop at the original trailhead.

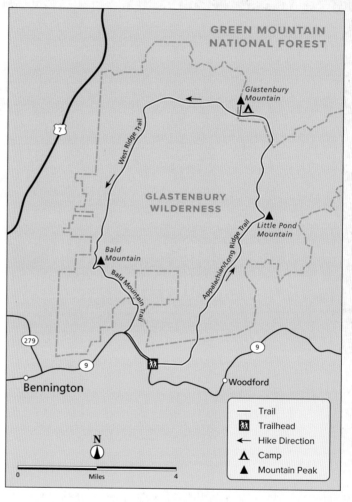

GREEN MOUNTAIN NATIONAL FOREST

Glastenbury Mountain

West Ridge Trail

GLASTENBURY WILDERNESS

Little Pond Mountain

Appalachian/Long Ridge Trail

Bald Mountain

Bald Mountain Trail

7

279

9

9

Bennington

Woodford

Legend:
— Trail
Trailhead
← Hike Direction
▲ Camp
▲ Mountain Peak

N

0 Miles 4

ALL THE EXTRAS

DON'T MISS THIS CAMPSITE: GODDARD SHELTER (MILE 9.3)

Many hikers will pull off the Appalachian Trail at the Melville Nauheim Shelter—let them. The simple (OK, dumpy) three-sided lean-to makes the Goddard Shelter seem almost palatial. With a more modest platform design, a large porch, a good roof, and a quick, 0.3-mile walk to this hike's finest view, Goddard is worth the effort to hike beyond the Nauheim. Once you're settled, continue gently uphill on the Appalachian/Long Trail and climb up the 50-foot-tall Mount Glastenbury fire tower. Atop the flight of steep, metal stairs, overlook a panorama where the setting sun tints fall foliage an even more brilliant gold.

KEEP YOUR EYES PEELED: WILDLIFE

On the West Ridge Trail, scan for clawed beech trees—markers left by territorial male black bears during past mating seasons.

EXTRA CREDIT: ADD A HIKE

At mile 11.8 (on day two), veer off the West Ridge Trail and take a 0.1-mile detour south to a pond bed where you'll find more prints from moose and deer hooves (especially at dawn) than boots.

West Ridge Trail

98: BACK TO NATURE
MOUNT GRACE,
MOUNT GRACE STATE FOREST, MASSACHUSETTS

With the nearby White and Green Mountains beckoning, Massachusetts hikers regularly skip over their home state's attractions in favor of the better-known summits to the north. It's a pity because some of New England's best hiking lies in the deep forests of the Bay State, where you won't find a peak over 2,000 feet. The old-growth woods in Mass's northern reaches drew wilderness pilgrims like Henry David Thoreau long before escapism was stylish—and this weekend-size slice offers the kind of lonely corridors and hidden waterfalls that can inspire another back-to-nature movement.

TRIP PLANNER

SEASON April to November

PERMIT None

CONTACTS Mount Grace State Forest, bit.do/mt-grace-state-forest & New England Trail, www.newenglandtrail.org

Photo: Melanie McManus

DISTANCE: 23 miles (point to point)

TIME: 2 to 3 days

DIFFICULTY: ★★

THE PAYOFF: Tick off a section of the New England Trail that meanders through an old-growth paradise.

TRAILHEAD: Mount Grace (42.6891, -72.3411); 8 miles north of Orange on MA 78

SHUTTLE CAR High Street in Troy, New Hampshire (42.8255, -72.1837); 4 miles northwest of Fitzwilliam on High Street

MILES AND DIRECTIONS

FROM THE MOUNT GRACE PARKING LOT:

1. Climb to the 1,621-foot summit on the **Mount Grace Trail,** stopping to savor the three-state view from the fire tower.

2. Turn north onto the white-blazed **New England Trail,** a patchwork of new trails, existing footpaths, and roads, as it descends over crumbling stone walls (old property lines) and weaves around and over small hillocks to Falls Brook near mile 11.9. (**Note:** The NET is constantly changing and receiving facelifts. Make sure you have the most up-to-date beta before heading out.)

3. Veer north, staying on the NET as it merges with the **Metacomet-Monadnock Trail** and leads into Troy.

4. Take Prospect Street less than a mile to your shuttle car.

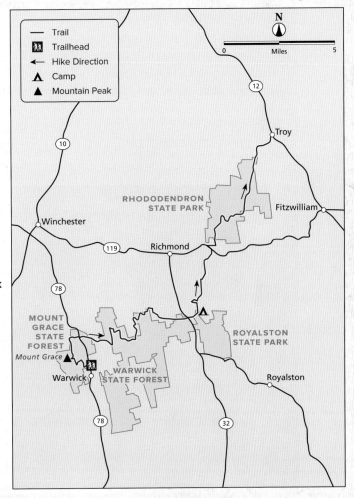

Legend:
— Trail
🚶 Trailhead
← Hike Direction
▲ Camp
▲ Mountain Peak

N

0   Miles   5

ALL THE EXTRAS

DON'T MISS THIS CAMPSITE: THE TRUSTEES OF RESERVATIONS (TTOR) SHELTER (MILE 11.9)

Campsites are hard to come by on this section of the NET—but that's OK because this shelter is ideally positioned near the midway point. It's a lean-to with three walls and four bunks, plus a loft, but you won't have to worry about sharing: Isolated from the Appalachian Trail corridor where most Bay Staters hike, it's blissfully quiet.

EXTRA CREDIT: ADD A HIKE

Before heading out on day two, venture south on a short, 0.3-mile detour from the TTOR Shelter to see Royalston Falls, a 45-foot plume that splashes through a narrow gorge into a shallow pool. The emerald mist will mesmerize, but take care: There's a steep pitch along the side, and moss can make the rocks slick. Heading back upstream, wade in a series of cool, calf-deep pools and look for two mini natural bridges, cleanly polished in the sandstone by time and the elements, as though punched by a wrecking ball.

Royalston Falls

Photo: iStockphoto

99: PRESIDENTIAL DEBATE
MOUNT CABOT, WHITE MOUNTAIN NATIONAL FOREST, NEW HAMPSHIRE

Blink twice: You won't find many hikers on Mount Cabot—and you won't find *any* cars. Some 60 miles north of the Presidentials and the people magnet that is Mount Washington, Cabot remains blissfully off the radar, despite its wealth of long-range views and early-changing leaves, plus a spiderweb of trails that make for any number of weekend-size loops. Climb to empty ridges and quiet pond campsites and you'll know the secret to solitude in the Whites: the Pilot Range.

TRIP PLANNER

SEASON June to November

PERMIT None

CONTACT White Mountain National Forest, www.fs.usda.gov/whitemountain

DISTANCE: 16.3 miles (loop)

TIME: 2 days

DIFFICULTY: ★★✦

THE PAYOFF: The northernmost 4,000-footer in the Whites is remote and crowd-free, while still offering the far-reaching views and heralded hardwoods of the Presidentials.

TRAILHEAD: Millbrook (44.5063, -71.3336); 18 miles northwest of Gorham off York Pond Road

◄◄ ──────────────────────────────── ►►

MILES AND DIRECTIONS

FROM THE MILLBROOK TRAILHEAD:

1. From the fish hatchery, head uphill on the **Mill Brook Trail** as the hardwood forest closes around you to mile 3.5.

2. Take the 1.2-mile out-and-back to the top of Rogers Ledge for a peekaboo view of Mount Washington 17 miles southeast.

3. Back at the junction, veer southwest on the **Kilkenny Ridge Trail** to mile 8.2, where another short spur (0.4 mile out and back) leads to The Horn, which protrudes into the sky like a rhino's spike and offers spin-around views across the Pilot Range.

4. Continue south on the Kilkenny Ridge Trail, which crosses The Bulge and Mount Cabot en route to a junction at mile 10.8.

5. Split east onto the **Bunnell Notch Trail** and coast 3.3 miles beneath leafy corridors to York Pond Road.

6. Track 2.2 miles around York Pond to close the loop back at the fish hatchery.

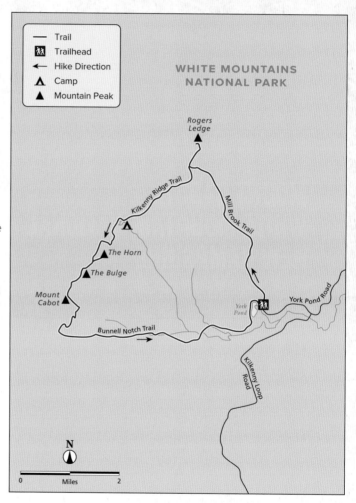

Adapted from text by Casey Lyons.

ALL THE EXTRAS

DON'T MISS THIS CAMPSITE: UNKNOWN POND CAMPSITE #5 (MILE 6.7)

Reach lily-padded Unknown Pond and pitch your tent in secluded site #5, roughly 300 feet inland from the eastern bank. (Bring rope to hang a bear bag.) At dusk, head to the shoreline as the bullfrogs begin their nightly concert, and, if the wind is calm, take in the reflection of 3,905-foot The Horn (day two's headline destination) and its forested contours in the pond's silvery waters.

KEEP YOUR EYES PEELED: FOLIAGE

At this latitude, the leaves change earlier than elsewhere in the range—but most hikers don't know that. While they're still waiting, head out by the second week of September, when the season's first reds, oranges, and yellows creep into the foliage of the Pilot Range. Grab the hike's best view from the airy overlook atop The Horn on day two (near mile 8.3).

EXTRA CREDIT: TAKE A BREAK

Stay awhile at the Mount Cabot Lodge, near mile 9.9 on this route. The four-sided, two-door shelter is pretty swanky for a backcountry hut (but Unknown Pond is prettier and quieter). Best bet: Enjoy lunch with your feet hanging off the deck.

Fall in the Whites

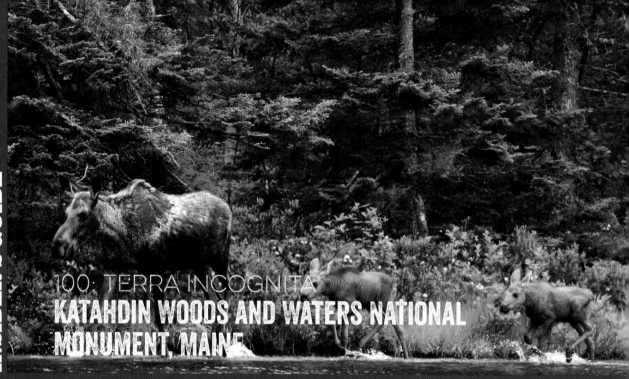

100: TERRA INCOGNITA
KATAHDIN WOODS AND WATERS NATIONAL MONUMENT, MAINE

We welcomed the Northeast's most pristine watershed to the national park system in 2016 with itchy feet. Now go see what the fuss is about. Hint: old-growth forests, craggy peaks, hidden waterfalls, and A-list wildlife. Local expert **Lucas St. Clair** delivers tips and trips for doing it up right. By Ryan Wichelns

THE INSIDER

What is now a national monument was until August 2016 Lucas St. Clair's backyard. "I spent my childhood canoeing, hunting, and fishing here," says the lifelong Mainer. In 2011, St. Clair took responsibility for the campaign to turn it into a park and spent his days showing it to congresspeople, National Park Service reps, school groups, and more. In the process, he's hiked, skied, and biked every inch of the park's trail system "and then some."

1. CASCADE HIKE

Waterfalls are a major part of Katahdin Woods and Waters, and according to St. Clair, the best is Orin Falls on the remote Wassataquoik (Wass-ata-cook) Stream. Take the only trail from Loop Road (between mile markers 15 and 16) and follow it 3 miles to the series of small drops and pools. Scout an established campsite along the riverbank because you'll want to linger: "I've walked a long way up and down that river," St. Clair says. "It's a spiritual place."

Adapted from text by Ryan Wichelns.

Photo: iStockphoto

2. BEST MULTISPORT TRIP

You could simply hike 1,942-foot Deasey Mountain—the monument's tallest peak—via the Katahdin Lake Trail and you wouldn't regret it, with its adventurous ford of the Wassataquoik and a trek through glacially carved hillsides. But you'd be missing out on a quintessential Maine multisport journey: "You should always start a hike in a canoe," St. Clair says. Put in at Lunksoos Camp and paddle 2 miles upstream on the East Branch of the calm Penobscot to the Big Seboeis campsite. Stash your boat and hike 4 miles on Old Telos Tote Road (which turns into the International Appalachian Trail) through a silver-maple floodplain and old-growth hemlocks to the bald summit. See forested Lunksoos Mountain (2.6 miles out and back from here), the ragged Traveller Range, and, of course, the Katahdin massif. Head back the same way.

3. TOP OVERNIGHT

Locals know the Appalachian Trail doesn't end at the Knife Edge. It keeps going 138 miles to Canada, bisecting Katahdin Woods and Waters. St. Clair calls the 27-mile section of the International Appalachian Trail (IAT) through the monument a classic: Start on the Loop Road and hike it north, taking the Katahdin Lake Trail (IAT) across the Wassataquoik and up Deasey (see "Best multisport trip," above). Drop down to the Lunksoos Lean-to at mile 12.9 before continuing 4.5 miles to Old Telos Tote Road, which parallels the East Branch. Still on the IAT, pick a campsite near a waterfall: 20-foot Grand Pitch (mile 23.4) or 15-foot Haskell Rock (mile 24.9). Next day, close out the hike at Haskell Gate.

4. WILDLIFE VIEWING

Black bears are a common sight when raspberries are ripe (July and August), but it's the moose that people come to Maine to see. According to St. Clair, you can find them just about anywhere. Even the 16-mile Loop Road is a hot spot for the ungulates. "They're so big, they can't plow through the dense forests," he says.

TRIP PLANNER

SEASON Year-round; expect snow October to April, but the roads and trails are skiable

PERMIT Required for backpacking (free); obtain from the Northern Regional Office of the Maine Fire Service in Ashland

CONTACT Katahdin Woods and Waters National Monument, www.nps.gov/kaww

ABOUT THE AUTHOR

Maren Horjus is the Destinations Editor at *BACKPACKER*. Her trips section, the Play List, which delivers more than 20 hikes from coast to coast in every issue, was a National Magazine Award finalist in 2016 and 2018. She has written for *Skiing*, *Mountain*, *Men's Health*, *Sports Illustrated*, and *SI Kids*, and she is the author of *Haunted Hikes* (Falcon). She lives in Boulder, Colorado.